The Ugly Truth About Milton Friedman

The Ugly Truth About Milton Friedman

by Lyndon H. LaRouche, Jr.
and David P. Goldman

The New Benjamin Franklin House
New York

Milton Friedman
The Ugly Truth About Milton Friedman
Copyright © 1980 by Lyndon H. LaRouche, Jr. and
David P. Goldman
FIRST EDITION
For information address the publisher:
New Benjamin Franklin House
Publishing Company, Inc.
304 West 58th St.
New York 10019

Library of Congress Cataloging in Publication Data
Goldman, David P.
   Milton Friedman—The Ugly Truth About Milton Friedman.
   Includes index.
   1. Chicago School of Economics.   2. Friedman, Milton, 1912-   3. Economics. I. LaRouche, Lyndon H., joint author.   II. Title.

HB98.3.G64   330'.092'4   80-20623
ISBN 0-933488-09-2

Cover and text design: James Montalbano
Cover photographs: Wide World Photos

PRINTED IN THE UNITED STATES OF AMERICA

To Jacques Rueff
In memoriam

Acknowledgments

The authors drew extensively from unpublished research drafts prepared by their collaborators at the *Executive Intelligence Review,* including exhaustive work by Kathy Burdman on the history of monetarism, and by Alice Roth, James Cleary, Carol Cleary, Susan Cohen, Richard Schulman, and Laurie Sloan among others.

The authors wish to thank Miss May Wu of the Lehrman Institute Library for the use of prepublication drafts of translations of Jacques Rueff's work, from the Institute's forthcoming publication of Rueff's complete works in English, and also thank our editor at Benjamin Franklin House, Linda de Hoyos.

Contents

Introduction: Friedman Is a Hoax ... 1

1. What Is Fascist Economics? 19
2. Rueff versus Friedman 61
3. The Fraud of Free Enterprise 93
4. Oxford Monetarism and
   Hitler's Vienna 141
5. Monetarism Invades America 169
6. The Undead of Economics 207
7. The Worst Economist in the World .. 231
8. The Basis of Real Economics 275

   Appendix: Interview with
   Milton Friedman on the
   Phil Donahue Show 305

   Notes 323

   Index 339

Figures

Figure 1 Manufacturing output versus energy flux density, 1954-1977
Figure 2 U.S. employment
Figure 3 Israeli exports and imports
Figure 4 Israeli inflation
Figure 5 Israeli balance of payments
Figure 6 Productivity and total debt
Figure 7 Reinvested profit since 1970
Figure 8 Free-energy ratio of the U.S. economy since 1970
Figure 9 Phase diagram of an economy
Figure 10 Productive fixed investment
Figure 11 Apparent energy efficiency in the U.S. economy
Figure 12 Actual energy efficiency in the U.S. economy
Figure 13 Nominal West German energy efficiency
Figure 14 Surplus available for productive investment (current trends)
Figure 15 Surplus available for productive investment (minimal survival conditions)
Figure 16 Free-energy ratio $S'/(C+V)$ (minimal survival conditions)

Illustrations
Between pages 140 and 141

Introduction: Milton Friedman Is a Hoax

> *Mr. Friedman can absolutely be counted upon to say that his theories were not given an adequate exercise. There is no doubting that he is correct. But it is possible that his theories suffer from the overriding disqualification that they simply cannot get a sufficient exercise in democratic situations—because it takes longer for them to produce results than the public is prepared to wait.*
> —William F. Buckley, Jr., in *National Review*, August 16, 1971

Milton Friedman's good repute among American conservatives is the result of a monstrous hoax. Now that Federal Reserve Chairman Paul Volcker has thrown the U.S. economy into a 1930s-level of depression by applying Friedman's monetary theories, and Ronald Reagan has embraced Friedman and his associates as advisers, Americans have two alternatives: either we will destroy the hoax, or the hoax will destroy us.

2 The Ugly Truth About Milton Friedman

Television viewers have heard Friedman's slick pitch on the recent public television series, *Free To Choose,* but they do not know the record of the man speaking. We will show, for example, that Friedman's role in General Pinochet's dictatorship in Chile was no side issue blown out of proportion by left-leaning opponents, but typical of the man's behavior for the last four decades. In particular, we will show that Friedman is no "American conservative," but the instrument of the remnants of the old Hapsburg aristocracy. What Friedman passes off as economics is, in reality, the theory that we fought the American Revolution to free the colonies from: the antigrowth doctrine of the British East India Company.

Milton Friedman's record makes his salesmanship for "free enterprise" over public television seem altogether less impressive.

Friedman is the international traveler who ordered the Chile dictatorship to reduce the consumption of its population in 1976, when average per capita food consumption was then the same as it had been in Hitler's concentration camps. He did so in the South American public press, as a matter of record—and then lied to American audiences about his true role in Chile after he was caught at it.

He is also the adviser to the Margaret Thatcher government in Great Britain, who turned that long-suffering nation into what is now called a "Once Industrialized Country," in the phrase of the London *Sunday Times.* Friedman's dictates to Britain, presented over British television and visits to 10 Downing Street, managed to raise that country's rate of inflation by a factor of four, from 6 percent to 22 percent a year, in the year since Thatcher took office. At the same time,

Britain's industrial production fell 8 percent, and British living standards fell by a sharper margin than during the 1930s.

This is the "monetarist experiment" that Friedman wants to impose on the United States.

Finally, Friedman is the Republican Party adviser who steered Richard Nixon and Gerald Ford into economic blunders that weakened the U.S. economy. He urged Richard Nixon into a disastrous money crunch in 1969, throwing the economy into recession and forcing the United States to sever the dollar's link to gold, an action Friedman had lobbied for. The abandonment of the gold standard has produced more inflation than any other American policy error. His friends William Simon and Alan Greenspan misled President Gerald Ford into the "whip inflation" morass that brought on the 1974-1975 recession and cost Ford the 1976 election.

Last and worst, Friedman is the adviser who persuaded Richard Nixon to forgo the draft in favor of the All-Volunteer Army. The result is that America now has an army 40 percent of whose soldiers are illiterate, and the majority of whom are chronic drug abusers. That should not bother Friedman; he has been demanding the legalization of all drugs, including heroin, since 1972. But he bears personal responsibility for undermining America's national security in a way the Soviet Union could never dream of doing.

Americans should have smelled a rat when Friedman began advocating marijuana decriminalization three years ago, and become more outraged when he demanded the legalization of heroin. In a television interview on April 15, 1980, Friedman declared:

"Even if on ethical principles, you believe it is right

4 The Ugly Truth About Milton Friedman

to prevent somebody else from smoking marijuana, as a matter of expedience, it's a terrible mistake. . . . I mean, it's a terrible mistake for society to render heroin illegal because that increases the harm which heroin does. . . . Why is heroin so expensive? Because it's illegal."

Accordingly, in his 1980 book *Free to Choose,* Friedman promotes Hong Kong, the world's opium capital, as the model for his version of "free enterprise." Friedman wrote:

"In today's world big government seems pervasive. We may well ask whether there exist any contemporaneous examples of societies that rely primarily on voluntary exchange through the market to organize their economic activity and in which government is limited. . . . Perhaps the best example is Hong Kong—a speck of land next to mainland China containing less than 400 square miles with a population of roughly 4.5 million people. Hong Kong has no tariffs or other restraints on international trade. . . . It has no government direction of economic activity, no minimum wage law, no fixing of prices. . . . It is somewhat ironic that Hong Kong, a Crown Colony of Great Britain, should be the modern exemplar of free markets and limited government."[1]

Hong Kong also pulls in $10 billion a year in revenues from the illegal heroin traffic, has one fifth of its population addicted to heroin, and boasts a $1 billion a year police bribery rate—more than the entire police budget—and has more prostitutes, pickpockets, muggers, and dope pushers per capita than any city in the world. Hong Kong's $10 billion annual take from the dope traffic is *twice* the size of the island's money supply.² To be sure, Hong Kong has no restraints on "international trade." According to every U.S. government agency and congressional investigation of the heroin traffic during the last fifteen years, Hong Kong is not only the center of the world's dope trade. It is also the center for financing opium production under the aegis of the Hongkong and Shanghai Bank, the island's central bank and the issue bank of its legal tender currency, the Hong Kong dollar. The Hongkong and Shanghai Bank is so notoriously corrupt that the New York State Banking Department refused to give it permission to buy a New York state bank, Marine Midland, in 1979—despite urgent pressure from the Carter administration. Hongkong and Shanghai moved into New York only after Carter's Treasury overruled the New York authorities.³

As Kalimtgis, Goldman, and Steinberg reported in the 1978 bestseller *Dope, Inc.*, Hong Kong's economy is not merely linked to the dope trade—it *is* the dope trade. Friedman did not mention that in his television broadcast from the island. Nor did he mention his role in an elite, secretive organization known as the Mont Pelerin Society, which met privately in Hong Kong in 1977.

Friedman has furthermore admitted, without the least sign of embarrassment, that his economic doctrines are a resurrection of those of Nazi Economics Minister Hjalmar Schacht. He endorsed Schacht's doctrines as applied to the 1930s German economy in his 1956 book *Studies in the Quantity Theory of Money,* and repeated his admiration for Schacht in the course of a 1978 radio interview in Atlanta, Georgia.

This tells us precisely who and what Milton Friedman

is. Of course, he did not sell himself to the Nobel Prize Committee all on his own. The hoax, known genteelly as "liberal economics," goes far beyond Friedman. On the record, Friedman cites his "free market" predecessors to be Adam Smith, David Ricardo, Jeremy Bentham, and John Stuart Mill. Every one of these individuals was a senior official of the British East India Company, which was conducting the aboveboard opium trade as the world's biggest business. Smith drew up the Company's plans for expansion into the great Chinese market; Ricardo sat on its board of directors; Bentham published the Company's official history; and Mill was chief of East India Company intelligence during the first Opium War.

Jeremy Bentham not only founded Friedman's school of monetarism, but also Friedman's gutter morality, known as "philosophical radicalism." Bentham expressed this in treatises in defense of usury, pederasty, and other forms of "libertarianism."

That is the philosophical radicalism that Friedman embraces in his 1962 book, *Capitalism and Freedom:*

"To the free man, the country is the collection of individuals who compose it, not something over and above them. . . . He recognizes no national goal except as it is the consensus of the goals that the citizens severally serve. He recognizes no national purpose except as it is the consensus of the purposes for which the citizens severally strive."

With this statement, Friedman has repudiated the principles of the United States Constitution in favor of the ideology of the British Empire builders who were bent upon destroying the young American republic.

Friedman then continues to define his brand of "politics": "It is extremely convenient to have a label for the political and economic viewpoint elaborated in this book. The rightful and proper label is liberalism.... Liberalism has, in the United States, come to have a very different meaning than it did in the nineteenth century or does today over much of the continent of Europe.... Because of the corruption of the term liberalism, the views that formerly went under that name are now often labeled conservatism. But this is not a satisfactory alternative. The nineteenth-century liberal was a radical, both in the etymological sense of going to the root of the matter, and in the political sense of favoring major changes in social institutions. So must be his modern heir."[4]

Yet, many conservatives—themselves committed to America's national purpose of economic and scientific development—continue to be duped by Friedman's lectures. There are three noteworthy ingredients in Friedman's presentation that work to perpetrate the hoax:

First, Friedman repeatedly stresses specific issues that are real issues in the experience of most of his credulous admirers.

Second, he uses homilies of a sort that appear plausible to his viewers, at least as long as the viewers are sufficiently ignorant of the ABCs of economics not to recognize the fraud involved.

Third, he reinforces the favorable impression produced by his time-tested lectern homilies by resort to wild lies, such as the lies we have identified in connection with Pinochet's Chile and the Hong Kong market.

8 The Ugly Truth About Milton Friedman

Friedman's rhetorical gifts are often admitted by his critics; the actual talent is a knack for unsettling the listener's belief in causality.

As Harvard Keynesian Paul Samuelson, the author of a standard textbook, commented on Friedman's habits: "Now I don't think Milton is a charlatan. He believes what he says at any time he says it. But he also has a very healthy respect for his audience. If you are a yokel, he gives you a hokum answer. If he is giving his presidential address [in his capacity as American Economic Association president], he states it more guardedly and more carefully. It is a matter of the style of the person."[5]

But Friedman never discusses actual economics. Therefore, as long as credulous viewers remain blind to the fact that Friedman never discusses actual economics, they tend to be hoodwinked into believing that Friedman is an economist. The effect is like the case of the pitchman's shell game, in which the suckers have been induced to forget all about the pea. The "pea"—actual economics—simply never appears. The credulous admirer of con man Friedman foolishly assumes that the "clever Friedman" has control of a "pea," which, in fact, never existed in that particular game.

In salesman's lingo, Friedman's economics is all "sizzle," without any distracting presence of "steak."

Thus Friedman "makes outrageous statements he doesn't believe and proposes policies that could never be carried out," Yale economist James Tobin complained during Friedman's tenure as economic adviser to the 1964 Goldwater campaign. Most of us occasionally get mad enough to say stupid things such as, "throw all the welfare bums into the street," or "I'm going to shoot that s.o.b. brother-in-law of mine," and so forth, without really believing them. But Milton Friedman, Nobel Prize winner and respected economist, is there to tell us that we are correct to make outrageously stupid statements!

Take his column in *Newsweek* magazine of March 24, 1980. He begins with an accurate statement: "President Carter's anti-inflation program is another in a long series of cosmetic measures designed more to quiet public outcry than to resolve our serious economic problems. That problem has two faces: inflation and declining productivity. Inflation has discouraged productive investment and fostered economic inefficiency. Declining productivity has contributed to inflation. We badly need a coordinated attack on both inflation and declining productivity." But Friedman concludes: "President Carter has not proposed a meaningful cut in spending. He has simply proposed a slightly smaller increase. We should be considering cuts of $60 billion to $100 billion in fiscal 1981 projected spending, not $14 billion."

What does Friedman want to cut from the budget? Cutting $100 billion means—as anyone would realize after a moment's thought—elimination of social security payments, elimination of welfare payments, veterans pay, and half the income support systems of the federal government. That means the murder of useless eaters on the Hitler model. No one is speaking hypothetically. Friedman's collaborators in the California tax revolt movement propose seriously that the unemployed should apply to local charities, that school can be taught in home basements, and that social services are superfluous in general.

10 The Ugly Truth About Milton Friedman

Does Friedman himself propose to murder some tens of millions of "useless eaters"? He merely wants to cut $100 billion from the budget.

Ending the phony debate

The time has come to stop using the despicable John Maynard Keynes as an excuse to tolerate Milton Friedman. We have not forgotten that Keynes, too, admired Hjalmar Schacht, and wrote in his introduction to the 1936 German-language edition of his *General Theory* that Germany's political system, under Schacht and Hitler, was ideally suited for the exercise of Keynes's theories.

We shall show in chapters ahead how interchangeable are the Keynesian and Friedmanite varieties of Benthamite "liberalism." Stanford University's Hoover Institution, Friedman's current place of employment and the front-ranking think tank for the Reagan presidential campaign, is stocked with both "conservative liberals" like Friedman and economist Martin Anderson, and "liberal liberals" like New York University's superannuated Marxist Sidney Hook.

The University of Chicago, home of Friedman's own teachers, was put in place as a project of Britain's socialist Fabian Society. The careers of two close friends, Friedman and his Chicago classmate Abba Lerner, demonstrate how identical the liberals are. Lerner, now a professor at Queens College in New York and one of America's leading Keynesians, is an unashamed totalitarian. In a debate with LaRouche on the Queens College campus in October 1974, Lerner passionately defended Nazi Hjalmar Schacht as a "great economist" whose economic policies should be viewed in isolation from Hitler's political approach—the same case that Friedman makes for Chile's Pinochet.

In 1946 Lerner published a treatise entitled *The Economics of Control,* advocating an explicitly totalitarian economy in which the state controls each facet of economic life. It was Milton Friedman who argued that Lerner's totalitarianism was only the mirror image of his own economics, that "totalitarian direction might achieve the same allocation of resources as a free price system," and achieve "a reasonable approximation of the economic optimum."[6] Friedman, in a published review of Lerner's book, gently chided his old college friend for underrating "the administrative problems of economic institutions," while insisting that the economic content of his and Lerner's proposals was indistinguishable.

Abba Lerner was prominently associated with the Initiatives Committee for National Economic Planning (ICNEP), a group of liberal economists headed by Milton Friedman's wartime supervisor, Wassily Leontief. At a 1975 press conference in New York City, Leontief and *Challenge* magazine editor Myron E. Sharpe distributed as their chief ICNEP policy document an article entitled, "The Coming Corporativism," published in *Challenge*'s March-April 1975 issue. "Corporativism" was Mussolini's phrase for his version of fascist economics. The authors of the policy paper, two British sociologists, stated: "What the parties are putting forward now is an acceptable face of fascism; because so far the more repugnant political and social aspects of the German and Italian regimes are absent or present in diluted form. *For consumers, there is bound to be a noticeable drop in living standards. . . .* Investment controls will certainly eliminate some of the trivia, gimmicks, and baubles of contemporary life, and probably a number of the joys as well." (emphasis added)

That is the sordid content of Milton Friedman's agreement with Abba Lerner.

The authors' qualifications

From the vantage point of the body of economic science available to America's founding fathers and to the Lincoln administration, Friedman's work is instantly recognizable as outright quackery. Economic science, as it was understood by George Washington's Treasury Secretary Alexander Hamilton, has a 2000-year history as the Queen of Sciences. It is the mastery of the means by which human society transforms nature to advance humanity. At bottom, only an audience deprived of knowledge of the ABCs of real economics will tolerate a Milton Friedman.

Lyndon LaRouche and his associates are not merely the continuation of that body of science, known throughout the nineteenth century as the "American System," but the originators of the most important advances in that science since the work of Alexander Hamilton. Among the world's leading policy-making circles and in Europe's public press, LaRouche is recognized as the "intellectual author" of the 1978 creation of the European Monetary System, the most important breakthrough in the field of public policy since the last war. The European Monetary System is the launching-pad for a system of gold-backed credit for the industrialization of the underdeveloped countries, and the cornerstone for what could be the greatest economic boom in history.

LaRouche shares responsibility for the architecture of the new monetary system with the late Jacques Rueff, President Charles de Gaulle's gifted economist, to whom we dedicate this volume. Although Rueff's thinking was not parallel to ours on every issue, he was the heir to the economic tradition of Benjamin Franklin's collaborators in France, the great economists and physicists of the École Polytechnique. Over a writing and public service career spanning six decades, Rueff fought for the idea that economics and physics are the same science, and that human society's ability to command nature in the form of economic science is the starting point of all physical science. A life-long associate of the great physicist Louis de Broglie, Rueff rose to international prominence as the economist of de Gaulle's economic miracle. Throughout the 1960s and 1970s, Rueff was the European antipode to Milton Friedman's proposal to reduce the international monetary system to "free market" chaos. When he met LaRouche in Paris in 1976, three years before his death, Rueff shared with LaRouche basic agreement on the content of the international monetary system that would emerge with the July 1978 Bonn agreement to create the European Monetary System.

Beyond this public policy role, LaRouche contributed a fundamental advance in the field of theoretical economics, making possible the application of American System principles to precise quantitative models of economic behavior. Alexander Hamilton had formulated the essential standpoint of the city-building school of economics in his 1791 *Report to Congress on the Subject of Manufactures:* the only measure of wealth is the increase in the productivity of labor, as a measure of man's command over nature. Smith, Ricardo, and the French physiocrats had described wealth as a collection of objects given by nature, fixed in character, and valued according to their scarcity (or according to the scarcity of the labor required to produce them, the so-called classical labor theory of value). Hamilton demonstrated that particular objects of wealth have value only as they contribute to increases in society's ability to create new value; the *invariant* measure of economic life is the rate of increase of the productivity of labor.

Friedman and the Keynesians concur in constructing "deterministic" mathematical models with the vicious prejudice that the productivity of labor is held fixed, or that the real economy is intentionally excluded from the system, as in Friedman's "monetary model." Since their models enhanced these economists' morbidly anti-growth outlook, the economics profession saw no problem here.

The fundamental problem of deterministic models, which all the monetarists ignored, is to make the productivity of labor—that is, *the rate at which the economy integrates new scientific advances*—the primary subject of investigation. The current prices of capital, consumption goods, and labor are derivative, continuously revalued as their contribution to an advancing economy changes.

In the early 1950s, LaRouche solved this problem of deterministic models in theory, by applying the great mathematical advances of the Göttingen school of nineteenth-century German scientists, principally Bernhard Riemann and Georg Cantor. Riemann and Cantor's work, the basis for modern mathematical physics, treats discontinuous change as the primary subject of mathematical investigation. Applied first to self-ordering physical processes in which higher levels of energy flow lead to higher-order geometries of physical organization, the Riemann method provided the necessary tools for the American System economic model.

LaRouche's method was realized in the form of a computer-based econometric model of the U.S. and other economies. Since its development in 1978, the LaRouche-Riemann model has proved to be the only successful predictive tool among the available computer models; but it is also a powerful tool for development planning. An application of the LaRouche-Riemann model to the problems of the development of India, published in the spring of 1980, attracted major international attention, and has already had a profound impact on development planning throughout the developing world.

The authors employed this unique advance in economic science to predict with great precision what the adoption of Milton Friedman's policies would do to the U.S. economy.

On October 9, 1979, Federal Reserve Chairman Paul Volcker announced that henceforward monetary policy would be conducted on Friedman's principles of stemming inflation through fiscal austerity. The LaRouche-Riemann model predicted that by the end of the year 1980, the Volcker measures would force a 15 percent drop in production. That projection has been completely borne out.

The Volcker policy has single-mindedly been committed to the purpose to uphold the mass of debt held by lower Manhattan and London and the federal government debt—at the expense of the productive economy. This is the same perspective as Adam Smith's, and is completely opposite to that of Alexander Hamilton.

Hamilton demonstrated that the single source of national wealth was the increase of productive skills of the citizenry. There is little question that today, without a major increase in our national productivity, this nation will die.

At the conclusion of this work, we will report the results of an authoritative computer economic analysis conducted by the authors demonstrating that a 3 percent annual rise in real social productivity is the minimum survival condition of the U.S. economy. Contrary to the fanatical delusions of Georgetown University and the Hoover Institution, no "Big Brother" seated at the control panel will be able to effect the required increase in productivity—which these men perceive to be necessary for a successful military build-up. Our continued existence as a nation hangs on the ability of our best citizens to mobilize the American population for science, on a scale far exceeding the enthusiasm for the NASA space program following the Russians' launching of Sputnik in 1957.

Real economics is first and foremost the science of the moral capabilities of the citizens of a republic. That is the lesson of the survival of the early republic under the economic guidelines set forth by Alexander Hamilton, the emergence of the United States as a great industrial power as a result of the policies of Abraham Lincoln, and the mobilization for World War II that pulled us out of depression in this century.

The same quality of mobilization must occur today—in opposition to the moral indifferentism of Milton Friedman et al. Our present generation of youth must find the moral resources to reject the countercultural hedonism that has already come close to destroying it, and become educated as the scientists, engineers, teachers, and skilled workers who will rebuild our economy. Nations do not stumble into productivity growth. This economic phenomenon takes place when entire populations raise their qualifications to produce the scientists, engineers, and skilled personnel required for the future.

There is no difference between the brutalized sheep of Lerner's "controlled economy," and the gratification-seeking hedonist of Bentham and Friedman. The citizen who is a docile sheep with respect to his responsibilities as a citizen will be a bestial hedonist in "private life." That the majority of the American population currently behaves in this fashion thins our prospects for continued national existence down to a slim margin.

By morality, we are not speaking of such nonsense as the "work ethic," but of the notion of causality, the fundamental principle of science. What is morality but a determination to judge the consequences of one's actions in the real world?

Milton Friedman is a moral obscenity, but his popularity is even more obscene. Whether or not Americans continue to tolerate him will say a great deal about whether America has the moral fitness to survive.

Lyndon H. LaRouche, Jr.
David P. Goldman
July 23, 1980

What Is Fascist Economics?

1

> *You want to prove that Milton Friedman is a fascist? It's easy. Quote him.*
> —Prof. Arthur B. Laffer of the University of Southern California, in conversation with the authors

Milton Friedman's public record defense of Nazi Economics Minister Hjalmar Schacht and his eerie justification of Hitler's economic methods published twenty-five years ago should have set off alarms in the minds of his readers. Statements of this nature are more than a reflection of the man's character. Fascist economics is the ultimate response, or "final solution," for an economy that monetarist mismanagement has thrown into apparently hopeless crisis. There is a thin line between monetarism in general and fascist economics as such. Among the leading monetarists, Friedman is the one with the least compunction about crossing that line.

Germany's economic breakdown crisis in 1933 was not, in fundamentals, far different from what the United

20 The Ugly Truth About Milton Friedman

States is experiencing now. Nine years before the great 1931 international economic crisis, Hjalmar Schacht had performed the misnamed "miracle" of ending the great hyperinflation of the early 1920s. What Schacht had in fact done was to negotiate credits from his friend Montagu Norman, the governor of the Bank of England, in return for handing over the German economy to London. Germany stopped investing in industry by written agreement with its British creditors and became a speculative fairground for short-term British capital. The international monetary crisis of 1931 brought the German economy down, and Hitler's SS became the bill-collectors for Germany's delinquent account, before it struck them that they could do some collecting on their own.

Nine years ago, the Nixon administration took Milton Friedman's advice and removed the link between the dollar and gold. The August 15, 1971 monetary debacle turned the American economy into a speculative fairground for the City of London. The devalued dollar ceased to be a vehicle for productive investment, and hundreds of billions of dollars piled up in the City of London, in the so-called Eurodollar market. Now valued at $1.2 trillion, larger than the U.S. money supply, the Eurodollar market is the primary cause of double-digit inflation in the United States.

Federal Reserve Chairman Paul Volcker, the Undersecretary of Treasury who fought for the end of the dollar-gold link in 1971, took Milton Friedman's advice once again in October 1979. Instead of concerning himself with interest rates in the future, Volcker announced in what the press called "the Saturday Night

Massacre" that the Federal Reserve would hold down the rate of growth of the money supply—period.

Now the American economy is suffering not merely a terrifying 15 percent per annum rate of decline of tangible output, but a massive financial crisis at the same time. Instead of the $40 billion deficit this fiscal year and the $16 billion surplus next fiscal year forecast in March by the Carter administration, the Treasury now officially projects a $100 billion deficit in the two fiscal years, not counting an additional $80 billion in so-called off-budget borrowing. In the official estimate of the White House, America cannot "afford" a recovery without a huge reduction in consumption.

America, like Germany in the 1930s, is undergoing a monetary crisis, but the monetary crisis is the form of a crisis in the underlying physical economy. Since approximately 1967, America's investment in both capital goods and labor has been insufficient merely to replenish our existing capital stock and skilled labor pool. The authors conducted a survey through the *Executive Intelligence Review* demonstrating that per annum capital investment was $50 billion short of the annual depreciation requirements of industry in 1979; the condition of the American labor force is a national scandal. Since 1971, the financial flow of capital has been concentrated into *nonproductive,* often speculative investment, under the policy slogan "post-industrial society." The rate of growth of demands for income in the form of debt service in the nation's economy (and internationally) has become an inflationary cancer, outstripping the economy's ability to produce real profit in the form of a surplus of tangible wealth.

22 The Ugly Truth About Milton Friedman

Monetarist economics invariably produces such crises by suppressing capital investment. At the point of crisis, the choices available are only two: Either the economy undergoes general financial reorganization in favor of relaunching the economy's productive potential, the solution associated with LaRouche and Jacques Rueff; or the economy must be cannibalized to protect the failing financial structure. Since the second option requires political methods that, as William F. Buckley said in 1971, "cannot get a sufficient exercise in democratic situations," we call that option by its German and Italian name: fascism.

Hjalmar Schacht did more or less exactly what Paul Volcker, under Milton Friedman's guidance, is doing now: impose a regime of "fiscal austerity" on the German economy, crush consumption, and maintain tight conditions on the credit markets. Neither Schacht nor his admirer Friedman makes an attempt to halt inflation. Their method is this: If, for example, there is an annual 10 percent inflation, then the economy must make up for that inflation by gouging an additional 10 percent each year out of the flesh and bone of the productive economy.

The analogy to this sort of method is given by the case of a loan-sharking victim. In a hypothetical case, illustrating the general principle encountered, a person with $20,000 earned income incurs $5,000 in debt service payment obligations to a loan shark. Unable to pay all of the $5,000, the victim "refinances" $2,000 of the debt service payment at 50 percent effective annual interest. He pays the $1,000 instead of the $2,000 portion of the $5,000; a total of $4,000. The following year, he owes

$6,000 in current debt service, instead of $5,000. The next year $7,000, and so forth.

That is Schacht's, and Friedman's, "monetarist" approach to "fighting inflation." That is the fascist economics policy Friedman applied to Chile under the Pinochet dictatorship—a dictatorship now contemplating ways for cutting out the growing ratio of "useless eaters" among its citizens.

What drives fascist economies in practice is the political economy of military power. Physically depleted economies are hollow shells from a military vantage point. A nation's capacity for warfighting in depth depends on its ability to deploy productive resources for military purposes. A healthy economy can afford even extraordinary levels of military expenditure; during the Second World War American home consumption actually rose, despite the enormous cost of military production and diversion of manpower into the armed services. Military production as such tends to expand the capital goods industries that are essential for improving the national stock of fixed capital, creating a "productivity spinoff" that benefits the civilian sector. That is also the experience, for example, of the National Aeronautics and Space Administration.

However, an economy depleted by Friedmanite methods cannot sustain military production in depth; it must rely on shallow "in-width" military production and *blitzkrieg* methods of war fighting. Fascist economies simultaneously loot their own productive base, while devoting massive amounts of resources to war-autarky expenditures. To ensure that "energy autarky" and military programs receive first access to limited supplies of credit, Schacht created an array of special financing institutions, including the infamous "Mefo-Institut," with the equivalent of unlimited check-cashing privileges at his Reichsbank. The Carter administration has done essentially the same thing through the Energy Security Corporation, the Synthetic Fuels Corporation, and other Schachtian "off-budget" institutions.

Friedman's defense of Schacht

Since the demise of the Nazi regime and the postwar studies of the Allied Strategic Bombing Survey, Friedman and other monetarists have devoted special attention to the Nazi economy, including the internal debates among its leaders. The centerpoint of this discussion is the 1938 economic crisis during which Field Marshal Hermann Göring dumped Schacht from the Reichsbank and economics ministry and took over plenipotentiary economic powers. The issue was whether the Nazi regime could continue to cannibalize its capital and workforce to produce weapons, as Hitler and Göring insisted it must, without leading to an internal economic collapse, as Schacht finally admitted it would. The Nazis obviated the internal effects of the crisis produced by five years of Schacht's "economic recovery" by conquering their neighbors. Gold from the Austrian central bank supported the decimated Reichsmark after the 1938 *Anschluss,* and the Nazi war machine temporarily thrived on Czech, Dutch, Belgian, and French plant and equipment, and on the 14 million slave laborers murdered at the workcamps.

What Is Fascist Economics? 25

The contenders in the current 1980 presidential race are committed to a "guns-not-butter" military economic program. Their economic advisers are currently reviewing German history of the 1930s to find potential exemplars and pitfalls. Whether the United States can throw its creaking plant and equipment and de-skilled industrial labor force into a military build-up is now a central topic of discussion at the Georgetown University Center for Strategic and International Studies, the Hoover Institution, and the various economics faculties now advising Republican Ronald Reagan. The old Schacht-Göring debate is playing itself out in what is known, through the press, as the "Team A-Team B" debate, following the labels of the competing intelligence evaluations groups that George Bush created during his tenure as director of the Central Intelligence Agency. "Team A" seeks to upgrade U.S. military capabilities, but without destroying the civil economy totally. "Team B," which includes Walter Rostow, James Schlesinger, and Harvard professor Richard Pipes, intends to gut social services and much of the civilian productive economy, while going over to a full-scale "war economy," in preparation for early war between the Soviet Union and the United States.

To a sane, moral person, the differences between Schacht and Göring are the equivalent of a factional debate between the eighth and ninth circles of Dante's Hell. Göring is arguably more satanic than Schacht, but it is Schacht's policies that made Göring's war machine possible.

Two standard works have come from the ranks of Field Marshal Göring's American admirers. One is *Germany's Economic Preparations for War,* by Rand

Corporation analyst Burton H. Klein, published in 1958 by the Rand Corporation.[1] The second is *Studies in the Quantity Theory of Money,* written two years earlier by Milton Friedman and colleagues.[2] The two works are complementary. Klein, drawing on similar conclusions reached earlier by the Strategic Bombing Survey, argued that Germany devoted insufficient resources to her war mobilization because of Schacht's unfounded concern over inflation.[3] Friedman and his graduate student, John J. Klein, attempt to demonstrate that Schacht's fears of an internal inflationary explosion were unfounded, because "the German economic controls system was successful not only in restricting individual spending but also in inducing individuals to hold their accumulating assets in the form of cash."[4]

The John J. Klein paper, entitled "German Money and Prices, 1932-1944," was written during the early 1950s as a doctoral dissertation under Friedman's direction at the University of Chicago. The 1956 volume also contains studies of hyperinflation in postwar Europe and in the American Confederacy, along with other studies of war-related economic breakdown.

Burton Klein was rather more overtly hostile to Hjalmar Schacht than were Friedman and his students, concluding:

"There is no doubt that without this concern for inflation, and without such an effective exponent of financial conservatism as Schacht, Germany would have had a larger rearmament. . . . Procuring additional funds by borrowing, it was thought, would destroy confidence in the economy and lead to an inflation. The fear of inflation weighed heavily in the policy decisions of the whole decade. The German leaders simply did not at this time understand the elementary economic lesson that a nation can finance anything which can be produced."[5]

The argument is certifiably lunatic, as we shall prove below: If a nation expends its entire investment resources on nonproductive expenditures, deducting the cost of those expenditures from the maintenance fund for the labor force and industrial plant, the consequences will be first hyperinflation and then breakdown.

But Milton Friedman's analysis, from the vantage point of the "quantity theory of money," goes even further off the deep end. Unlike Burton Klein, he ignores the physical problems of wringing war materiel out of a depleted economy, and adopts a single criterion for the success or failure of the Nazi economy: whether it succeeded in maintaining price stability. What is remarkable, the paper concludes, is that the Nazis managed to hold the increase of wholesale prices between 1932 and 1944 to a mere 22 percent, or less than 2 percent per year, despite the fact that the money supply rose over the same period by 437 percent.

In *Studies on the Quantity Theory of Money*, Friedman states point-blank that Nazism worked:

"Germany did not choose to pay for its increased expenditures by taxation. Nor did it urge individuals to invest in government securities. It did, however, borrow heavily from the German banking system. To avoid a price boom, and simultaneously to have ready access to the credit market, the German government imposed economic controls. First wage, price, and credit controls and then rationing. Eventually Germany became a directed economy.

"The objective of such controls is the restriction of

spending on the part of individuals, so that individual spending will increase less rapidly than the quantity of money. Such a policy, if rigorously enforced, should restrain a rise in the price level. *As indicated earlier, this policy appears to have been successful in Nazi Germany.*"[6]

Friedman's explanation for this "success" is horrifying. In his "quantity theory," the effect of Nazi territorial annexations is to reduce the problem of excess money creation, by spreading the same amount of money over a larger population! "The Reichsmark was made legal tender in Austria in April, 1938; in Sudetenland in October, 1938; in Memel territory in March, 1939; in the Free City of Danzig in September, 1939; in East Upper Silesia in September, 1939; in the Annexed Eastern Provinces in November, 1939; in Eupen, Malmedy, and Moresnet in June, 1940; in Luxembourg in February, 1941; in Alsace and Lorraine in March, 1941; in Carinthia, Carniola, and Lower Styria in June, 1941; and in Bialystock in January, 1942. The above areas were directly incorporated into the Reich. The Reichsmark was also made legal tender in the Protectorate of Bohemia-Moravia concurrently with the Czech koruna."[7] Carefully noting these events, Friedman concludes, "For the purposes of this study it has been assumed that the amount of money issued for the newly annexed areas was the same percentage of total hand-to-hand currency as the population of their areas was of the new total population; this assumption is then used to estimate the stock of money in the territory of 1937 Germany."[8]

In their perverted way, John Klein and Milton Friedman are making a correct point: The annexations did buttress the value of the Reichsmark, which, in 1938, stood on the verge of inflationary collapse. However, it was not the fact that the Reichsmark went out of "old Germany" into new populations, but the fact that new populations were brought into Germany in cattle cars, that prevented the Nazi economic system from breaking down.

In the "Blitzkrieg" economy, where existing (and antiquated) industrial plant spews out "production in-width" of existing technological models, the only economic recourse is the cannibalization of the workforce. That is the content of the downward revision of the German money supply statistics to take into account annexed populations, which Friedman et al. factor into the Nazis' "success."

In an October 15, 1941 remark to his Berchtesgarten cronies, Hitler put Friedman's arguments in a slightly more honest fashion: "Even to Schacht," Hitler said, "I had to begin by explaining this elementary truth: that the essential cause of the stability of our currency was to be sought for in our concentration camps."[9]

Having proven that Nazi policies worked by virtue of the stability of the wholesale price index, Friedman and his coauthors prefer Göring to Schacht, and prefer Albert Speer, who replaced Göring's stooges at the economics ministry in 1942, to Göring. They quote favorably the evaluation of the Strategic Bombing Survey that the Göring economics ministry "expressed the general attitude that sacrifices of the civilian population should be kept at a minimum. It tried to equilibriate the divergent claims of the industrialists, the military, the gauleiters. . . . High cost firms were protected, production of *superfluous civilian goods* continued, and scarce materials allocated to nonessential programs."[10] Therefore, Friedman writes:

"German authorities realized after the Battle of Stalingrad in December 1942, that current economic policies were not resulting in the production of armaments sufficient to insure success in the new phase of the war. For this reason a New Ministry of War Production was created. Albert Speer as its head had almost unlimited control over the industrial resources of Germany. His assistants for the most part were young managers of efficient business enterprises. At this late date industrial capacity could not be expanded. The only alternatives were either to restrict civilian consumption or to improve the use of existing industrial capacity. He took the latter course and achieved significant increases in armaments production."[11]

Precisely how Speer accomplished this, Friedman does not report: The 250 percent increase in arms production Speer accomplished between 1942 and 1944 was the result of the most systematic collection and mass murder of slave laborers in human history.

Speer rejected the crude mass extermination program Göring had proposed under the code-name "Green File," in favor of more efficient methods of working slave labor to death. Göring's secret orders had stated: "Many tens of millions of people in the industrial areas [of Russia] will become redundant and will either die or have to emigrate to Siberia. Any attempts to save the population from starving to death by bringing in surplus food from the black soil region can be made only at the expense of feeding Europe. They undermine Germany's ability to hold out in the war.... There must be absolute clarity on this point. From this fact there follows forcibly the extinction of industry as well

What Is Fascist Economics?   31

as of a large percentage of the human beings."[12]

Before Stalingrad, the Nazis had permitted the death by starvation and related causes of 3,000,000 of the 3,800,000 Russian prisoners of war taken. Despite post-1942 efforts to rationalize the mass murders to achieve maximum benefit for the war economy, the Speer ministry had to contend with a perpetual labor shortage until 1944, when the machine collapsed, as Konstandinos Kalimtgis has documented. In a 1975 study of the Nazi economy, Kalimtgis concluded that "historians who clamor about the Nazis' inefficiency in exploiting their conquered assets are perhaps even more psychotic than the Nazis who carried out the crime."[13]

Speer's own evaluation of his efforts treats the Nazi war machine as a failure. In his memoirs, Speer reported, "Even at the height of military successes in 1941 the level of arms production of the First World War was not reached. During the first year of the war in Russia production figures were a fourth of what they had been in the autumn of 1918. Three years later, in the spring of 1944, when we were nearing our production maximum, ammunition production still lagged behind that of the First World War—considering the total production of Germany at the time with Austria and Czechoslovakia."[14]

But Speer had less to do with the failure of Nazi policy than did Hjalmar Schacht, whose "recovery" program of 1933-1938 dug the ground from under the German economy.

Economists like Milton Friedman and Burton Klein who wish to defend the *feasibility* of Nazi economic policies reach the same conclusions as the Strategic Bombing Survey (which was staffed by liberal economists among whom were John Kenneth Galbraith, Wassily Leontief, and Cambridge University's Nicholas Kaldor). The conclusion: The Nazis tolerated too high a level of civilian production. The report of the Strategic Bombing Survey, which was the source book for Burton Klein, Milton Friedman, and the "Team-B" proponents, concluded: "Germany entered the war with a 'guns *and* butter philosophy.' "[15] This is a lie, as any honest examination of the statistics will confirm, and an extremely revealing lie.

No prominent American will publicly endorse fascism. That is an unpopular position, although nearly all of the "Team B" gang privately endorse Nazi methods as the best means of achieving the kind of military build-up they want. American fascists do not argue that fascism is *good,* but only that fascism *works.* To maintain this conclusion in the face of the evidence, they must argue that the enormous inefficiencies in the Nazi economy were simply a matter of misadministration and policy errors, and, implicitly, that they could do it better. This could turn out to be the last delusion American policy-makers ever have.

The German war mobilization misfired because of endemic shortages of skilled labor. It did not occur to Schacht, nor to his modern disciples, that labor requires investment no less than industrial plant, and that failure to meet the investment requirements of labor power leads to consequences not much different from deterioration of the capital stock. Real wages in Germany in 1933 were roughly half of their 1929 level. The Labor Front fixed wages at that low level, but in fact reduced them through unemployment insurance; *Wintershilfe* and other payroll deductions, including "retirement insurance"; Labor Front dues; and the notorious people's car (Volkswagen) swindle. Wage reductions of this sort and the deterioration of consumer goods (*ersatz* goods) kept living standards down throughout the 1930s at levels substantially below those of 1929, and 1929 levels were significantly below those of 1913. An entire generation of Germans—those aged twenty-one or younger at the time Hitler seized power—had grown up in relative poverty, marked by long periods of mass unemployment and near-starvation. Germany entered the 1930s missing an entire generation of skilled labor.

The defenders of Schacht and Göring must thus go to ridiculous extremes to explain away the Nazi economic crisis as excess consumption. For example, Schacht's (sympathetic) biographer Edward Norman Peterson wrote in 1954: "Despite the cries of Hitler that he was waging a 'Total War,' Germany was making less of an economic effort than any of her opponents. There was no 'total mobilization'; civilian goods were restricted only to a moderate extent. Any serious restriction began only in 1942, when the war was three years old. Total employment increased by 8 million or 30 percent between 1930-1939. This was not fully mobilized, not even unduly concentrated on war production. Civilian consumption in 1939 at the outbreak of the war was above the 1929 level and it had fallen only slightly by 1941."[16] Peterson cites *total* civilian consumption figures in the same breath he reports that 8 million people entered the labor force! The increase in overall consumption was entirely due to expansion of the labor force; per capita income remained at roughly half the 1929 level.

The only mystery is how Friedman, Klein, and other

Schachtians could fail to make the connection between the already abysmal consumption levels of the Third Reich and the tendency of Nazi industry to disintegrate. Between 1933 and 1939 enrollment in technical schools, the equivalent of our engineering schools, fell from 20,474 to 9,554. The quality of graduates declined even further. At the skilled operative level, apprenticeship programs became a national scandal. In one test of 400 apprentices in Hamburg, three quarters of those tested failed to capitalize proper names, and an equal number could not spell the name of Goethe. The Nazi Labor Front attempted, without success, to prevent industrialists from raiding each other's skilled labor with under-the-table wage bonuses. Like today, demand for skilled labor was highest in the military industry sector, and skilled labor shortages therefore had their greatest impact on military production. The Third Reich inherited an exhausted, impoverished population from the dead Kaiserreich and the Weimar Republic, and suffered the consequences.

It must be added that Nazi educational methods, which placed primary emphasis on physical education and second on "racial science," did not contribute to the cognitive powers of the population. But at least German youth did not have to contend with rock music and marijuana, the most efficient methods of killing a population's cognitive powers.

Before judging the statistics concerning German technical school graduates, the American reader should consider that the number of doctorates in physics awarded in the United States in the past ten years has also fallen by half. Despite a 7 to 8 percent (actually closer to 10 percent) unemployment rate, America currently has a serious skilled labor shortage. For every four positions opening for machinists today, only one qualified machinist is graduating from apprenticeship programs, and the same pattern applies in other job categories.

No world war, no punitive reparations payments did this to us. The long-term application of Friedmanite economics has done to the United States approximately what the First World War and the Treaty of Versailles did to Germany.

The Schachtian dictatorship today

It would be dangerous to imagine that Paul Volcker's command over the United States' credit system is anything less than a dictatorship, or that his policy objectives are any different from those of Hjalmar Schacht.

Two pieces of legislation—the 1969 Credit Control Act and the Omnibus Banking Bill of 1980—establish the Federal Reserve and its chairman, Paul Volcker, as an economic dictatorship capable of rule by decree. On March 16, 1980, President Carter invoked the Credit Control Act of 1969, which was drafted at the time by the predecessor organization of the Federal Emergency Management Agency. This legislation gave the Federal Reserve the power to control or prohibit every transaction in the banking system down to the level of the corner savings and loan association, to fix interest rates, to stop foreign money transfers, to allocate credit to the borrowers it chooses, or any other action the Fed requires.[17] Strictly speaking, the Federal Reserve and

Paul Volcker have more power *on paper* than any central bank and its governor at any previous time in modern history, including the tenure of Hjalmar Schacht at the Reichsbank.

All the possible powers under the Credit Control Act have not yet been invoked. But the effect of the formal use of this legislation for the first time since August 15, 1971, when the United States removed gold backing from the dollar, combines with the Omnibus Banking Bill sponsored by Rep. Henry Reuss (D-Wisc.) and signed into law by President Carter on March 31, 1980, to give the Federal Reserve awesome power.

The content of the Reuss legislation is, first, to eliminate the differences between commercial banks and savings institutions, by phasing out the "Regulation Q" differential between the interest rates they may pay on deposits; to undermine the 1954 McFadden Act ban against interstate banking, which protects regional banking institutions from predatory takeovers by large money-center banks; and to give the Federal Reserve additional powers to raise compulsory reserves from banks that have left the Federal Reserve System. Under the sweeping 1969 legislation, the Federal Reserve can do whatever it wants. Even more, the Federal Emergency Management Agency, under the limitless powers of the National Security Act of 1947 (the legislation that created the Central Intelligence Agency and other such entities), can take over and run banks, merge banks, collapse banks, or create banks the moment the President declares a "national banking emergency."

Except for the possible intervention of FEMA, the remaining supports of the Volcker credit dictatorship have been discussed extensively in the public press. To be more precise, they have been widely misrepresented as measures to control inflation by halting the rate of growth of the money supply, in accordance with Milton Friedman's doctrine that the rate of expansion of the money supply determines prices. On that level, Volcker has indeed brought the rate of increase of the money supply down from about 10 percent prior to his October 7 announcement of tight money, to between 3 and 4 percent during the first few months of 1980, the range recommended by Friedman for the past thirty years. However, the rate of inflation *doubled* by February 1980, from about 11 percent to about 20 percent, a pattern identical to that of every other period when Friedman's recommendations were adopted in an industrial country.

There is no direct connection between the rate of inflation and money supply growth. *Inflation is determined by the way the expansion of credit affects the economy's productivity,* or by the extent to which new credit is applied to productive rather than nonproductive uses. Credit expansion to build corporate headquarters, gambling casinos, or weaponry is inflationary, while credit to finance investments in new productive facilities at state-of-the-art technology is counterinflationary. The final chapter of this book will treat this question in depth. Suffice it for now to emphasize that the cause of the gross divergence between the rate of money supply growth (itself a poor measure of the rate of credit expansion) and the inflation rate has nothing to do with the time delays that Friedman and his followers predict between the imposition of tight money policies and the reduction of inflation rates.

Volcker's measures absolutely do not represent a

tight credit regime as such, but a two-tier credit regime that favors nonproductive investments above all others. In combination with an unpleasant (and little-discussed) feature of Carter's budget program known as "off-budget" financing, the Federal Reserve has effected a shift of about 15 percent in the composition of total industrial output from productive to nonproductive categories.[18] In precise parallel to 1933-1938 Germany, the reduction in output in productive categories has occurred mostly in consumer goods industries, and the increase in nonproductive categories has occurred in military-related industries or investment in "energy self-sufficiency" (the same as Schacht's "autarky").

The only difference worth mentioning is that while Schacht took office some years after the onset of the depression, with the collapse of the consumer goods industries ready-made, Volcker needed to engineer a collapse of the consumer sector in order to carry out the same shift in composition of the economy's total output.

In more detail: the most important categories of consumer durable goods are residential construction and autos. In September 1969, their combined value of output was $150 billion at an annual rate. That figure had dropped by half as of March 1980. From a September 1979 level of 2 million housing starts per year—less than the absolute minimum replacement level for the existing housing stock of 2.5 million units per year—housing starts have fallen by two thirds, the sharpest drop since World War II. Auto production has fallen by slightly under 20 percent at this writing, although the daily reportage of auto layoffs is so continuous that the decline will undoubtedly go much further. These industries rely on an orderly flow of consumer credit in the form of mortgages and installment loans. Volcker pulled the bottom out from under them.

First, the record-breaking interest rate levels achieved during March 1980, including a 20 percent prime rate that exceeds any rates in the recorded history of the republic, sucked funds out of the financial institutions that provide consumer credit. Whether or not the savings banks, which are losing deposits at the rate of several billion dollars a month, will survive 1980 without mass bankruptcies is now a matter of Paul Volcker's largesse. Whatever becomes of these institutions, which will lose an estimated $4 billion on their profit-loss accounts in 1980, they have left the lending markets. Mortgage credit is available only at interest rates in excess of 14 percent, and is usually not available at all. The finance companies, including those attached to Ford Motor Company and Chrysler Corporation, which provide funds to auto dealers for installment loans, are in the same position. The bankruptcy rate among auto dealers is higher than that among professional gamblers. Volcker's direct order to the banks to reduce the availability of consumer credit through the commercial banking system has succeeded in cutting the 1979 rate of bank lending to consumers in half.

Americans lost 8 percent of their purchasing power between March 1979 and March 1980, the largest drop in real income levels since the Great Depression. This was only the first of Volcker's shocks. Since consumer purchasing power is proportional to the output of consumer goods, the drop in 1980 will be at least as large, and possibly twice as large. We are moving into the range of income-reduction that German consumers suffered between 1929 and 1933.

As noted, the prospects for our youth, even discounting the ghettoized hell to which most minority youth are assigned, do not bear favorable comparison with those of German youth in the early 1930s.

It would be a devastating mistake to treat these events as mere symptoms of a classical depression. In that sense comparisons to the American Great Depression of fifty years ago are misleading. Statistical comparisons prove that there is a fundamental difference between the 1980 situation and previous industrial declines. For example, in the biggest postwar decline, between September 1974 and March 1975, the rate of decline of the consumer goods industries was slower than during the comparable period of 1979-1980. Auto production fell by approximately the same amount, with roughly the same number of auto layoffs, but housing starts fell by only 20 percent, a mere third of their fall during the first six months of 1980. Yet the industrial production index, a handy rough measure of real economic activity, declined by 15 percent. That is, when the big consumer goods sectors dropped off, industries stopped making investments, and orders for capital goods plunged; the suppliers of the consumer industries in primary metals, rubber, and construction materials dropped off; and the entire economy shrank in roughly the same proportions.

During the seven months after Volcker's recession trigger in October 1979, however, despite the record decline of the consumer goods industries, total industrial production did not fall. Capital goods output only fell after March 16, 1980, when Volcker imposed credit controls affecting the total volume of funds banks were permitted to lend.

What is important is that those seven months saw a shift in the composition of the American economy. To the extent that consumer goods had fallen, other goods had been produced in greater quantity. Every sector to benefit was related to either war preparations or the equivalent—Carter's "energy independence" program.

The auto industry profile shows why production of capital goods had risen, in most cases, despite the elimination of housing and auto, two of the economy's biggest sectors. During the next five years, the three major automakers—Ford, General Motors, and Chrysler—will spend $60 billion to retool their assembly lines for smaller, "fuel-efficient" cars. Even in inflated 1980 dollars, this is the most extensive investment program the auto industry has adopted since the heyday of the 1920s. At its conclusion they will not produce more cars, or better cars, but only cars that consume less gasoline.

As a senior Ford Motor Company official complained in a conversation with the authors, government regulations prevent Ford Motor from going into the nuclear power business; if Ford invested the $20 billion required to produce fuel-saving cars in nuclear power plants, it would save the country a great deal more oil, and make a great deal more money. Instead, automakers must retool under orders from the Environmental Protection Agency, if they wish to do business five years from now. They may not be able to sustain this rate of investment, for the simple reason that Chrysler (and possibly Ford) are likely to go bankrupt. Chrysler has already failed to obtain the commercial bank support demanded by Treasury Secretary G. William Miller as a condition for the federal loan guarantees it needs to

42   The Ugly Truth About Milton Friedman

stay in business. Ford lost $1 billion in domestic operations, barely breaking even through foreign profits, during 1979. This year it will lose a great deal more and make less money abroad. Chrysler's business may be restricted to its one big government contract—tank production—and Ford may soon be in the same situation.

Aerospace is also booming, with the largest order-book in history. Most of this is not Pentagon orders, but, under national security legislation, all civilian aircraft must now be built readily convertible for military usage. Production is so high that the leading aircraft makers report endemic shortages of skilled labor, machine tools, ball bearings, electronic components, specialty metals, and other goods from the upper end of the technology spectrum. The demand for electronic components is so intense that their manufacturers—on orders from the Department of Defense—have already begun to suspend production of consumer items such as electronic games in order to meet military-related aerospace orders. Equally intense is the demand for machine tools, whose manufacturers are swamped with a three-year backlog of orders. In the past, the auto and aerospace industries combined bought about 12 percent of the nation's output of machine tools. Now they are absorbing more than 25 percent of machine tool production, to service the programs ordered by the Carter administration.

Overall, these and similar military and "energy independence" programs have produced a swing of about 15 percent from consumption into investment, setting the trend demanded five years ago in *Challenge* magazine under the rubric, "The Coming Corporativism:

Fascism With a Democratic Face." The economy is already running into extreme shortages in every field requiring advanced labor skills and high-technology products. In the strictest economic terms, America is becoming a fascist economy.

At the administrative level, Paul Volcker already has more authority under the Credit Control Act of 1969 than Schacht ever enjoyed. His power is supplemented by a group of specialized financial institutions that operate off the federal budget, allocating credit to various forms of war preparedness. Off-budget financing is not in principle fascist; it began under the New Deal as a Rooseveltian method of channeling credit to depressed sectors, including agriculture and housing. During the 1970s, the off-budget agencies did relatively little mischief, the worst of which was support for the secondary-market real estate bubble through the government-sponsored housing program. Under off-budget financing, the Government National Mortgage Association, the Farm Credit System, and various other entities borrowed from the capital markets under federal guarantee, making their operations indistinguishable from the deficit financing of the Treasury itself.

By the fiscal year 1981 budget, the volume of such financing approached $80 billion, making somewhat ironic the Carter administration's claim to having introduced a balanced budget. This time the housing agencies found their borrowing quotas cut by $10 billion across the board. In their place, the administration programmed an additional $10 billion in borrowings by the Energy Security Corporation, newly created to finance "energy independence" efforts, including synthetic fuels plants, solar power, and the oil reserve pumped into the Louisiana salt domes. Additional borrowing authority appeared for aerospace, railroads, and other military-related industries.

These numbers are relatively small, but promise to balloon enormously. As cited earlier, Carter's proposed $80 billion in synthetic fuels plants is still under congressional debate. But the expected designation of "energy production" as a military requirement under legislation sponsored by Rep. Moorehead of Pennsylvania would permit the Federal Emergency Management Agency, the moment Carter or his successor declares emergency conditions, to ensure that no resources are allocated until the synfuels program has had its fill. In this event the entire $80 billion price tag would be added to the off-budget agencies' borrowing.

Schacht invented this kind of "off-budget" financing in 1934, through the creation of two dummy corporations, the Public Employment Co. and the Metallurgical Research Co., or "Mefo-Institut." Between 1934 and 1937, the Mefo-Institute guaranteed 12 billion Reichsmarks of bills in payment of war production. Technically, Schacht was permitted to buy bills of exchange due for collection in return for Reichsbank cash—a normal central banking function—only on a short-term basis. Mefo-bills' payment schedules were extended to five years. With a government guarantee, the Mefo-bill was the equivalent of cash, except that it earned interest like any commercial paper.

Thus Mefo-bills both circulated among manufacturers and contractors as a means of payment for war production, or were held as an interest-bearing asset by industrialists and banks. As more of this paper cascaded onto the German money market, commercial and savings banks were ordered to invest 30 percent of their deposits into Mefo-bills; securities frozen during the 1929-1931 collapse were "unfrozen" on condition of reinvestment into Mefo-bills; and municipalities, insurance companies, and others were compelled to place almost all their cash balances into Schacht's armaments scrip.

Altogether, Schacht managed to finance half of all military production expenditures in this fashion between 1934 and 1937. The scale of the operation is staggering. Mefo-bills, which were a cash equivalent, grew by 12 billion marks, more than the 9.3 billion mark growth in what Friedman calls the money stock—currency plus bank deposits![19] Factored into the money supply figures, the rate of money supply growth during Schacht's tenure at the Reichsbank was an inflationary 17 percent per annum.

Among other drawbacks, Friedman's "quantity theory" analysis of Nazi Germany is incompetent. However, as Schacht demonstrated, money supply bears no necessary relation to anything. *Schacht compensated for the explosive growth of Mefo-bill financing by shrinking general availability of credit, throwing all available credit into the weapons drive.*

In his valedictory speech as Reichsbank president November 19, 1938, Schacht described the measures he took to "control the course of the expansion of credit."[20] They included limitations of security issues by private firms to clear the capital markets for the Mefo-bills; draining funds from the money markets through the issue of special Gold Discount Bank bills, what we would now call "open market operations"; and direct controls over bank lending. He did not go as far as Milton Friedman, who wants the total elimination of the credit-creating powers of commercial banks, but he did succeed in draining all net available funds into rearmament.[21]

However, Schacht observed that the prospects for success of this operation ended when no additional real economic resources were available for diversion into arms manufacture: "The spring of 1938 signified a new period in our financial policies because then the German economy had reached the condition of full employment. As soon as a national economy had taken up the last available working resources and all available materials, every further credit expansion would not only be senseless but destructive."[22] Hitler's response we cited earlier.

The only real difference between Schacht's Mefo-bills and Carter's off-budget securities is that Schacht, fearful of a panic, kept the size of Mefo-bill issuance secret. Details of the Carter administration's financial operations are available in *Special Analyses of the Budget of the United States,* published by the Office of Management and Budget.

Volcker's aim is to repeat Schacht's achievement, as described by Milton Friedman in *Studies on the Quantity Theory of Money:* to maintain gigantic nonproductive expenditures while preventing an inflationary collapse of the monetary system. Inherently, war production, especially *blitzkrieg* production in-width at a stagnant level of technology, is violently inflationary. Production of energy at costs several times in excess the cost of nuclear-generated electricity is also inflationary, for two reasons. First, the energy-price requirements to finance high-cost energy raise the base rate of inflation through pass-ons of energy prices. More fundamentally, the high-cost energy programs generate inflation by sabotaging capital formation throughout the economy.

Synthetic fuels, secondary oil recovery methods, oil-shale production methods, coal mining of the conventional sort, coal-slurry pipelines, solar power, and other high-cost methods have an incredible appetite for capital goods. These capital goods must be taken away from other sectors. Since the American economy is already running a net deficit in investible goods—that is, it is burning up more of its plant and equipment than it replaces each year—the effects of massive investment in high-cost energy methods would be catastrophic. The result is that the collapse of industrial efficiency throughout the economy due to Schachtian investments lets loose a hyperinflationary tendency.

Despite the *tendency* toward hyperinflation under fascism, it is possible to suppress inflation, at least for some period of time, as Milton Friedman said in his now-classic study of Nazi economics. In a 1976 discussion with LaRouche, the French economist Jacques Rueff proposed an alternative definition of fascist economics as *"inflation turned inward against the economy,"* leading to the same conclusion as LaRouche's different approach. Instead of absorbing the consequences of massive nonproductive spending through increasing price levels, the Nazi economy absorbed these consequences by cannibalizing the economy's own flesh and bone, turning inflation inward. Rueff's definition is precise and correct, and stands in striking contrast to Milton Friedman, who leaves the consequences for the real economy out of his analysis altogether.

In his 1964 book *The Age of Inflation,* Rueff wrote that Hitler ironically found the magical cure for inflation that governments sought:

"In reality, only one man succeeded in coming to terms with inflation—Hitler. He understood that inflation destroys the ties that bind man's desires to reality, and, in so doing, transforms their freedom into a terrible menace to the social order. To save the social order, he sacrificed freedom. By subjecting individual conduct to strict control, he restrained people from utilizing that part of their purchasing power which exceeded the value of the purchaseable wealth. In this way he was able to distribute generously the means of buying goods which did not exist. He turned this lie into a system of government."[23]

Hjalmar Schacht was a monumental liar—witness his performance in the dock at the 1948 Nuremberg War Crimes Tribunal. But Milton Friedman makes him look like a man of integrity. The two factions among the Nazi economic planners (and their present-day disciples) can be characterized as those who merely want to lie to the public, in the deeper sense of Rueff's analysis, and those who want to lie also to themselves.

In his memoirs, Schacht wrote: "The unlimited increase in Government expenditure brings the national finances to the verge of bankruptcy despite an immense taxation screw, and as a result is ruining the Central Bank and the currency. There exists no recipe, no system of financial or money technique . . . to check the devastating effects on currency of a policy of unrestricted spending. No central bank is capable of maintaining the currency against an inflationary spending policy on the part of the State."[24]

To be more precise, Schacht should have said, "capable of so doing for any length of time." He managed to do it by "turning inflation inward against the economy" for some four years. Rueff's analysis establishes the point of failure of Nazi economic policy as the point of exhaustion of real economic resources. No sane person could view the matter any other way. Even Hjalmar Schacht understood this, only making the blunder of trying to explain it to Hitler and Göring.

In a certain way, Milton Friedman takes real economic resources into indirect account, by factoring in the slave populations of Nazi-conquered Europe to "adjust the money supply figures." But he insists that real economic resources had nothing whatsoever to do with the problems of the Nazi economy. He argues that the Nazis permitted civilian economic activity "to operate in a leisurely, semi-peace fashion," and that they failed to "restrict civilian consumption" until efficiency expert Albert Speer took over.[25]

One critical instance of lying by omission must be cited in Milton Friedman's account of Nazi economics. Jacques Rueff pointed it out, with some bitterness: "Contrary to general belief, Dr. Schacht did not invent Hitler's monetary policy."[26] Germany's British and American creditors, Rueff reported, "advised Germany to suspend its foreign commitments and authorized it to put into effect, with the blessing of its creditors, the system that was to enable Dr. Schacht and Hitler to finance war preparations and finally unleash war itself."[27]

Rueff's insight is of the greatest importance. Negotiations for what was called the Standstill Agreement of

1931—which prevailed throughout the 1930s and allowed Germany a moratorium on foreign debts—were an amicable exchange between the London, New York, and German branches of the Warburg and Schroeder banking houses. Paul Warburg, the "father of the Federal Reserve System," and German resident Max Warburg, who remained Schacht's deputy at the Reichsbank until 1938, had jointly made the decision in 1931 to deny Germany further credits and precipitate the great 1931 European banking crisis. The Morgan-influenced American Secretary of State, Henry Stimson, proposed the 1931 moratorium in a way that ensured Hitler's ascendancy in Germany. Max Warburg's collaborator Schacht emerged as the political fixer in German politics, with sufficient clout to tell industrialists who gathered to hear Hitler's exhortations, "Und nun, meine Herren, an die Kasse" ("And now, gentlemen, take your checkbooks out"). Industrialists' levies for Hitler were paid into secret accounts at the Schroeder Bank. Germany's British and American creditors were the underwriters for the Nazis' rise to power.

Through the looking-glass with Milton Friedman

If, as an intellectual exercise, we asked the reader to construct an "economic theory" that could describe Nazi economics as a possibly "successful" system, he would probably start this way: The first condition of this new economic theory would have to be that the real economy never has to be taken into account, and the second condition would have to be that the theorizer can define "reality" to be whatever he wants it to be whenever he wants it to be that way.

You have now grasped the essence of Milton Friedman's economic theory.

The preceding documentation of the facts of the matter is indispensable background to any useful discussion of Milton Friedman's theoretical views as such. In his published output, Friedman carefully distinguishes between his "popular" books such as *Capitalism and Freedom* or *Free to Choose*, and his technical works, including *Studies in the Quantity Theory of Money*, *Essays in Positive Economics*, *A Monétary History of the United States*, and *Milton Friedman's Monetary Framework*. The technical works are unreadable academic jargon that virtually no one reads. However, Friedman sets forth a theory capable of predicting the success of the Nazi system, and the above description of that theory is no exaggeration.

Friedman's early notoriety as a "theorist" sprang from an essay published in 1953 in *Essays in Positive Economics*, entitled, "The Methodology of Positive Economics." He insisted there that his approach was "positive," which he said meant "objective," while everyone else's was by implication "normative," that is, shaped to fit preconceived conclusions. "Friedman's strong implication was that economists who disagreed with him were guilty not only of questionable values or political purposes but also of an unscientific method, a neglect of 'positive economics,' " rankled *New York Times* economics writer Leonard Silk after Friedman was awarded the Nobel Prize.[28] Silk continued: "The most controversial part of Friedman's concept of positive economics was still to come. For it was not merely

52   The Ugly Truth About Milton Friedman

that the validity of hypotheses could be tested by the accuracy of their predictions; rather, this was the only way they could be evaluated. To judge a hypothesis by the realism of its assumptions would be illicit. Thus, he contended, it is wrong to reject the hypothesis of free-market price determination in an industry if it turns out on inspection that the industry is not perfectly competitive; what matters is whether prices are set as if there were perfect competition. Friedman went so far as to make a positive virtue out of 'unrealistic' assumptions."

Let us quote what Friedman had to say on the subject:

"In so far as a theory can be said to have 'assumptions' at all, and in so far as their 'realism' can be judged independently of the validity of predictions, the relation between the significance of a theory and the 'realism' of its 'assumptions' is almost the opposite of that suggested by the view under criticism. *Truly important and significant hypotheses will be found to have assumptions that are wildly inaccurate descriptive representations of reality, and, in general, the more significant the theory, the more unrealistic the assumptions (in this sense).* The reason is simple. A hypothesis is important if it 'explains' much by little, that is, if it abstracts the common and crucial elements from the mass of complex and detailed circumstances surrounding the phenomena to be explained and permits valid predictions on the basis of them alone. *To be important, therefore, a hypothesis must be descriptively false in its assumptions;* it takes account of, and accounts for, none of the many other attendant circumstances, since its very success shows them to be irrelevant for the phenomena to be explained." (emphasis added)[29]

What Is Fascist Economics? 53

If the "predictive value" of theories were the only thing by which to judge them, Friedman has a great deal of wrong predictions to explain, including that Nixon's tight money policy would ease inflation (it did not), that Britain's 1979 tight money program would ease inflation (inflation quadrupled), that application of his free-market principles by the Begin government would reduce Israeli inflation (inflation became so bad that the government will issue a new currency), that oil prices would fall shortly after 1974, and so forth. Friedman has the worst predictive record in the economics profession, itself notorious for failed predictions.

But that is not the important point here. Friedman is making a statement in the tradition of the Bertrand Russell-Ludwig Wittgenstein positivists, restricting the pursuit of knowledge to abstract and arbitrary juggling of empirical data. But not even one of the most extreme Vienna positivists would ever argue that some simple extrapolation of a tendency one chances to hit upon in a data series proves any hypothesis, merely because some other data collected in the future happen to fit into the linear extrapolation trend. In any event, Friedman never succeeded once in explaining anything in this fashion, as readers who have puzzled through *A Monetary History of the United States* well know. It takes a while to sink in, but Milton Friedman means precisely what he says about the realism of assumptions, namely, "the more significant the theory, the more unrealistic the assumptions."

Friedman *does* exactly what he advises. He treats the Nazi economy in terms of monetary flows only, in order to reach the conclusion that Schacht and his successors

54 The Ugly Truth About Milton Friedman

acted correctly, except to the extent they permitted excessive consumption. No special acumen for number-juggling is required to accomplish this. All that is needed is to adopt any arbitrary criterion after the fact, "abstract the common and crucial elements from the mass of complex and detailed circumstances surrounding the phenomenon to be explained," and array the statistics accordingly. Without attributing undue merit to the economics profession, which after all made Friedman the president of its association a decade ago, it is safe to say that Friedman is exceptional in making the most extreme form of radical nominalism the *stated* principle of his methodology. "Words mean what I want them to mean," said Humpty-Dumpty to Alice, but without the unctuous claim that this represented the most objective of all sciences.

What precisely is it that Friedman claims to have achieved as a theoretical economist? In a Mad Hatter's "debate with his critics" published by the University of Chicago in 1970, Friedman stated his claim to fame to be a method of describing economies *in monetary terms only,* without reference to the problem of real economic growth. This is what stands behind Friedman's assertion that the Nazi economy was "successful" from the standpoint of monetary analysis. Waspishly, Friedman accused his critics of misunderstanding him by falsely assuming that he was talking about real economic growth, whereas the "quantity theory of money" has nothing to do with anything but money and prices:

"We have always tried to qualify our statements about the importance of changes in M* by referring to

---

* *Friedman's symbol for money supply.*

their effect on *nominal* income. But this qualification appeared meaningless to economists who implicitly identified nominal with real magnitudes. Hence they have misunderstood our conclusions.

"We have accepted the quantity-theory presumption, and have thought it supported by the evidence we examined, that changes in the quantity of money as such in the long run have a negligible effect on real income, so that nonmonetary forces are 'all that matter' for changes in real income over the decades and money 'does not matter'.... I regard the description of our position as 'money is all that matters for changes in *nominal* income and for *short-run* changes in real income' as an exaggeration but one that gives the right flavor of our conclusions."[30]

The context for this extraordinary statement was an Alice-in-Wonderland exchange with Keynesian James Tobin (who served on John Kennedy's Council of Economic Advisors) and various others. Tobin and the Keynesians do not come off looking too well either—from the standpoint of the intelligent layman who expects economists to tell him how the economy works. Friedman's idea is that if you dump more money into the system, people will spend it and prices will go up:

"The quantity theory of money takes for granted ... that there is a fairly definite real quantity of money that people wish to hold under any given circumstances. Suppose that the nominal quantity that people hold at a particular moment of time happens to correspond at current prices to a real quantity larger than the quantity that they wish to hold. Individuals will then seek to dispose of what they regard as their excess money balances; they will try to pay out a larger sum for the purchase of securities, goods and services, for the repayment of debts, and as gifts that they are receiving from the corresponding sources . . . which will lead to a bidding up of prices and perhaps also to an increase in output."[31]

That is, if you hand more money around, people will go out and spend it, and prices will rise. Friedman's bone of contention with the Keynesians is their argument that output would go up instead of prices, that "quantity was the variable that adjusted rapidly, while price was the variable that adjusted slowly."[32] Keynes also added a long and involved argument that under some conditions, such as the Great Depression of the 1930s, people will refuse to spend their excess cash, no matter how much is floating around. Keynes said this would happen because of "overinvestment" in useful production. Investments would not make a profit any longer, as people would hold onto their cash or its close equivalent—short-term government securities; Keynes called this "absolute liquidity preference." His well-known remedy was to have the government spend it for them, although *not* on anything useful, because that would make matters worse. The government should spend money on nonproductive things, such as digging holes in the ground, according to the British epigram, "Two pyramids, two masses for the dead are better than one; but not so two rail lines from London to Birmingham."[33]

In the Friedman-Tobin debate, equations fly back and forth like cow pancakes. Friedman insists that "prices adjust more rapidly than quantities, indeed, so rapidly that the price adjustment can be regarded as instantaneous." Tobin replies that the "Phillips Curve" sets the "trade-off" between prices and quantity: "A large fraction of the profession is preoccupied with theoretical and empirical investigations" of whether prices or output go up when you dump in more money.[34]

Friedman correctly points out that neither he nor the Keynesians have what he calls the "missing equation" that tells us what the relationship might be between prices and real economic activity. That is true; the "Phillips Curve" that the Keynesians proudly hailed in 1970 said that prices went up when unemployment went down and prices went down when unemployment went up. In these years of combined depressed real economic activity and high inflation, the discredited "Phillips Curve" has disappeared from the academic journals and the financial pages.

The remedy Friedman proposes to the terrible predicament of the economics profession, which admittedly could not find any relationship between prices and output, is breathtakingly simple: ignore the problem altogether. That is no exaggeration; he says it.

Friedman proposes "*bypassing* the breakdown of nominal income between real income and prices and using the quantity theory to derive a theory of nominal income rather than a theory of either prices or real income."[35] This works out nicely, Friedman discovered. "One finding that we have observed is that the relation between changes in the nominal quantity of money and changes in nominal income is almost always closer and more dependable than the relation between changes in

58 The Ugly Truth About Milton Friedman

real income and the real quantity of money or between changes in the quantity of money per unit of output and changes in prices."[36]

"Nominal quantity of money" means how many dollars are sloshing around, and "nominal income" means how much money individuals get, regardless of how much this money can buy. Friedman says that there is a "close and dependable" link between these two things, a conclusion that does not seem particularly striking. Note that he says that the relationship between money and prices and money and output is *not* so dependable—although he does not say so in his *Newsweek* columns or in his television programs.

Where his peers in the academic world were concerned, Friedman's famous assertion that changes in the money supply cause changes in prices fell by the wayside on the last page of his magnum opus, *A Monetary History of the United States*.[37] Friedman could not find any consistent behavior for what is called the "velocity of circulation" of money during the entire postwar period. The way the "quantity theory of money" is supposed to work, Friedman reports, is according to a turn-of-the-century formula penned by Yale professor Irving Fisher, now best-known for a prediction in mid-1929 that the stock market rise proved that the United States would have permanent prosperity from then on.[38]

The formula reads $MV=PT$, where M is money supply, V is its velocity (how fast people spend it), P is the price level, and T is the amount of goods available per unit of time. It says that if there is more money and people spend it faster, prices will rise.

The "bogey" variable is the *velocity of circulation,* or *V.* Monetarists, from Jevons and Marshall a century ago to Friedman now, have put tomes of statistics through analysis in an attempt to explain why *V* goes up or down—without measurable success. Friedman admitted as much in his *Studies in the Quantity Theory of Money* and later in his 1963 monetary history, finally giving up the attempt in his 1970 "debate" with his Keynesian opponents.[39]

In conclusion, that leaves us with a theory that says that if there is a lot of money about, individuals are likely to have a lot of it; the "theory of nominal income." It should not be a surprise that Friedman's academic opponents do not come outright and say that all of Friedman's theories are irrelevant, boring nonsense, considering the quality of their own opposing theories, although they have occasional fun pointing out Friedman's record of off-the-mark predictions.[40]

At the outset, we answered the question "What is fascist economics?" by analogy to loan-sharking methods—the looting of the flesh and bone of the economy to maintain the value of paper claims to income. Milton Friedman's personal contribution to fascist economics adds another dimension to this answer. British System, or monetarist, economics will invariably create monetary crises. The instinctive response of British System economists is to force negative growth policies onto already depleted economies to defer, but in reality worsen, the monetary crisis. The consequences of repeated looting of real economic resources are, as Hitler put it, to base "the stability of our currency" on "the concentration camps."

60 The Ugly Truth About Milton Friedman

Not every public figure or economic policy-maker committed at a given moment to monetarist principles is a fascist; the fascists distinguish themselves by making their irrationalism a matter of pride. That is what makes Milton Friedman so evil. It is not merely that the inner content of his economics is fascist, but that he demands the destruction of every criterion of reason that might hold us back from the horrifying final consequences of his policies.

Rueff versus Friedman

2

> *The truth is that the public interest is not, as is widely believed, the sum of private interests, but its opposite. Consequently, the real political problem is finding a system whereby the general interest can prevail against the aggregate of individual wills.*
> —Jacques Rueff, 1964

France's brilliant monetary economist, Jacques Rueff, is known in the United States as an opponent of John Maynard Keynes, but not of Milton Friedman, his opponent in a twenty-year struggle over the future of the international monetary system. More importantly, the American conservatives who have expressed their high regard for Rueff do not understand his accomplishments, and, in their ignorance, what has been lost is the knowledge of how "American System" economics works.

Rueff towered above the squabble between the "monetarist" and "Keynesian" versions of British System economics, and located himself in the continuity of

Benjamin Franklin's collaboration with the founders of the École Polytechnique. As the author of President de Gaulle's great launching of the French economy in the years after 1958, he emerged at the end of a long career not only as an economist of great stature, but as one of America's best friends abroad—the persistent critic of America's self-destructive course.

It is not outrageous to identify Jacques Rueff as a "protectionist" in the American System sense of the word. His objective was to design the credit system to protect the productive sectors of the economy from speculative abuses through misuse of the public credit. Specifically, the task of monetary policy is to bind the individual will to the national purpose, by identifying the prosperity of the individual with the economic growth of the nation, "finding a system whereby the general interest can prevail over the aggregate of individual wills." Bitterly opposed to the Keynesian mode of government intervention, which breeds inflation by promoting nonproductive investment, Rueff wielded power as de Gaulle's economic plenipotentiary as a *dirigiste* in the tradition of Jean-Baptiste Colbert.

In modern form, Rueff's economics are an extension of Alexander Hamilton's 1790 *Report on Public Credit.* The state must destroy speculation in its public debt, Hamilton wrote, because "being only an object of occasional and particular speculation, all the money applied to it is so much diverted from the more useful channels of circulation . . . [and is] a pernicious drain of our cash from the channels of productive industry." The task of monetary policy is to ensure that sufficient credit resources are available to "the channels of productive industry," to "enable both the public and individuals to borrow on easier and cheaper terms," said Hamilton.[1]

American System economics is a moral science. The standard for judging alternative policies is their impact on the moral and intellectual powers of the population. For Hamilton, Mathew and Henry Carey, Friedrich List, and other leaders of the American School, economics was the science of nation-building. For them, as for de Gaulle and Rueff, the republican nation-state was the vehicle for the perfection of its citizens, for the continuous enhancement of their ability to master science and culture. The task of the nation-state is to protect the resources of its citizens, not the least of which its public credit, from their internal and external enemies. The Careys and List fought successfully for trade protection, against Great Britain's attempts to undermine American and German industrialization through commercial war. Rueff, who dissolved many of France's trade barriers into the European Economic Community founded by de Gaulle and West German Chancellor Konrad Adenauer, was no less a "protectionist" in his campaign to destroy speculative encroachment on the French, and later the international, monetary system.

Rueff demanded that competent monetary policy ensure that public finances follow the development of real economic resources. The potential for economic growth—namely, the surplus of goods available for investment into new production—must be matched to the pool of credit that will finance these investments. But this credit pool is made up of the savings of thousands of households and corporations. If government policy has cheated citizens by investing their savings nonproductively, thereby creating inflation, they will refuse to invest, unless Hjalmar Schacht and men in black uniforms are there to make such saving and investment compulsory.

That is the situation de Gaulle faced after his dramatic accession to power in 1958, averting a fascist coup in preparation. The Algerian war (which de Gaulle quickly ended) and other nonproductive government excesses had left France with the weakest currency among the major European nations, high and rising inflation, and a $2.5 billion budget deficit—huge relative to the size of France's economy and then-prevailing currency values. The reaction of the French population to creeping economic disaster was predictable; fleeced many times in the past, they behaved like scared sheep. French citizens either sent their capital abroad in the form of purchases of stronger currencies, or, more importantly, buried it in the ground in the form of gold. The "lying" monetary policy of the French government had turned the "individual wills" of French citizens into those of raving anarchists. Private gold hoards alone were estimated at 3,000 tons, or $2.5 billion at the then $35 per ounce gold price—about equal to the 1958 budget deficit.

The emergency plan Rueff drew up for de Gaulle—and de Gaulle acted upon—did not propose to reduce inflation through fiscal austerity, but through *increased investment* in the productivity of the French economy. The possibility of breaking the inflationary cycle in such Promethean fashion—to use Rueff's word for his approach—could never occur in the irrational mind of a Milton Friedman. The plan worked because Rueff convinced the French population that it *would* work, in one of the most striking calls to action issued by any government. His task force at the French finance ministry wrote in 1959:

"The history of France has entered upon a new phase. The wave of productivity upon which she has risen will, within a few years, create a young country, facing the future with eagerness, and once more equal to the highest destiny. In an inspired effort of anticipation—by an unprecedented economic expansion—the country has already prepared the means of its recovery.

"But the growth achieved has not yet nearly reached the level called for by the nation's responsibilities.

"If it were desired merely to maintain the existing level of development of an increased population, it would be necessary to invest immense sums in schools, in infrastructural development, in construction of housing and in job opportunities.

"Yet to do no more than this would be to remain hopelessly inadequate to the task. To accomplish the task would mean, in the course of the coming years,

- To develop the Sahara;
- To raise the standard of living of the peoples that have lately reaffirmed their loyalty to and confidence in France;
- To modernize the national defense;
- To develop and convert power installations so as to retain the benefits of technological progress;
- To continue modernization and growth of productive plant in the spheres of agriculture, industry, and commerce;
- To improve facilities for scientific research;
- To expand medical and hospital services;
- To foster the advance of social welfare by all suitable means.

"At the same time France is under a basic imperative

to remedy, without delay, the housing crisis that is undermining her social structure, freezing the distribution of labor in a manner highly injurious to industrial progress, inflicting cruel and unjust suffering on wide sections of the population and turning them into confirmed enemies of the social order.

"For many years to come, all France's problems will be problems of investment. France will not be taking full advantage of the opportunity that offers unless these are successfully solved, not in a spirit of apathy and decadence, but with the dedication called for by the task to be accomplished and by the greatest rewards to be won."[2]

From his command post in the finance ministry, Rueff used the same method as Lyndon LaRouche in campaign appearances before "town meetings" during the 1980 presidential primary campaign: appeal to the morality of the population. The most criminal facet of inflationary economic policies is their effect on the moral outlook of the population, breeding an everyman-for-himself outlook. France underwent in 1958 the same kind of crisis the United States is going through now. British System economic mismanagement leads to a threshold of economic breakdown. The crisis is resolved either by Schacht's blackshirt methods, or by throwing out the British System. But that cannot be done simply by putting the right policies on paper. As Rueff knew, the first step is to correct the damage done to the moral powers of the population. Once the population is committed to an economic program founded on science and technology, economic recovery is possible. That was the cutting edge of Rueff's plan to break the inflationary cycle.

The immediate problem was the enormity of the French budget deficit. Rueff threw out all the mystical nonsense about "balanced budgets" and "inflationary government spending" now circulated in the United States by Friedman and his dupes. He noted, with some scorn, that while Anglo-American economists call a deficit whatever the government spends in excess of tax revenues, French economists are concerned only with spending in excess of what the government can tax *or borrow*.[3] If the government can finance expenditures by convincing savers to buy its securities, it is not in deficit. "We have inflation because there are not enough savings on the market; and there are not enough savings on the market because there is inflation. The problem is to get out of this vicious circle.... The way to do it is create a situation of certainty that the public expenditure will in no case exceed the cumulative sum of receipts from taxation and savings."[4] But Rueff did it not by cutting expenditures, but by increasing savings.

"We have been told that our plan was a deflationary one," his finance ministry report continued. "This was a dreadful lie; the [1959] budget in its present state includes 28 percent more investment than the 1958 budget and, as a result, we are going to be able to carry out all the tasks which had been written into our budget, in other words, the building of schools, housing, the development of atomic energy, our energy policy in general, the equipment of our nationalized industries, the equipment of Algeria, all the projects of the Economic and Social Development Fund, which will be carried out according to plan."[5]

Getting the savings to invest in these projects was a trivial matter, said Rueff, once the population believed that the economy was on the road to higher productivity. "The supply of savings on the market—whether derived from current savings or from savings previously hoarded—is by no means unchangeable. It is controlled by individual decisions, and especially by the responses of savers to the monetary outlook.... Investment of a small share of [the hoarded gold] in French securities would substantially expand possibilities of issue on the market, and would, other things being equal, contribute decisively to the solution of our investment problems."[6] He was right. Within the next year, the Banque de France took in 150 tons of gold, which hoarders gave up in return for sound Treasury securities.

Both Friedmanite "fiscal conservatism" and Keynesian "fiscal stimulus" will fail, Rueff repeated until his colleagues understood it. "At present, concern for lessening the deficit in public finances takes the form of penurious restriction on the amount of investments undertaken by the Treasury. And yet that amount is never limited sufficiently to arrest the process of progressive deterioration characteristic of inflation; the limitation is sufficient, though, to prevent contemplation of all the increased investments that the present situation requires. A chasm yawns between the jealously restrained and hotly debated investments we appropriate to plans of modernization or to housing construction programs, and the recovery that would be made possible by restoration of a real money market. All the past experience goes to show that so far from sacrificing investment, an end to inflation would call forth those financial resources essential to the joyful accomplishment, without glum negation, without paralyzing distinctions, of the tasks with which circumstances are confronting France."[7]

Stopping inflation—by increasing investment in productivity of labor and eliminating unproductive spending—"will promptly bring abundant repatriated capital into the financial market, lower all interest rates—especially long-term rates—significantly, and thereby expand capacity for public or private credit."[8]

Rueff's package became law on December 7, 1958. By March, $600 million of French savings held abroad had returned to the French money markets. Inflation fell during 1959 to 4 percent—about half its previous level. France's foreign payments balance corrected from a $100 million deficit in 1958 to nearly $2 billion in surplus the next year. Industrial production rose by 12 percent. All in all, the economic results of 1959 were the best since Liberation. "Some of our early critics, when confronted with actual facts, called this a miracle," Rueff wrote ten months after his program went into effect. "The speed of change was so surprising that they insisted it was the result of exceptional circumstances. I beg to differ. Everything that has taken place in France in economic and financial terms since January 1959 is absolutely normal. All the results recorded since then have been the direct and unavoidable consequences of the reforms of December 27, 1958."[9]

The method of the American System

From this account, it is clear how far Rueff stands above the mindless quibbling over monetary technicalities we reviewed at the conclusion of the last chapter. The debate between Friedman and the Keynesians over whether fiscal and monetary stimulus will increase production or increase prices is irrelevant. High rates of economic growth based on investment in new technologies are "absolutely normal," Rueff demonstrated. The only issue in monetary policy is to see to it that the monetary system and the real economy are in alignment, that credit flows to productive investments.

LaRouche's economic methodology defines with rigor the need for industrially oriented credit expansion through sound national banking practices. Although Rueff, in reaction to the spread of Keynes's influence in the 1950s and 1960s, expressed great caution against money expansion of the Keynesian variety, he was in agreement with LaRouche on this point.

Following the principles of national accounting universally accepted until the advent of John Stuart Mill and subsequent chicanery in the economics profession—LaRouche analyzes the value of the economy's tangible output in terms of the reproduction costs of capital and labor inputs at the economy's existing scale, or constant capital (C) and variable capital (V); the overhead costs of the economy, including education, health, national security, as well as various forms of unneeded waste, or d; and a surplus of tangible output above overhead expenses, or $S - d$, or S'.

Contrary to the Malthusians and Milton Friedman, the production and subsequent productive investment of S' is not a privilege but a fundamental condition of continued economic existence. That margin of society's resources available for employment of additional population or more productive employment of the existing workforce, defined by S', represents more than simple economic growth at existing technological levels. The mere growth of an economy within a fixed technological mode—something that never occurred and could never have occurred for any significant period of economic history—would rapidly produce a crisis of scarce resources. The more successful a given technological level, the more rapidly it exhausts the materials that that level of technology defines as resources. What the Club of Rome argues to be a "final solution" for economic growth is the perpetual challenge to science of the past 10,000 years of economic history. Without successively defining domestic animals, water power, coal, oil, and nuclear fuels as power sources, the human species would have ceased to exist long ago.

The relevance of this to monetary economics is direct and immediate. New technology can only be introduced into economies through state-directed creation of credit, under the national banking systems first invented by the nation-builder Jean-Baptiste Colbert in the seventeenth century, and subsequently refined into the modern form by Alexander Hamilton in his 1790 *Report on the Public Credit*. The monetary equivalents of our divisions of the gross tangible output of an economy—C, V, d, and S'—are *not necessarily* in direct correspondence with the actual produced wealth. In general terms:

Constant capital = total purchases of raw and intermediate materials, and manufacturing and other equipment;

Variable capital = total wages of goods-producing workers;

d = total interest, rent, profit and salaried income of nongoods-producing workers;

S' = all households' savings plus corporate profits, also called corporate savings.

Savings are the national fund for investment. By centralizing these savings, the equity markets and financial institutions provide capital to corporations and entrepreneurs to purchase those goods corresponding to S' for new investment. However, even under conditions of relative prosperity, the unconsumed portion of monetary income, or savings, is inferior to the total volume of tangible output available for new productive investment. Under conditions of rapidly rising labor productivity, through the absorption of new technologies into the production process, the total output expands faster than savings available either as risk-capital, or equity, or loan-capital. Various anarchistic radicals take this to imply some fundamental "contradiction" in capitalism, in the form of the silly "buy-back" problem that states that the capitalist pays workers less than the value of the goods they produce, thus making the workers unable to buy back the product of their labors.

In fact, competent national banking policy works to add a margin of state-created fiat credit to the pool of savings, corresponding to the amount of S' produced in excess of savings. Central banks create money by purchasing government securities or commercial paper in return for the fiat currency of the central bank. Under capitalist finance, the central bank works in cooperation with private commercial banks, purchasing either their holdings of government securities or other paper. In the United States this is "discount window borrowing" at the Federal Reserve. However, central banks must be cautious, ensuring that the bank notes printed are used to purchase capital goods for expanding production. If such fiat money were distributed in some other way, it would tend to inflate the currency, with only some portion of that inflation offset by capital purchases.

As long as the state creates money through lending by national banks to purchasers of productive capital, no error is introduced. If the investment is sound, the wealth put into circulation by the new production will exceed the money created to enable the investment. Rueff's emphasis on these points is entirely correct. He insisted that the central bank must limit its expansion of credit to "real bills," that is, to commercial paper representing an exchange of useful goods. "There can be no inflation as long as the quantity of currency in circulation is proportional to the total volume of desired cash holdings. In other words, as long as any increase in the money supply is desired [for circulation of real wealth], it has no effect on prices. There is no inflation as long as the money supply reflects a need for more liquidity."[10]

Rueff's treatment of the investment problem during the 1958 crisis is in harmony with LaRouche's statement of the need to keep interest rates significantly below the average rate of profit, so that interest costs as such do not inhibit long-term capital investment and penalize risk-capital in favor of debt-capital. As the 1958 "miracle" showed, by ensuring that state finances contribute to productive investment and penalize nonproductive investments, the aggregate of produced wealth rises faster than payments obligations, reducing inflation. This permits industrial investors to attract an orderly flow of savings at low interest rates.

In a capitalist economy, there are two "rates of profit": the rate of profit on capital, and the rate of creation of free energy in the form of tangible wealth. The first is measured by the prevailing rate of interest and rate of return on industrial equity, adjusting for risk and liquidity. The second is expressed by the term $S'/(C + V)$, or the amount of investible surplus produced in any given period divided by constant plus variable capital expenditures, or economic maintenance costs. *Inflation occurs when demands for revenue on the part of paper capital exceed the "real" profit in tangible terms of the economy.* Since interest rates reflect inflation, inflation becomes self-feeding at the point that interest rates rise above the rate of return available to industrial equity—precisely the formula Keynes proposed in order to restrict industrial investment.

The introduction of new technology is the means by which tangible profit may rise at a faster rate than paper profit. The contraction of equity investment thus puts the economy into a spiraling industrial decline. Conversely, investment policies that channel available capital into realization of new technologies produce a fall in the general price level, the "typical" condition of the U.S. economy during the late nineteenth-century industrial boom.

The contrary argument, which Milton Friedman plagiarized from opium-trade economist David Ricardo, insists that money expansion must remain fixed in all cases. In particular, it militates against the mere possibility of credit expansion through a private banking system, through so-called 100 percent reserve banking, a favorite Milton Friedman prescription since 1947.[11] Only under extraordinary conditions would the available supply of savings be sufficient to reinvest the margin of expansion of total output, or S', *under conditions of fixed technology.* Introduction of new technologies, which increase *the rate of increase* of economic expansion, would be flatly impossible, according to Friedman. In opposition to Rueff, the Chicago School and its Vienna School counterparts demand a Malthusian regime of zero technological growth, under the pretext of opposing "inflationary" credit expansion.

Credit expansion of the nonproductive, Keynesian variety is inflationary; but the monetarist effort to turn this possibility into an argument for the end of Hamiltonian national banking is a fraud.

At the height of his career, Rueff grounded his economics in Charles de Gaulle's political leadership, and this is the explanation for why his economic policies worked. Economics is a moral science, whose success depends upon rallying the population to that sense of national purpose that Friedman scorns as unnecessary. The tradition upon which the American System rests, is that tradition of nation-builders that sees economics as the science of uplifting the moral and intellectual powers of the population. This includes the Carey-List faction of economists in the United States and Germany a century ago; the French nineteenth-century economists Claude Chaptal and Charles Dupin; Louis XIV's finance minister Jean-Baptiste Colbert; and the "American faction" of Benjamin Franklin's European collaborators. LaRouche's conception of economics as physics—through which the enhanced mental powers of mankind are mediated—prevailed among the leading French economists of the American Revolution years, including Lazare Carnot, Gaspard Monge, and their students of the École Polytechnique. Rueff, whose closest intellectual collaborator was the great French physicist Louis de Broglie, argued passionately for the identity of moral and physical science:

"If the moral order is the outcome of an orientation of the behavior of a human being with regard to himself and the order of law—mainly of his behavior in relation to other human beings—then the economic order is the result of the orientation of the behavior of human beings in the administration of their earthly habitat, including its planetary and possibly its stellar extensions—that is to say, all the goods the universe has placed at their disposal."[12] Man transforms the universe through "Promethean intervention," Rueff wrote.

Rueff conserved for modern France the great tradition of Carnot's students Charles Dupin and Claude Chaptal. These economists took Carnot's definition of higher forms of self-organization of energy in physics as their starting point, drawing on Alexander Hamilton's concept that the sole measure of wealth was the rise in the productive powers of labor. Dupin wrote in 1827:

"I call productive powers the unified powers of men, of animals and nature, applied through labor in agriculture, manufacture, and trade. These powers do not stand still; they grow with the rise of peoples and decline with their fall. In the case of our country I have tried to measure not their present value, but their rate of growth, which must be the gauge of all our hopes. . . . These powers have no pure material and physical effect: their regulator, brake and accelerator are human spirit, patience, and will power. For this reason, the capacity for reason and morality of peoples is necessarily and in the closest possible way connected with their productive and commercial powers."[13]

One can see Rueff nodding in agreement with Forbonnais, the chief economic theoretician of the "American party" in eighteenth-century France:

"Only credit which is actually directed toward the production of real income is worthy of the name wealth. Properties which bring forth no annual production incorporate only a sort of wealth that draws income, but is not wealth in its real meaning; we will call such properties 'commodities.' For this reason land that does not produce and industry that does not manufacture, that is, bring new wealth into circulation, are not real wealth; they merely represent commodities which might indeed be transformed into wealth, if they are set into motion."[14]

The entire success of Rueff's 1958 program is based on a comprehension of the difference between productive and nonproductive investment. That Rueff did not solve the problem of deterministic models of economic growth, which began with LaRouche's 1951 work on the implications of Riemannian mathematics for economic science, is beside the point for our purpose here; we will present LaRouche's solution, with the results of the LaRouche-Riemann computer-based economic model, in the final chapter.

What is more important is Rueff's role as an international statesman during the 1960s and 1970s, in the cause of a new world monetary system. Again, Rueff's role stands in the tradition of the "Grand Design" of his predecessors, including Chaptal and Dupin, whose work was determining for the success of Friedrich List's German *Zollverein* (Customs Union) and the exponential growth of German industry.

The monetary system: the crux of the issue

The year 1958 marked a turning point in the postwar period, in which de Gaulle's coming to power was an international event of the greatest importance. De Gaulle and Rueff brought France into economic alliance with Konrad Adenauer's West Germany in the European Common Market, the foundation of a new Grand Design for world economic development and international security. Rueff's reforms and the Common Market created an economically strong Europe and a bloc of strong European currencies for the first time since the end of the Second World War, at the same time that the U.S. dollar began to show the weakening effects of the flawed international economic policy America had adopted under the Truman administration. The American payments deficit and sterling and dollar crises of the 1960s led in a direct line to the catastrophic events of August 1971, when the Nixon administration removed gold backing from the dollar.

To Rueff, this consequence was the foreseeable result of the defects in the International Monetary Fund-centered monetary system, and he fought for its reform until the end of his life. Others foresaw the demise of the dollar, from the City of London and Wall Street side, but thought it untimely to announce prematurely that "controlled disintegration of the international monetary system is a legitimate objective," as the New York Council on Foreign Relations did at length in a 1979 study. There is one exception: From the early 1950s onward, Milton Friedman demanded "controlled disintegration" of the monetary system, specifying the unfortunate steps that President Nixon would take in 1971.

With hindsight, we know that only two paths could emerge from the unstable trajectory of the monetary system founded at Bretton Woods in 1944: The Grand Design of de Gaulle, Pope Paul VI, and LaRouche; or the "controlled disintegration" project of the Anglo-

American financial oligarchy. These two policies now coexist, embodied in the European Monetary System and the International Monetary Fund, in a situation of dual power. Retrospectively, the monetary history of the 1960s was a debate between Rueff, LaRouche, and others in one camp, and Milton Friedman in the other. Although Friedman comes from the "mainstream conservatism" of Wesley Clair Mitchell and Arthur Burns—later we will show what a hoax this is—he has carved out a role as a "fringe element" who blurts out policies that his more "respectable" colleagues do not wish to state.

The Marshall Plan, as Secretary of State George Marshall first envisioned it, was to carry out Roosevelt's threat to dismantle the British Empire and replace it with a regime of American-sponsored world development. It became the 180-degree reverse in implementation. The State Department Policy Planning Staff turned effective control of the plan over to Britain, and diverted the largest single share of Marshall Plan aid, $3.4 billion of the $14 billion total, to London.[15] Instead of piercing the boil that the pound sterling left on the international monetary scene after the war, the Marshall Plan, as well as the International Monetary Fund, bailed out the sterling monetary area, building into the monetary system a detonator for the exchange crises that exploded in the late 1960s.

The Marshall Plan undermined the dollar's long-run stability by intentionally *restricting* American exports to war-stricken Europe. Europe was compelled to rebuild, in some cases literally, out of its own rubble. The Marshall Plan's official target was to reduce European imports from the United States to $2.7 billion for 1952-1953, against $3 billion in 1938—at the trough of the Depression—and $6.7 billion in 1947. Under the direction of British treasury official Sir Eric Roll, Harlan Cleveland (now chairman of the Aspen Institute), and George Kennan's State Department planners, the Marshall Plan succeeded in reducing America's exports to trifling levels compared to those of other industrial countries. Britain offered America the status not of a world industrial power but of a rentier.

After the European currency devaluation of 1947 (begun by the British with the secret connivance of the American Treasury) and the postwar collapse of European wage-scales, American investors could buy capital and labor in Europe at roughly one-quarter the comparable American prices (although at considerably lower productivity levels). Private capital, not industrial exports, flowed across the Atlantic to Europe; most American exports were food or coal supplies.[16]

Simultaneously, the International Monetary Fund, the central monetary institution formed at Bretton Woods, imposed a "fiscal austerity" regimen on developing nations, preventing them from absorbing large-scale American industrial exports, which would have implied trade deficits forbidden under the IMF's Rules of Agreement.

America became a continental, not a world, industrial power, hemmed in by the postwar monetary blueprint authored by John Maynard Keynes, Britain's negotiator at Bretton Woods. From a position of unchallenged strength at the war's end, the American dollar became a deficit currency by 1958 and a bankrupt currency in 1971. The era of dollar weakness began as soon as

Europe, by virtue of enormous and prolonged sacrifice, recovered from the war, despite the flawed Marshall Plan.

The dollar's obituary was already the subject of memoranda among Marshall Plan economists in 1950, when Robert Triffin, the bright young man of the "Austrian School" of von Hayek and von Mises, became Special Advisor on Policy, Trade and Finance to the Economic Cooperation Administration, the government agency that administered the Marshall Plan. Under him worked Milton Friedman, newly notorious for his extreme monetarist views. Triffin, a Jesuit-trained Belgian, came to the U.S. government via Harvard University. He became the leading postwar proponent of Keynes's original scheme to eliminate the dollar as an international currency altogether, in favor of a "one-world" currency like the present Special Drawing Right controlled by the International Monetary Fund. Friedman, his consultant, took the apparently opposite, but actually compatible position that chaos should be allowed to take its course, in a memorandum later republished as "The Case for Flexible Exchange Rates."[17]

Under what were considered normal conditions until 1971, central banks maintained the respective prices of their currencies against each other and against an international standard, gold. World trade necessitates such stability. If the values of currencies shifted continuously, exporters, importers, and international investors would have no way of knowing what the future price of the currencies they are to be paid in would be, except through enormously expensive hedging operations. But Friedman insisted that chaos should be the acceptable norm of economic affairs, and nations should accept that notion by abandoning fixed rates:

"The nations of the world cannot prevent changes from occurring in the circumstances affecting international transactions. And they would not if they could. For many changes reflect natural changes in weather conditions and the like; others arise from the freedom of countless individuals to order their lives as they will, which it is our ultimate goal to preserve and widen; and yet others contain the seeds of progress and development. The prison and the graveyard alone provide even a close approximation to certainty."[18]

In particular, Friedman justified the floating rates regime on military grounds: "A really serious rearmament drive is almost certain to produce inflationary pressure, differing in degree from country to country because of differences in fiscal structures, monetary systems, temper of the people, the size of the rearmament effort, etc. With rigid exchange rates, these divergent pressures introduce strains and stresses that are likely to interfere with the armament effort."[19]

Friedman cannot be accused of lack of foresight here. America formally agreed to end the world role of the dollar in 1965, after Treasury Secretary Henry Fowler told Lyndon Johnson that if he wanted to finance the Vietnam War, he would have to junk the dollar for the IMF's Special Drawing Rights, historian William Wiseley reported. Wiseley noted maliciously that Britain's Field Marshal Lord Carver persuaded the United States to get into Vietnam in the first place. Vietnam did not create the 1960s dollar crisis any more than the Algerian conflict created the French franc crisis of 1958, but it did provide the final blow.

Friedman added to this prescription in late 1968—when he began to advise Richard Nixon, the President-elect—that the United States should eliminate gold from the monetary system, and "set the dollar free by stopping pegging the dollar." He told an American Economics Association conference gleefully, "Each of these steps is within the unilateral control of the U.S. No other country can by its action prevent us from taking them."[20] The most Europe could do in response to shotgun monetary diplomacy, Friedman suggested, was "to try to set up a kind of gold bloc whose currencies would be linked at fixed rates to one another but fluctuate as a group vis-a-vis the dollar." In August 1971, to the disbelieving outrage of the Europeans, Nixon took Friedman's advice, at the urging of then Undersecretary of the Treasury Paul Volcker.[21]

Friedman's vision of a "gold bloc" in Europe accurately describes the first, present phase of the European Monetary System, which European leaders envision as "the seed-crystal of a new world monetary system." In effect, Friedman boasted that European monetary stabilization efforts could be contained to that continent, and that the American policy of "controlled disintegration" would prevail in world affairs.

Jacques Rueff was determined that this would not happen.

Instead of abusing the dollar's international acceptability as a reserve currency by running continuous payments deficits, he argued in a June 1961 essay in the Paris daily *Le Monde* that the United States should pay its foreign obligations in gold. Rueff did not suggest that the United States should give up its gold stocks (as it did, in fact, give up half of them before 1971). He instead proposed an increase in the gold price relative to all currencies, which would enable America to meet its foreign obligations in gold. The contents of the *Le Monde* article, which Rueff had earlier sent to President de Gaulle in memorandum form, set off an international controversy that lasted throughout the 1960s. Until LaRouche's 1974 "Golden Snake" proposal, which projected what later became Phase One of the European Monetary System, Rueff was the authoritative spokesman for the politics of the Grand Design in the monetary sphere. Relative to LaRouche's more comprehensive formulation of the required new international monetary system, Rueff's plan was simple, but no less effective. The United States was an underexporting nation, Rueff wrote, and required a discipline by which to correct the tendency toward rentier status of the postwar period.

Emphatically, the problem was not excess money supply creation: "Internal credit expansion has not been the main fault of the system. The main fault of the system has been the gold-exchange standard," the system by which America could compel other central banks to treat its IOU's as the equivalent of gold.[22] The problem could not be dealt with by tightening domestic money conditions in the United States: "It would be much more complex than is generally recognized in the over-simple contentions based on the quantity theory of money," Rueff said disparagingly of Friedman's argument.[23] The Friedman method of dealing with excessive credit creation "aims at offsetting in one single operation the cumulative effect of excess purchasing power, often of protracted duration . . . in every circumstance, if it is to be effective, it must bring on a deflation of considerable magnitude. It subjects the economy to a sort of shock treatment and has a painful impact."[24] This must be avoided, Rueff wrote. In particular, "in no case" should there be a decline in wages.[25]

Therefore, Rueff proposed a rise in the gold price, combined with the obligation to meet international deficits through gold transfers, to enable (and compel) the United States to make sufficient resources available for export—the point of the entire proposal.[26] The effect would not be a Friedmanite deflation, but would be "slow and gradual . . . hardly perceptible from the social point of view."[27] The Rueff plan had nothing whatsoever to do with the "invisible hand" regulator in British economists' depiction of the nineteenth-century gold standard. On the contrary, "due to the substantial credit margin they involve, monetary systems based on gold are endowed with considerable flexibility and afford broad opportunities for contracyclical action by the monetary authorities."[28] The gold standard is the proper framework for government intervention into the economy in a system of sovereign nation-states.

De Gaulle made the Rueff plan official French policy at a February 4, 1965, press conference, at which the French President proposed a rise in the gold price that would permit the United States to meet its foreign obligations—which grew during the 1960s to a swollen $61 billion—in gold. This provoked hysteria in London and Washington. The London *Economist* sent economist Fred Hirsch to Paris to interview Rueff a week later.

The secret of de Gaulle's ability to terrorize London on this score is that the Rueff plan was *not*—as the

London *Economist* and the American press lied—mere French anti-Americanism. On the contrary, as Richard Nixon came to understand too late, it was the only policy suited to American's national interest. In no way did the U.S. balance of payments deficit benefit the United States. It benefited London. Dollars leaking abroad were jobbed out through the Eurodollar market—the market in foreign-held dollars—by British banks. The Eurodollar market, which eventually grew to over $1 trillion, gave the bankrupt City of London a new lease on life. During the 1950s, when American payments were still strong, the once-great City of London was a virtual ghost town, in which fewer than one dozen foreign banking institutions did business. Despite liberal infusions of Marshall Plan and International Monetary Fund assistance, the dying British pound could not survive as an international lending currency, especially after Eisenhower and Khrushchev jointly crushed Prime Minister Anthony Eden's Suez adventure in 1956.

The miraculous rebirth of the City, and its ten-year evolution into the world's biggest banking center, began with the U.S. payments deficit. Anglophile Secretary of the Treasury C. Douglas Dillon and his Undersecretary Robert V. Roosa presented the British with an extraordinary gift in 1962: They concocted a means of making it more lucrative to hold dollars in London than in New York, thus underwriting London's return to financial power. This was the Interest Equalization Tax, which penalized American loans to foreigners. Nominally a way to stop the outflow of dollars, the tax simply enabled dollar-holders to earn a premium by lending them out from London, free of tax.

The growth of British banking business that resulted was so rapid that in his 1968 pitch for throwing out gold, Milton Friedman could tempt American bankers with the prospect that "the Eurodollar market will shrivel and New York will become in the final decades of the twentieth century what London was in the final decades of the nineteenth century."[29] As we shall see momentarily, New York got the shaft after gold went.

The Eurodollar market was a highly leveraged, rapid-turnover racket of the sort that the British have run since the 1773 crisis shifted the Amsterdam capital market to London.[30] Its existence and de Gaulle's international development objectives were incompatible. But the de Gaulle policy of industrializing the developing sector was the policy Franklin Roosevelt had proposed—to Churchill's mortified objections—at the 1944 Casablanca conference.

As LaRouche demonstrates in a forthcoming textbook, *Mathematical Economics,* the extension of industrialization at the highest levels of technology is the least-action path of development for the industrial countries themselves. By introducing high-technology industry into the so-called Third World, and bringing the developing countries' populations into the industrial labor force, the advanced sector countries cheapen the cost of their imports from these countries, through the rise in the productivity of labor in the developing sector. In somewhat fragmented form, this is the policy Japan has followed with respect to Taiwan and South Korea, investing heavily in shipbuilding, steel, and construction, and obtaining future imports of Japan's own requirements in these areas at low cost.[31] Enunciated by de Gaulle, the strategy for international development was the content of Pope Paul VI's encyclical *De Populorum Progressio (On the Progress of Peoples),* incorporating the policy elements that took their most elaborated form in LaRouche's 1975 International Development Bank proposal.[32]

Industrializing the developing sector, however, was not the objective of the 1944 Bretton Woods system. By 1965 and 1968, meetings of the International Monetary Fund had turned into scenes reminiscent of Western-movie saloon fights. The Anglo-Americans, following Johnson's capitulation to Secretary of Treasury Fowler's 1965 advice, proposed getting rid of both the dollar *and* gold, in favor of some form of international paper standard, along the lines of the original Keynes (later Robert Triffin) proposal cited above. This plan, still fought out bitterly at the most recent IMF meeting in Hamburg on April 26, 1980, would make the International Monetary Fund a world central bank with explicit or implicit powers to dictate financial policy to every capitalist country—in the way it already does to Third World countries.

The differences between this arrangement and the Milton Friedman plan, which would leave the International Monetary Fund with the only important base of power in the storm of "floating exchange rates," are trivial. The content of the international monetary debate must be sought at the level of international trade and development policy. The British and their American friends insisted upon maintaining British imperial policy of enforced colonial backwardness and investment in raw materials extraction rather than industry. The European faction, led by de Gaulle and Pope Paul VI, and for which Jacques Rueff was chief economic theoretician, insisted on financial arrangements conducive to long-term, large-scale international development lending. Gold standard stability is the indispensable condition for long-term capital provision to the developing sector.[33]

France's representative to the IMF, Finance Minister Michel Debré, blocked the British plan until late in 1968. Then, in a virtual repeat performance of the Jacobin riots in 1789, when Lord Shelburne's agents Marat and Danton unleashed the gigantic destabilization of Britain's enemy France,[34] British-controlled anarchists initiated the May 1968 events, which weakened de Gaulle's political authority. NATO intelligence-controlled sections of the French Communist Party around Louis Althusser, anarchist ideologues like Jean-Paul Sartre, and the directly British-controlled Situationist International, combined to initiate a short-lived general strike.

The collapse of the French franc that September undermined de Gaulle's ability to guide international monetary affairs, and it was the unpleasant job of a new finance minister, Valéry Giscard d'Estaing, to go to the International Monetary Fund and make a temporary peace with the British. De Gaulle's ouster and the accession of Willy Brandt's Social Democrats to power in West Germany put the world on direct course toward the August 1971 debacle, and postponed the international development strategy for another decade.[35]

How much the United States lost when its great wartime ally and postwar friend Charles de Gaulle departed office is not understood by most Americans. President Nixon is one of the few who had an inkling; he saw the postwar political leadership of the West "in the shadows of those two giants, Eisenhower and de Gaulle."[36] Despite Nixon's great personal regard for de Gaulle, his comprehension of what the French President and his adviser Rueff represented was subliminal.

How little Nixon understood is evident in his decision to make Milton Friedman the guiding economic policy voice of the first two years of his administration, until Friedman's money program had put the United States into deep recession by 1970. But Nixon carried out the full Friedman program on August 15, 1971, with the addition of the wage-price controls demanded by "populist monetarist" Henry Reuss.[37]

What is of greater importance here is that we honor this nation's debt to Jacques Rueff, emphatically because the United States must now make its final choice between Friedman's "controlled disintegration" and the Grand Design for international development Rueff worked to formulate. There is a continuum between the Grand Design to break Hapsburg rule and Jesuit control over Europe at the time of Henri IV and his great minister Sully; the collaboration of French minister Colbert and the German scientist and diplomat Gottfried Wilhelm Leibniz at the close of the seventeenth century; the plans of Benjamin Franklin and the "American faction" around French Foreign Minister Vergennes; the efforts of the American Cincinnatus Society and John Quincy Adams in common with Lafayette and the brilliant students of Lazare Carnot; and the Grand Design of Rueff, Pope Paul VI, and LaRouche today. The fiber of this continuity is the science of economics, defined as the self-development of man's command over nature, to which LaRouche contributed the unique solution of a deterministic mathematical description of self-developing economic processes. The work of Rueff demonstrates how fraudulent are the pretensions of Milton Friedman to speak on the subject of economics.

How it happens that the likes of Milton Friedman have the opportunity to make such pretensions over public television is a different question, which we now proceed to answer.

The Fraud of Free Enterprise

3

> *I need not mention the difficulty of detecting a falsehood in any private or even public history, at the place where it is said to happen; much more when the scene is removed to ever so small a distance. Even a court of judicature, with all the authority, accuracy, and judgement, which they can employ, find themselves often at a loss to distinguish between truth and falsehood in the most recent actions. But the matter never comes to any issue, if trusted to the common method of altercation and debate and flying rumors; especially when men's passions have taken part on either side.*
> —David Hume, in "On Miracles"

Milton Friedman, in a February 1980 commentary in the *Times* of London, traced his spiritual ancestry to David Hume, who, two centuries earlier, had formulated a quantity theory of money identical, as Friedman noted, to the Chicago School's. Friedman's testimony in this case is perfectly accurate but incomplete. David Hume did not invent the profession of lying, but he did

94 The Ugly Truth About Milton Friedman

his best to turn it into a science, as he states in the passage cited above. For two centuries, what has come down to us as "British System economics" is not economics at all, but the art of professional lying as a means of social control. As a liar, Milton Friedman is a mediocrity. But he stands on the shoulders of great predecessors. He has inherited a method that, in the extreme form he represents it, leads to explicitly fascist economics.

We will encounter the following noteworthy lies throughout this presentation:

1. That "British System economics" stands for "free trade." In the Orwellian translation, British "free trade" means trade warfare, as Hume and Adam Smith directed it against the young American Republic, and against industrial republics since then.

2. That "British System economics" derived from a British-centered Industrial Revolution. The financial basis of the British Empire throughout the nineteenth century was the opium trade, which also gave personal employment to Adam Smith, David Ricardo, Jeremy Bentham, James Mill, John Stuart Mill, Benjamin Jowett, and John Ruskin. Except for temporary advantages gained through trade war, Britain's industrial capabilities were behind those of France starting in the 1780s.

3. That British System economists were men of science and reason. They were, according to all contemporary accounts, the sort of kooks the average person would avoid on the street. There was Hume, dying of obesity; Adam Smith, who lived until his death in his mother's house in Edinburgh; Jeremy Bentham, shut up at home, the "Hermit of Queen Square Place,"[1] talking a queer Newspeak language comprehensible only to a

The Fraud of Free Enterprise 95

few disciples; James Mill, driving his son John Stuart Mill to an early nervous breakdown through strict enforcement of Aristotle's program of education. Worst of all, there was John Ruskin, the Oxford guru of a generation of British imperialists and Cambridge economists, immersed in occult practices, celibate after a terrifying wedding night, and the inspiration of the decadent Pre-Raphaelite group of artists. The greatest progress the British System has made is to find a spokesman who would not violate the sensibilities of decent people on sight, unattractive as Milton Friedman is.

The same characterizations apply to the Austrian School of monetarists who later joined forces with Chicago in the Mont Pelerin Society and among whom can be numbered such types as Friedrich von Hayek and Ludwig von Mises. These products of the Viennese salons at the turn of the century are the men who trained Milton Friedman's teachers, including the founder of the National Bureau of Economic Research, Wesley Clair Mitchell. Rubbing shoulders with the Austrian economists were Ernst Mach, who insisted that thought in the physical sciences could have no relationship to the physical universe; atonal composer Arnold Schönberg, the founder of "modern music"; pornographic playwright Frank Wedekind, author of the "Lulu" plays; Wagnerian visionary Theodore Herzl, figurehead of the Zionist movement; and a host of abstract painters, bizarre poets, and crank scientists who made period Vienna a synonym for a terminally decadent society. The Austrian economists were rustic noblemen patronized by Empress Elizabeth, the sponsor of the Viennese counterculture.

These are the ghosts who howl in the background every time Milton Friedman offers his "free enterprise" homilies on television.

Momentarily, it will become clear to the reader why economics has always been presented as the most arcane science. Throughout its history, and particularly since John Stuart Mill, British economics strove to eliminate from consideration what Alexander Hamilton and his American System successors identified as the subject of economic science—the transformation of man's power over nature through technology. To extirpate this notion, the British economists have insisted upon two premises: that the individual is an unchangeable creature of passions, and that the physical universe is a fixed "equilibrium" system not susceptible to alteration by human intervention. Adam Smith, Hume, Ricardo, and their immediate successors were willing to say so bluntly, as were the Viennese economists, who claimed that economies do not produce wealth but only redistribute whatever nature chooses to provide. Friedman and his colleagues merely rule the issue of the real economy out of consideration to begin with.

The monetarists have thus applied themselves to writing justifications for the most repugnant policies, beginning with the defense of the opium traffic by Smith, Bentham, and Mill, and continuing through to Friedman's shameless defense of Hitlerian economics.

At different periods we find the same set of principles and the same set of economists defending apparently opposing policies, such as the combination of Fabian socialist anticapitalism and Friedmanite anticapitalism that has prevailed at the University of Chicago since its founding in 1892. This is no question of conflicting policies or principles. The shock of seeing Milton Friedman in his true light should be sufficient to scare away the idea that we are dealing with normal questions of scientific investigation that can be settled among rational people. British System economics is a cult whose proper origins go back to the Cult of Apollo at Delphi and its agent, Aristotle, the spiritual father of British economics.

The opium base of British economics

The narcotics traffic is the best reference point for the descent into the moral netherworld, for two reasons. First, it brings us full circle from East India Company employees Adam Smith and the Mills to Milton Friedman, the advocate of Hong Kong as the present-day model of "free enterprise." Second, it sets the record straight concerning the real content of British System economics.

The British Empire was founded on the opium trade, as Kalimtgis, Goldman, and Steinberg document in *Dope, Inc.*[2] All the talk about Britain's industrial prominence has no basis whatsoever in fact. Britain's share of world industrial production began to decline sharply in the mid-1840s. By the end of the nineteenth century, Britain was importing half again as much as it exported—£450 million in imports against £300 million in exports. It made up the difference on dope. In 1890, the value of the British opium revenues in China alone equaled the entire home trade deficit! Gross revenues from the opium traffic averaged two thirds of the total volume of exports from Britain between 1840 and 1890.

Measured in millions of burnt-out lives, the sum is staggering.

The numbers by themselves do not convey how critically dependent the British Empire was on dope. All British trade rested, especially before the American Civil War, on an opium-based cycle of trade: Britain imported cotton from American plantations in the South (which it financed and ultimately backed during the Civil War); turned the cotton into textiles in British mills; exported the textiles to India in return for opium, which British merchants then sold to China. By 1850, cotton textiles accounted for 40 percent of British exports. India alone absorbed fully one sixth of these cotton exports and one eighth of total British foreign sales. India, in turn, depended on opium for 30 percent of its own exports, the majority of which went to China. The remainder of its exports were distributed among different categories of agricultural products, such as cotton, sugar, raw silk, and indigo. In British India, taxes on the opium trade provided almost 20 percent of total government revenues by 1880—the largest single source of government revenue excepting land. The proceeds financed the largest standing army in the world next to Russia's.

That the British banking system still controls an international dope trade now valued at about $200 billion (roughly the same proportion of world trade that dope occupied under British colonial rule in 1880) has been documented at length in *Dope, Inc.* The lurid facts concerning dope's pivotal position in British finances throughout the nineteenth century are a simple matter of officially released trade statistics.

England did not merely go into the dope trade after the American Revolution; the dope trade took over England. Lord Shelburne, the British prime minister who concluded peace negotiations with America after Britain was beaten at Yorktown, staged a virtual coup d'etat in 1783 that brought into power the financial and political faction that had conducted the opium traffic in its early stages since the seventeenth century.

Shelburne's power bloc in the 1783 coup, which brought William Pitt the Younger into power for twenty years, rested on the combined aristocratic and religious orders on the continent: The Order of St. John of Jerusalem and the Society of Jesus grouped around the Orléans family, and the East India Company in London, reorganized by Francis Baring.

Shelburne derided as a "Venetian dogeship" (Disraeli's words) the Hanoverian monarchy and the old Glorious Revolution families who had dreadfully bungled the American Revolution. In the chaos that followed the Yorktown defeat, he employed the best contemporary intelligence and dirty-tricks organization to take England back from them. "He maintained the most extensive private correspondence of any public man of his time," Benjamin Disraeli wrote. "The earliest and most authentic information reached him from all courts and quarters of Europe; and it was a common phrase, that the minister of the day sent to him often for the important information which the cabinet itself could not command."[3] Shelburne was chief of the British Secret Intelligence Services, and his key operative during the 1780s and 1790s was Jeremy Bentham.

On the way Shelburne had bought the services of the

young Bentham and two Scottish scribblers, David Hume and Adam Smith, whom he sent to France for Jesuit training and then put on retainer to create a "theory" of free trade, which meant in England the narcotics trade. The principal objective of the Shelburne gang was the elimination of potential rivals among industrial republics, and their method was trade warfare under the name "free trade."

David Hume, who spent ten years as Shelburne's official representative in France, learned the art of lying during a 1734 internship at the Jesuit monastery at La Flèche in France, the same monastery where René Descartes, the founder of so-called enlightenment philosophy, was educated a century earlier. Hume reported to his biographers that his greatest insights into the human mind arose from the nature of miracles allegedly performed at the Jesuit monastery: They were obviously fraudulent, but *impossible to prove fraudulent*.[4] From this experience came Hume's first book, *Treatise on Human Understanding* (1734), a report to an English-speaking audience on Jesuit methods of mind control.

At the time, the Jesuits represented the purest continuation of the tradition of the Delphic Cult of Apollo, which in turn drew on the "secrets" of the great myth fabricators, the priesthood of Babylon. Hume reported excitedly that no matter how atrociously absurd, "miracles" can be sold to the suckers on the P. T. Barnum principle: "The many instances of forged miracles, and prophecies, and supernatural events, which, in all ages, have either been detected by contrary evidence, or which detect themselves by their absurdity, prove sufficiently the strong propensity of mankind. . . . There is no kind of report, which rises so easily, and spreads so quickly, especially in country places and provincial towns. . . . When afterward the [wise and learned] would willingly detect the cheat, in order to undeceive the deluded multitude, the reason is now past, and the records and witnesses, which might clear up the matter, have perished beyond recovery."[5] If you give enough hokum to the yokels, in Paul Samuelson's quip about Milton Friedman's method, the sheer mass of their stupidity will outweigh any later attempt to prove you wrong.

Hume set out to prove the axiom true. On his return to England, he enlisted Adam Smith, his fellow Professor of Moral Sciences at the University of Edinburgh and "dearest Friend,"[6] in the literary hoax of the century: the Ossian epic.[7] Now obscure, Ossian was the founding document of what would be called the Nazi race mythology, a forged tale of Teutonic greatness in the Scottish isles 2,000 years ago. Allegedly collected from fragments preserved orally among Scottish tribesmen by an obscure Scottish parson, James Macpherson, the volume first appeared in English in 1765. The Viennese Jesuits had a German edition out three years later, thoroughly duping the Goethe circle in Germany, and becoming the antecedent for the ugly race fantasies of the German romantic movement around Richard Wagner.[8] Macpherson was Hume's shill, and Hume and Smith created a national scandal by sponsoring Macpherson in his literary "miracle."

From his deathbed, Hume had a good laugh at those he had duped. In a confession published after his death, he wrote, "I think the fate of this production the most curious effect of prejudice, where superstition had no share, that ever was in the world. A tiresome, insipid performance; which, if it had been presented in its real form, as the work of a contemporary, an obscure Highlander, no man could ever have had the patience to have once perused, has, by passing for the poetry of a royal bard, who flourished fifteen centuries ago, been universally read, has been pretty generally admired, and translated, in prose and verse, into several languages of Europe."[9] He admonished the supposed translator Macpherson: "Let him now take off the mask, and fairly and openly laugh at the credulity of the public, who could believe that long Ese epics had been secretly preserved in the Highlands of Scotland, from the age of Severus till his time. The imposition is so gross, that he may well ask the world how they could ever possibly believe him to be in earnest?"[10]

The next great Scottish hoax, for which Ossian was mere preparation, was *Wealth of Nations,* Adam Smith's supposed economic masterpiece.

Hume and Smith's contact point in France was the Temple, the Paris headquarters of the Order of St. John of Jerusalem, a chivalric secret society that still occupied the island of Malta as a sovereign fiefdom. The Order owned enormous amounts of property, about one sixth of all clerical lands in France, and a large proportion of the real estate of Paris. Centered in the Genoese nobility, the Order of St. John absorbed the elder, military-oriented sons of the Pallavicini and Orléans families, while younger sons out of the line of primogeniture entered the Society of Jesus, making the two organizations branches of the same entity.

Hume's personal patron while in France, where Hume served as British Foreign Minister Shelburne's envoy from 1766 to 1767 and unofficial envoy at other times, was the Grand Prior of the Order of St. John, the

Prince de Bourbon Conti. Prince Conti succeeded as Grand Prior the Duc d'Orléans, who later financed the mobs that burned the Bastille.[11] Conti's personal librarian, the Abbé Blavet, popularized Hume's writings in France and wrote the first French translation of *Wealth of Nations*.

The Scottish pipeline into the Orléans family and the French branch of the Order of St. John had been established at the turn of the eighteenth century, when the remnants of the exiled Scottish Jacobites—the faction that opposed the 1688 "Glorious Revolution" against the Stuarts—settled in France. Their leading political spokesman in early eighteenth-century England, Lord Bolingbroke, fled to France after he was accused of supporting the 1715 Highlands uprising, and spent the remainder of his life under Orléans sponsorship. Shelburne and his Jacobite father-in-law John Carteret, continued Bolingbroke's efforts to take England back, concluding in the Shelburne coup of December 1783. As Benjamin Disraeli wrote a century later:

"Lord Shelburne adopted from the first the Bolingbroke system; a real royalty, in lieu of the chief magistry; a permanent alliance with France [with the Orléans family] instead of the Whig scheme of viewing in that power the natural enemy of England; and above all, a plan of commercial freedom, the germ of which may be found in the long-maligned negotiations of Utrecht, but which, in the instance of Lord Shelburne, were soon in time matured by all the economical science of Europe."[12]

The "economical science" Shelburne employed did not start with Smith and Bentham, who worked on the

Shelburne payroll, but with the Order of St. John's group of pet intellectuals, the physiocrats. Sorting out physiocratic writings is a thankless task, because the French writers combined the most extreme zero-growth, anti-industrial attitude with obligatory references to concepts developed by the French humanist economists. We do not hear of Jacques Rueff's forbears Forbonnais, Trudaine, and others among Benjamin Franklin's intellectual collaborators in France, only of Quesnay, Mirabeau, and the other physiocrats, due to the pernicious fraud of Hume and Smith, and Karl Marx's credulous perpetuation of that fraud.

Strictly speaking, the physiocrats were the spokesmen for Chinese "oriental despotism" in economics, the same viewpoint that now lauds agrarian backwardness in Maoist China. They rewrote Chinese zero-growth economics into European terminology, based on Chinese texts brought back to Europe by the Jesuits' mission to China. The famous author of the *Tableau Economique,* François Quesnay, who served as physician to Madame Pompadour, began his writing career with a study of the Chinese model, *Despotism in China.* Even Franklin's friend Anne Robert Turgot, whose fall as France's finance minister made the 1789 French Revolution inevitable, gobbled up the sinophile currents that swept France. His major economic treatise, *Reflections on the Formation and the Distribution of Wealth,* was written in 1776 for two Chinese who had been brought to France by the Jesuits, and who were to return to Canton to correspond with the Jesuits on "Chinese literature and science."[13] Voltaire, Rousseau, Diderot, and the entire Enlightenment mafia became rabid sinophiles. According to a French historian, "China, to judge from the number of citations, seemed more in favor than England itself."[14]

The physiocrats drew three principal notions from the work of Confucius, Mencius, and the Chinese sages: first, that the universe was a fixed entity that underwent yin-yang cycles of expansion and contraction but could not develop; second, that *laissez faire,* or free enterprise, among the prisoners of this fixed universe would sort out economic matters by itself; and finally, that land was the source of all wealth by gift of nature. Man can distribute this value, but not create it.

Smith made these alien notions the core of his *Wealth of Nations.* In fact, he did not bother to rewrite some of the physiocratic treatises he had obtained during a ten-year sojourn in France prior to the 1776 publication of his book. Entire sections of *Wealth of Nations* were plagiarized from Turgot's *Reflections,* as the French economist and chemist Du Pont de Nemours noted bitterly some years later.[15]

Smith could not bring himself to insist that *all* value came from nature, which the Austrian School economists were to do later, but argued that a special sort of value comes from nature, which human effort could never match:

"No equal capital puts into motion a greater quantity of productive labor than that of the farmer. Not only his labouring servants, but his labouring cattle, are productive labourers. In agriculture too nature labours along with man; and though her labour costs no expense, its produce has its value as well as that of the most expensive workmen.... The labourers and labouring cattle, therefore, employed in agriculture, not only occasion, like the workmen in manufactures, the reproduction of a value equal to their own consumption, or to the capital which employs them, together with its owner's profits; but of a much greater value.... No equal quantity of productive labour employed in manufactures can ever occasion so great a reproduction. In them nature does nothing; man does all; and the reproduction must always be in proportion to the strength of the agents that occasion it."[16]

Alexander Hamilton devastated this view in his 1791 *Report to Congress on the Subject of Manufactures*:

"But while the *exclusive* productiveness of agricultural labor has been ... denied and refuted, the superiority of its productiveness has been conceded without hesitation. As this concession involves a point of considerable magnitude, in relation to maxims of public administration, the grounds on which it rests are worthy of a distinct and particular examination. One of the arguments made use of in support of the idea may be pronounced both quaint and superficial. It amounts to this—That in the productions of the soil, nature cooperates with man; and that the effect of their joint labor must be greater than that of the labor of man alone. This, however, is far from being a necessary inference. It is very conceiveable, that the labor of man alone laid out upon a work, requiring great skill and art to bring it to perfection, may be more productive, *in value,* than the labor of nature and man combined, when directed toward more simple operations and objects; And when it is recollected to what an extent the Agency of nature, in the application of mechanical powers, is made auxiliary of the prosecution of manufactures, the suggestion, which has been noticed, loses even the appearance of plausibility.... Another, and that which seems to be the principal argument offered for the superior productiveness of Agricultural labor, turns upon the allegation, that labor employed in manufactures yields nothing equivalent to the rent of land; or to the net surplus, as it is called, which accrues to the proprietor of the soil. But this distinction, important as it has been deemed, appears rather *verbal* than *substantial*."[17]

In his first major work, the 1759 *Theory of Moral Sentiments,* Smith set forth the principle of "moral indifferentism" that underlies "free enterprise" in a way that left nothing for Milton Friedman to add:

"The administration of the great system of the universe ... the care of the universal happiness of all rational and sensible beings, is the business of God and not of man. To man is allotted a much humbler department, but one much more suitable to the weakness of his powers, and to the narrowness of his comprehension; the care of his own happiness, of that of his family, his friends, his country.... But though we are ... endowed with a very strong desire of those ends, it has been intrusted to the slow and uncertain determinations of our reason to find out the proper means of bringing them about. Nature has directed us to the greater part of these by original and immediate instincts. Hunger, thirst, the passion which unites the two sexes, the love of pleasure, and the dread of pain, prompt us to apply those means for their own sakes, and without any consideration of their tendency to those beneficent ends which the great Director of nature intended to produce by them."[18]

In the *Theory,* Smith tried to impose a "self-regulating" system of moral affairs on his Benthamite creatures of passion by arguing that since one of these passions is the desire to be admired by others, everyone will do the things that cause others to admire them, in a sort of feedback mechanism. Seventeen years later he transferred this mechanism to economics under the famous rubric, the "Invisible Hand."

To Shelburne, Smith's economic theory was a minor fringe benefit of the Jesuit connection to China; of overriding importance was the link to the opium trade. That was a matter of survival. Shelburne devised two grand, interlocking strategies for the British Empire: the "peaceful" takeover of the United States through the weapon of "free trade," and the launching of the opium trade on a massive scale. The first was the content of declared and undeclared war between Britain and the United States until the United States slowly succumbed in the years before World War I. Before that happened, the second provided the sustenance of the City of London and allied European financiers.

Shelburne's reorganization of the East India Company into a looting organization that rivaled Hitler's SS, and the subversive "free trade" flank against the United States, both emerged as policy proposals in *Wealth of Nations* in 1776. Smith blasted the East India Company's practice of "ordering a peasant to plough up a rich field of poppies and sow it with rice or some other grain," in order to maintain high opium prices in the existing restricted markets. Smith argued instead that the opium market had to be extended on a large scale. The East India Company itself had been doing business in dope since 1717, but faced considerable restrictions on the expansion of the trade, notably the Chinese emperor's ban on opium imports.

The Fraud of Free Enterprise

Since the establishment of the first Jesuit mission in Peking in 1601 (coincidentally the year of the East India Company's founding), the Jesuit missions held the key to Asian trade. The Jesuits reached the orient after the first Portuguese trade and military inroads at the end of the sixteenth century, and achieved positions of immense influence in China and in India, then under the Mogul empire, when the first large-scale cultivation of opium is recorded officially. After the 1644 overthrow of the Ming Dynasty by the Manchu, the Jesuits persuaded the new Chinese court to eliminate all Western contact but theirs. When Dutch traders drove the Portuguese out of Asian trade, their negotiating partners for matters of Chinese trade were the Jesuits. The Portuguese, and later the Dutch, took over the centuries-old dope-trading routes once plied by Arab and Indian traders, including opium trade between Canton, China's key port city, and Portuguese-controlled Macao. The Dutch later negotiated an opium monopoly for the entire northern part of the Indian subcontinent with the Jesuit-influenced Mogul court. The monopoly included Bengal, Bihar, Orissa, and Benares, and permitted the Dutch traders to force-draft Indian peasants to produce opium in exchange for taxes paid to the Mogul court. In turn, the Dutch used opium as a medium of exchange for spices in the East Indies; the great Chinese market that sustained the British opium trade was still closed off to them.

By 1659, the opium trade had become second only to the spice trade. A century later, the Dutch were shipping more than 100 tons of opium per year to Indonesia. Apart from the immense financial benefits of the traffic, the Dutch found opium "a useful means for breaking the moral resistance of Indonesians who opposed the introduction of their semiservile but increasingly profitable plantation system. They deliberately spread the drug habit from the ports, where Arab traders used opium, to the countryside."[19]

Britain's East India Company muscled into the opium trade only after the British military victories in India in 1757, which put Bengal under British rule. However, the British administrations in Bengal of Robert Clive and later of Warren Hastings ran the opium monopoly on behalf of East India Company officials, who lined their pockets on the side. The Indian fortunes of individual "company servants" became immense, and among other things provided the biggest slush fund in eighteenth-century politics short of the rotten boroughs and George the III's personal patronage.

The East India Company, which had paid the costs of the military expeditions without seeing any of the profit from the resulting opium monopoly, was on the edge of bankruptcy from the late 1760s until its reorganization under Shelburne in 1784. The company was restructured along the lines Adam Smith proposed in a paper prepared at Shelburne's instigation for an East India Company "Commission of Investigation" in 1772. Repeatedly the East India Company had to apply for a parliamentary bailout, and the collapse of its shares triggered the 1769 financial crisis.

Throughout the Revolutionary War period, the East India Company was not an agency of the British monarchy but a leech on it, benefiting the financial faction that ultimately consolidated around Shelburne. The expenses of the Revolutionary War brought England to the poorhouse door by 1783, the year of the signing of the Treaty of Paris with Franklin. Britain's national debt had swollen to the then-stupendous figure of £240 million, and debt service consumed more than half of all government tax revenues. Worse, Britain lost most of the European market in staple items such as linens, textiles, and ironware to France, which also threatened to take over the Atlantic trade with the new United States under a project devised by Hamilton and Lafayette. Loss of control over trade financing would have toppled the pillar on which the entire British national debt rested. Shelburne, standing behind the ministry of the twenty-two-year-old William Pitt, set out to break the French, expand the opium traffic, and subvert the United States—all in the name of "free trade."

First, Shelburne struck an alliance with the East India Company faction around Laurence Sullivan, whose son had subcontracted for the private opium monopoly in Bengal; Francis Baring, the Anglo-Dutch banker prominent in the Atlantic trade; and the head of the monarchy's patronage machine, John Robinson.[20] The combined slush funds of the monarchy and the East India private fortunes were sufficient to outweigh the impressive patronage powers of the Glorious Revolution's landed families. In mid-December 1783, Shelburne made George III an offer he couldn't refuse, and the king appointed William Pitt First Treasury Lord. Shelburne himself was too hated—his nickname was "the Jesuit of Berkeley Square"—to take office after his brief term as prime minister two years earlier. Slush fund manager John Robinson drew up a list of every member of the British Parliament by political affiliation and purchase price, with a bottom line figure of slightly under £200,000 for the lot. East India Company officers marshaled by Laurence Sullivan paid up, and Shelburne bought the 1784 election for William Pitt.

Pitt's first major piece of legislation was the 1784 East India bill, which made the East India Company in effect a department of the British government, under a Board of Control. Scottish mafioso Henry Dundas, Pitt's secretary of state, directed the Board of Control, and in 1787 wrote a master plan to extend the opium traffic into China. Dundas, an early patron of Adam Smith, was the uncle of Robert Dundas, the infamous Lord Advocate of Scotland, whose "clearances" of the Scottish Highland population inspired the phrase "Sheep eat men."[21]

Blitzkrieg against France

Merely surviving the 1780s, however, required the first major exercise in Smithian trade warfare, against France, which had experienced a stupendous growth spurt under the administration of Louis XV's great Colbertian administrator Daniel-Charles Trudaine. Although hampered by poor internal communications, French industrial production surged to the point where, by the end of the American Revolution, France's steel output was almost twice the British level, and French traders dominated the Iberian, Italian, and German markets. But France's great weaknesses were poor transport—compared to England's natural maritime advantage—and a financial system dominated by Genevan and Dutch financiers, whose representative was Jacques Necker, the finance minister at the time of the Revolution.

Louis XV's death in 1775 weakened the hold of the *Colbertistes* and strengthened the hand of the Orléans group, the ally of the Geneva bankers. Pressed by Talleyrand, who was starting his career at the French treasury, and the younger Mirabeau, son of the physiocrat economist and a picaresque figure during the Revolution, France fell for Shelburne's ruse in 1786. The Pitt government offered France a "free trade" treaty, opening France up to British textiles in return for promised British markets for French wines, and the further promise of a system of trade treaties that would enhance the French position in German and Russian markets, a slant devised by Mirabeau. Immediately after France signed the treaty, British exporters dumped masses of textile products in the French market, provoking economic chaos and mass unemployment. Even though French textiles were at the time produced at higher labor productivity and lower cost, British control over trade financing and merchant shipping allowed British manufacturers to temporarily undercut French prices. At the same time, Pitt lowered tariffs on wine imports from Portugal to below the level that the French treaty had set for French wine imports, enabling cheap Portuguese imports to take the English market away from French vineyards. France's internal finances collapsed, and Genevan financiers made Necker's appointment as finance minister a condition for a rollover of the French national debt.

Necker, in turn, demanded that Louis XVI convene the Estates General, the assembly of the French nation, in order to raise the additional taxes required to meet French debt service to Geneva. Mobs paid and armed by the Duc d'Orléans, the former Grand Prior of the

Knights of St. John who had hosted Smith and Hume in Paris through the 1760s and 1770s, constituted the force that stormed the Bastille, and threw France into the chaos of the Jacobin terror.

Shelburne exerted his influence on the collapse of France through his Secret Intelligence Service operative Jeremy Bentham. Bentham, who adapted Smith's bestial theory of "moral sentiments" into a would-be "moral calculus," had the opportunity to put his views into practice from 1789 onward.

Bentham had moved onto the Shelburne payroll and into Shelburne's house in 1782 as the "Jesuit's" personal secretary and librarian. Through Shelburne, Bentham met Mirabeau—the inside man of the 1786 trade treaty—who arranged the translation of Bentham's leveler ravings into French almost before the ink had dried.[22] By 1788, translation was no longer necessary—Bentham had begun writing his tracts in French.[23] Bentham rushed copy into terrorist Jean-Paul Marat's "revolutionary" newspaper, *L'Ami du Peuple,* by special boat to France. Marat, the mob leader who personally insisted upon the murder by guillotine of every leading French scientist, including the chemist Lavoisier, had spent ten years prior to the Revolution under Shelburne's personal tutelage.[24]

The Jacobin mob represented the ideal type of Bentham man. A "philosophical radical," Bentham threw out Smith's idea that moral society operated under some sort of internal controls. "Nature has placed mankind under the governance of two sovereign masters, pleasure and pain," Bentham wrote; "it is for them alone to point out what we ought to do, as well as to determine what we should do."[25] Bentham insisted that there could be no restrictions to human bestiality. His most notorious exercise in favor of the principle of utility, which says roughly, "If it feels good, do it," was an essay in defense of pederasty.[26]

Although he acknowledged Adam Smith's authority in economic matters, Bentham's first published tract on economics was his 1787 *Defence of Usury,* which lambasted Smith's cautious endorsement of usury laws in *Wealth of Nations.* Usury laws, Bentham said, violate Adam Smith's own precept that the individual is the best judge of his own interest, and if individuals want to borrow at any rate they choose, that is their business. After reading the pamphlet, Adam Smith told Bentham: "The work is one of a superior man. He has given me some hard knocks, but in so handsome a manner I cannot complain."[27] Bentham immediately celebrated the outbreak of the Revolution by organizing a cheering section for Marat called the English Jacobins.

Until 1794, when Lazare Carnot and his allies finally drove the Jacobins from power, France was in ruins. Shelburne and Bentham had bought Britain time to lick its wounds from the Revolutionary War and prepare the expansion in the Far East. In the years from 1786 to 1800, Britain grasped the control over international trade that it retained through the end of World War I. Actual British exports grew only marginally. However, British reexports of goods produced in other countries and sold by British middlemen grew exponentially. If anything, total world trade volume declined during the period due to the destabilization of France. However, Britain's share of it, particularly the German, Italian, and Russian markets seized from France, more than doubled.

The subversion of America

If it were not for the passage of the Constitution of the United States in 1789, Shelburne's more ambitious project—the financial reconquest of the United States—would have succeeded. Smith urged the colonies, in his *Wealth of Nations,* not to enter into manufacturing, and above all not to keep British goods out:

"It has been the principal cause of the rapid progress of our American colonies towards wealth and greatness, that almost their whole capitals have hitherto been employed in agriculture. . . . Were the Americans either by combination or by any other sort of violence, to stop the importation of European manufactures and by this giving a monopoly to such of their own countrymen as could manufacture the like goods, divert any considerable part of the capital into this employment, they would retard instead of accelerating the further increase in the value of their annual produce, and would obstruct instead of promoting the progress of their country toward real wealth and greatness. This would be still more the case, were they to attempt in the same manner to monopolize to themselves their whole exportation trade."[28]

This position, adopted by David Hume's admirer Thomas Jefferson, is fraudulent on Smith's part. Nowhere in *Wealth of Nations* does he remonstrate against British prohibitions against American manufactures, which already threatened to outstrip British productivity a quarter-century before the American Revolution. Shelburne wanted to keep the United States an agrarian protectorate. The major policy objective toward America that Smith enunciated was to compel Americans to pay the British national debt. The entire concluding chapter of *Wealth of Nations* is a tabulation of the taxes that Smith suggested could be imposed on American produce, from timber to tobacco. The bottom line was an annual take of £15,900,000—the total debt service owed on Britain's national debt at the time Smith wrote.

Smith had attempted, as adviser to Chancellor of the Exchequer Lord Townsend, to push such taxes through, and therefore had a direct role in forcing the American colonists to fight for their independence. The concluding paragraph of Smith's book complains that past British governments had failed to realize sufficient revenues from the colonies even to compensate for military expenditures there:

"The rulers of Great Britain have, for more than a century past, amused the people with the imagination that they possessed a great empire on the west side of the Atlantic. It has hitherto been, not an empire, but the project of an empire; not a gold mine, but the project of a gold mine; a project which has cost, which continues to cost, and which, if pursued in the same way as it has been hitherto, is likely to cost immense expense, without being likely to bring any profit." If Britain cannot loot the colonies, it should permit them to separate, "and endeavor to accommodate her future views and designs to the real mediocrity of her circumstances."[29]

In fact, two British factions—for different reasons—encouraged the American revolutionaries in open defiance of the Tory cabinet of Lord North. The old Glorious Revolution Whigs, under Lord Rockingham, found themselves in a bitter patronage contest with the monarchy, and cheered anyone who seemed likely to

118 The Ugly Truth About Milton Friedman

embarrass George III or break his power. Shelburne, under the slogan "We prefer trade to dominion," also opened contacts with the revolutionary leaders, believing that trade warfare would be more effective than military warfare. Great Britain, Smith had argued in *Wealth of Nations,* "would not only be immediately freed from the whole annual expense of the peace establishment of the Colonies, but might settle with them such a treaty of commerce as would effectually secure to her a free trade."[30]

Smith's encomium had been the subject of a series of velvet-gloved offers from Shelburne, starting during the 1767 government of William Pitt's father, Lord Chatham. Shelburne faced adamant demands from the Americans for the westward expansion of the settlements, prohibited except for areas of Georgia and Florida in the south, and Nova Scotia in the north. Shelburne himself, at the head of the Board of Trade at age twenty-six, had written the prohibitions against western colonization. The intent of the restrictions, according to historian Vincent Harlow, was to subvert the development of colonial manufactures, ensure that future colonization did not interfere with the British fur trade, and, above all, to prevent the expansion of the New England colonies' republican form of government.[31] As a concession, Shelburne offered in 1767 to permit three new settlements along the Illinois and lower Mississippi rivers, all the while continuing with his plan to develop the St. Lawrence River and Great Lakes as British continental waterways for British markets. He proposed to finance the scheme by permitting large land speculators to purchase immense tracts of land, in imitation of the plan his great-grandfather, economist William Petty, had devised a century earlier for the Herditary Revenues of Ireland.

At the 1782 peace negotiations in Paris, Shelburne offered the Americans "self-governing" dominion status with commercial union—which both the victorious revolutionaries and British West Indian interests, who stood to lose by the arrangement, rejected, bringing down Shelburne's short-lived ministry.

The content of Shelburne's offer became evident in the struggle for control of Atlantic shipping that followed the Treaty of Paris. Britain's Navigation Acts gave British ships a monopoly over Atlantic trade until the Revolution. Even afterward, Britain continued to dominate not only the Atlantic but also American seacoast trade, while American ships were prohibited from trading in British ports. Under the Articles of Confederation, the federal government, such as it was, had no authority to retaliate against this open form of trade warfare. Individual states, especially Rhode Island and the New Englanders, made special deals with Britain to the disadvantage of the American nation, so that no common front could be formed. As soon as the Constitution was ratified in 1789, one of the first actions of the new Washington administration was to prohibit British ships on the American seacoast routes. American superiority in shipbuilding technology asserted itself, and by the end of the century, 90 percent of Atlantic shipping was under American control.

"Free trade," the contemporary equivalent of "free enterprise," was a lie concocted by Shelburne's hired scribblers Hume, Smith, and Bentham. Shelburne's first efforts at ruining the United States with this lie did not succeed. But his persistent efforts to infiltrate American political circles paid off. Shelburne maintained correspondence with Thomas Jefferson's political lieutenant, Arthur Lee, for some years after the Revolution. Jefferson himself, who supported both the British free trade and anti-industry doctrines throughout his life, maintained a friendship and correspondence until his death with Adam Smith's successor at the University of Edinburgh, Dugald Stewart, the man who trained Britain's Opium Wars prime minister, Lord Palmerston. Jefferson's Vice-President, Aaron Burr, asked Jeremy Bentham to write the constitution for his projected break-away empire in the Louisiana territories; when Aaron Burr went to England after his trial for treason, he lived with Bentham.[32]

Starting in the second decade of the nineteenth century, Britain's most important tool for cracking open the United States was the opium trade. The British banking families, including the Barings, who had intermarried with the Philadelphia Binghams, cut some Boston merchants in on the lucrative China traffic. John Jacob Astor was trading opium as early as 1816, by special arrangement with the East India Company; Aaron Burr was Astor's personal attorney, and Astor provided the funds for Burr's escape to England after Burr murdered Alexander Hamilton in 1801.[33]

The Boston "Brahmin" families, the backbone of the "Cobden Clubs" free trade movement during the nineteenth century, made it into the mainstream of the opium traffic. William Hathaway Forbes, of the Boston family, achieved sufficient prominence to join the founding board of directors of the opium trade's central bank, the Hongkong and Shanghai Bank, two years after its founding. The Cabots, Lodges, Forbes, Cunninghams, and other leading Boston merchant families made their initial fortunes through Russell and Co., whose principal lines of business were West African slaves and opium to China.[34]

Shelburne and his successors bought themselves an American clique, through the resources of the East India Company. These were the bitterest enemies of the Lincoln faction in American politics and of the Lincoln economists, Mathew and Henry Carey. One of Carey's associates, economist Jacob Patton, wrote in 1887:

"By far the most persistent and the most powerful antagonist of our mechanical industries is the famous 'Cobden Club.' Ever since its formation it has been popular with the ruling classes in England, counting among its members a year or two since twelve cabinet ministers out of fourteen, and all the great Secretaries of State, from the Prime Ministers down to those of the colonies, and also other prominent men in Church and State, besides manufacturers and owners of the soil."[35]

Patton continued: "England was an oppressor of the trade and mechanical industries of the American colonists, and only encouraged them in producing the raw material. . . . Lord Brougham in his place in Parliament after the Treaty of Ghent was signed, announced that 'it was well worth while to incur a loss upon the first exportation of goods in order by the glut to stifle in the cradle those rising manufactures in the United States which the war had forced into existence, contrary to the nature of things . . . a Parliamentary commission in 1854 spoke of the losses their manufacturers sustained in foreign markets.' Thus 'to overwhelm all foreign competition' and then 'step in for the whole trade when prices revive.' "[36]

"Before the civil war," Patton reported, "one of the largest establishments in England for rolling iron had an agency in the City of Boston. The duties in railroad iron at that time—under the tariff of 1846—were quite low, and our railways were supplied partly from domestic mills and partly from those in England. The latter firms systematically kept lowering their prices. Meanwhile the American mills, the weaker first, were compelled to shut down ... and when the last one succumbed, the news was sent to England, and with it also the statement 'that there was no longer any danger from American competition.' The reply immediately came back, 'advance prices,' and in less than a year the price of English rails to American consumers had increased about 100 percent."[37]

The new East India Company

Free trade was the official doctrine of the East India Company, but for reasons other than the obvious. Opening the Chinese market required seventy years of subversion and two Opium Wars.

In 1787, when Secretary of State Henry Dundas circulated his blueprint for the taking of China, Britain was neither prepared nor able to use the military methods of 1840 to impose the opium traffic on China against the edicts of prohibition of the Chinese emperors. As a crown corporation, the East India Company could not do opium business in its own name. It required a set of "cut-outs," or intermediaries, who would conduct the exports of opium from India to China on the company's covert behalf. The penny-ante efforts of the pre-Shelburne East India Company had no part in the bigger scheme of things, as Adam Smith wrote in *Wealth of Nations:*

"The servants of the company have upon several occasions attempted to establish in their own favour the monopoly of some of the most important branches, not only of the foreign, but of the inland trade of the country.... In the course of a century or two, the policy of the English company would in this manner have probably proved as completely destructive as that of the Dutch. Nothing, however, can be more directly contrary to the real interest of those companies considered as the sovereigns of the countries which they have conquered.... It is in [the sovereign's] interest, therefore, to increase as much as possible that annual produce. But if this is the interest of every sovereign, it is peculiarly so of one whose revenue, like that of the sovereign of Bengal, arises chiefly from a land rent. That rent must necessarily be in proportion to the quantity and value of the produce, and both one and the other must depend upon the extent of the market."[38]

With the connivance of Dundas, Francis Baring, the banker who remained Shelburne's closest political ally, financed a network of "agency houses," which by the 1790s controlled the Indian interior trade, the Canton trade, and most government contracts.[39] Jardine Matheson, the king of the nineteenth-century opium trade was already in operation; Jardine still manages heroin traffic out of Milton Friedman's Hong Kong today.[40]

"Thus the chain of commodity-exchanges, linking England, India, Southeast Asia and China, was developed and diversified through a strange marriage of convenience between a monopoly corporation [the East

India Company] and an elaborate and exclusive form of private enterprise," wrote historian Harlow.[41]

Gradually, the functions of the East India Company diverged into the official crown administration of India, and the network of private dope traders that ultimately formed the Hongkong and Shanghai Bank in 1864. British traders shipped opium to China in open violation of imperial prohibition, as a "free enterprise" activity in which official British hands were clean. But when China attempted to crack down on the out-of-control dope traffic in 1840, Prime Minister Lord Palmerston, who had received the wisdom of Adam Smith at Edinburgh University from the hands of Dugald Stewart, declared the first Opium War against China.

By the 1830s, opium was the largest commodity in international trade.[42]

From dope to Malthus

The East India College at Haileyburg, the training center for Company officials and Indian civil servants, became the clearinghouse for the next generation of British economists, including James Mill, his son John Stuart Mill, David Ricardo, Parson Thomas Malthus, and aging Jeremy Bentham, their intellectual leader until his death in 1821.

Malthus, the inventor of body-count economics, is most important; his theory of population was adapted by Ricardo into a generalized theory of political economy. As a young Oxford divinity student waiting for appointment to a Church of England sinecure, Malthus was called to public life by William Pitt. The first great financial crisis of the war with Napoleon which had broken out in 1796, had ruined British finances, compelling the Bank of England to suspend for fifteen years the convertibility of the pound sterling into gold. By 1800, social conditions had deteriorated to the point that expenditures under the Poor Law, a rudimentary form of welfare, exceeded £2 million per year, a staggering sum for the times. Pitt encouraged the 1798 publication of Malthus's *Essay on Population,* which was understood at the time as a frank apology for the extermination of "useless eaters." John Maynard Keynes, in his biographical sketch of Malthus, reports:

"In dropping his new Poor Bill, Pitt, who in 1796 thought that a man had 'enriched his country' by producing a number of children, even if the whole family were paupers, had stated in the House of Commons that he did so in deference to the objections of 'those whose opinions he was bound to respect,' meaning Bentham and Malthus."[43]

Poor relief was eliminated. "Malthus's *Essay* is a work of youthful genius," Keynes commented.

Malthus and Bentham's argument was, of course, that population must grow faster than the increase in the food supply, and therefore will be restrained by famine, pestilence, and war. A more obvious lie has not been told by any economist since. In a country like the United States, where 2.5 percent of the population produces half again as much food as is needed for the entire population, it is outrageous to speak of "fixed natural resources." That has not prevented the Club of Rome, the World Bank, and other professed adherents of Malthus from perpetuating the lie.

Proposing to eliminate large portions of the world's population through war, pestilence, and famine qualified Parson Malthus for the Chair of History and Political Economy at the East India Company's Haileyburg training center. He sent a generation of Malthusians into controlling positions of the narcotics traffic in Asia. Malthus, in his 1819 *Principles of Political Economy,* elaborated his population program into a generalized zero-growth approach to industrial economies.

He began by admitting that his murderous population theory was, after all, a hoax: "The millions in capital which have been expended in drainings" of agricultural land "and in the roads and canals for the conveyance of agricultural products, have tended to raise rather than lower profits; and millions and millions more may yet be employed with the same advantageous effect."[44] In other words, capital investment lowered the price of grain relative to the virtual depression period in which Malthus wrote his original *Essay on Population.* As a result, the cost of *subsistence* wages fell, and industrial profits rose. This, of course, was the opposite of what Malthus and David Ricardo had predicted would happen.

The fact that Malthus so casually qualified his population theory merely draws attention to the more fundamental issue: In the tradition of David Hume, he was a liar, who spun out "economic theories" according to Hume's principle of the "undetectable lie." As Keynes noted, Hume was Malthus's fairy godmother.[45]

Speaking for the East India Company's looting program in Asia, Malthus was committed to the defense of zero growth. When the British experience of 1800 to

1820 failed to corroborate his earlier prediction of mass starvation, Malthus revised his population principle for application to industry in general. So what if profits rose, Malthus asked. Manufacturers would merely have to reinvest them, and as they did, the competition of many capitals in the same industrial fields would drive profits down just as surely as would a rise in wages due to more costly, scarcer grain.[46] For that reason, it was useless to attempt to import cheap grain to meet the subsistence requirements of the Lancashire textile workers who spun cotton for the Indian market at pennies per day:

"Our present body of manufacturers, when they call for imported corn, think chiefly of the additional demand for their goods occasioned by the increased imports [which would supposedly cheapen the cost of wages], and seem quite to forget the prodigious increase of supply which must be occasioned by the competition of so many more workmen and capitals in the same line of business."[47]

No matter what you do, Malthus expounded in his *Principles,* profits will fall, economic growth will cease, and society will settle into a permanent equilibrium, enforced by war, famine, and pestilence.

Malthus was joined at Haileyburg in 1819 by James Mill, a protégé of Jeremy Bentham, who assumed the post of Assistant Examiner of India Correspondence, that is, second-in-command of East India Company intelligence. Mill had spent the past dozen years under company contract writing the standard text for East India Company operations, *A History of British India.* The *History* called for the end of restrictions against

British textile exports to India, and the expansion of India's opium exports, both of which occurred within a decade of the book's release.

Two central themes pervaded Mill's book. First, following Malthus, Mill distorted Indian history to argue that the Indian economy had been stagnant and unchanging since the time of Alexander the Great, and therefore was fair game. Second, he invented an incredible legal argument for the seizure of all Indian property by British dope dealers: The Mogul emperor, said Mill, owned all land, and no institution of private property existed prior to Britain's presence in India. The East India Company, therefore, should claim the same rights as the Mogul empire!

In point of fact, total economic stagnation occurred in only one period of Indian history—the rule of the British Empire. "The British were the first conquerors of India who showed gross indifference to public utilities," wrote the great economist Rosa Luxemburg. "Arabs, Afghans, and Mongols had organized and maintained magnificent works of canalization in India; they had given the country a network of roads, spanned the rivers with bridges and seen to the sinking of wells. . . . The East India Company which ruled India until 1858 [before the Crown took over direct rule] did not make one spring accessible, did not sink a well, nor build a bridge for the benefit of the Indians."[48]

James Mill rose rapidly to the position of Chief Examiner of Indian Correspondence, the head of East India Company operations in London. Jeremy Bentham, who adopted Mill as his disciple in 1808, said happily, "Mill will be the living executive—and I shall be the dead legislative of British India."

As Bentham slowly went mad in middle age, Mill mediated between the old goat and the outside world. Bentham "came to write in a language which grew more and more obscure, and he made for himself a new terminology which he might indeed call 'natural' in contrast to the 'technical' terminology which was in use in the courts, but which in reality constituted a new technical terminology,"[49] a kind of Orwellian Newspeak. "It was to James Mill that this hermit, this maniac, owed the fact that he became the popular chief of a party that was half philosophical and half political," wrote Bentham's biographer.[50]

David Ricardo, who sat on the Court of Proprietors (board of directors) of the East India Company, had arranged for Mill's appointment as Chief Examiner, and Mill returned the favor by conducting a two-decade-long propaganda campaign on behalf of Ricardo that manufactured the latter's reputation as a "classical economist."

Ricardo, the "father of the quantity theory of money,"[51] is the most direct link to Milton Friedman. Unlike Friedman, however, Ricardo was—as a major stockholder and theoretician for the East India Company—concerned with real economics, to the extent of specifying what wealth was available *to be looted*. This is the origin of the "theory of differential rent" that American System economist Henry Carey devastated some forty years later. Ricardo offered this theory in his *Principles of Political Economy and Taxation,* which appeared a year after Malthus's work, as a set of policy recommendations for the Indian, and secondarily the British, tax system.

The rent theory proceeds from Malthus's population argument. Increasing population, Ricardo wrote, will outstrip available resources of food. Therefore, additional land must be brought into cultivation. However, since the best land is presumably put under cultivation first, the additional food requirement means putting inferior land under the plough. The cost in terms of the labor of producing food on inferior land is, of course, greater. Therefore, the price of grain must rise to meet the higher production costs of the last land brought into cultivation. What of the landowners who are lucky enough to hold land more fertile than the average? They also sell their grain at the higher price. In addition to the normal profits they always obtained on capital invested in agriculture, they receive a premium, or rent, according to the differential fertility of their land.

Like William Petty and Adam Smith, Ricardo was sufficiently concerned with the requirements of financing the British national debt and the Indian administration costs that he specified sources of tax revenues. He grudgingly distinguished between nonproductive and productive labor, and recommended taxing rental income as an unearned, nonproductive revenue. Malthus, in his textbook, also recommended that Indian tax policy should impose rent according to the differential fertility of land. But, in the case of England, Malthus remonstrated against taxing rents, precisely because they *were* unproductive! Since continued productive investments would supposedly lead to a fall of profits and the end of economic growth, Malthus argued, the only means of postponing economic crisis was to siphon capital off into nonproductive consumption, such as into the consumption of landlords and of parsons like himself! As Keynes later wrote, this was the origin of Keynesian economics.[52]

Several rungs down the Darwinian ladder, the Ricardo-Malthus debate was repeated dully in the exchange between Milton Friedman and James Tobin reviewed in Chapter 1. What makes both sides of the argument so grossly fraudulent is that it occurs in an imaginary zero-growth universe, in which improvement in technology has been eliminated. Under East India Company rule, such a zero-growth regime existed in India, as indeed it did in every area under British colonial rule. As American economist Henry Carey pointed out, the application of technology to agriculture eliminates the so-called differential rent entirely.[53] Land improvements made during the period between the publication of Malthus's *Essay on Population* and Ricardo's *Principles of Political Economy* made nonsense out of differential rent at the very moment that Ricardo was preparing to preach the doctrine.

Ricardo's economics in practice

Only to the extent that India under the East India Company was a laboratory for zero-growth doctrines does Ricardo's theory have any more to do with the real world than Friedman's. The doctrine itself, whatever vessel it is dished into, is no different than the doctrine that Aristotle put forth in *The Politics*. Aristotle denounced the view of Solon, the builder of Athens, that "no bound is set on riches for man."[54]

"But the best is," Aristotle wrote, "that the wealth should be provided at the outset by nature. For it is a function of nature to provide food for whatever is brought to birth, since that from which it is born has a surplus which provides food in every case. We conclude therefore that any form of money-making that depends on crop and animal husbandry is for all men in accordance with nature. Money-making then, as we have said, is of two kinds; one which is necessary and acceptable, which we may call administrative; the other, the commercial, which depends on exchange, is justly regarded with disapproval, since it arises not from nature but from men's dealings with each other. Very much disliked also is the practice of charging interest; and the dislike is fully justified, for interest is a yield arising out of money itself, not a product of that for which money was provided. . . . Of all ways of getting wealth this is the most contrary to nature."[55]

That, in the words of the greatest professional liar of all time,[56] is the quantity theory of money. Ricardo's "quantity theory," introduced in the Bullion Debates of 1810, had precisely the same content as Milton Friedman's. Friedman, in his 1956 study of the Nazi economy, praised Hitler for holding down the rate of money creation by adding to the *population* under Nazi rule, and therefore spreading the volume of money over a larger number of users. Friedman left out of his account the fact that most of these users were headed for the gas ovens. Ricardo proposed to peg the value of the pound sterling in terms of gold to the rate of opium addiction in China. Both Friedman and Ricardo use as window dressing the following simple-minded tautology proposed by David Hume:

"It seems a maxim almost self-evident, that the prices of everything depend on the proportion between commodities and money, and that any considerable alteration on either has the same effect, either of heightening or lowering the price. Increase the commodities, they become cheaper; increase the money, they rise in value. As, on the other hand, a diminution of the former, and that of the latter, have contrary tendencies."[57]

Hume's seeming tautology is an outright fraud. Ricardo was as much of a fraud as was Milton Friedman on the matter of the money supply of the German Nazi economy. However the essential fraud of the quantity theory of money has to do with monetarism's insistence on leaving the real economy "out of the system," in Milton Friedman's phrase.

Ricardo took this to ludicrous extremes, beginning with the so-called Bullion Debates of 1810, when the Benthamites employed hearings in the British Parliament on the then-explosive inflation crisis to sound out Ricardo's "quantity theory." Fifteen years of the Napoleonic Wars had broken the British economy; only ten years earlier William Pitt had ordered the starvation of useless eaters rather than pay poor relief. Ricardo proposed drastic reductions of money in circulation, in other words, a credit contraction by the Bank of England. Since the supply of goods had contracted, due to chronic poor harvests and other factors, Ricardo argued that the problem was an excess of commodities relative to goods!

"England, in consequences of a bad harvest, would come under the case of a country having been deprived of a part of its commodities, and, therefore, requiring a diminished amount of circulating medium. The currency which was before equal to her payments would now become super-abundant and relatively cheap."[58]

In the thick of wartime, Ricardo, with the enthusiastic backing of Mill and Bentham, demanded that the Bank of England limit the circulation of its currency to its war-starved gold reserve. One historian describes the predicament:

"British agriculture approached collapse, for its output was no longer required for Wellington's armies. Doubtless a demobilized man will eat as much as a soldier, but no Waterloos depended upon his nourishment. Domestic trade moved in rhythm with agriculture. Thousands of traders found oblivion in bankruptcy. The commercial discounts of the Bank of England, which had amounted to twenty million pounds in 1810 and which had been fifteen million in 1815, fell to four million by 1817. . . . Industrial shutdowns coupled with demobilization brought into being an army of unemployed estimated at half a million, and threw into high relief social inequalities which war-time prosperity had concealed. . . .

"The stockjobbers, headed by the Ricardos, who had been playing the market for a fall against firms more successful in securing government contracts, had long been for resumption. The Bullion Report of 1810, prepared under their auspices, furnished apparently scientific proofs that the money market could be stabilized on a gold basis."[59]

Ricardo's point was not the gold standard as such, but a deflationary collapse of the domestic economy. In 1819, Ricardo prevailed, through legislation put through Parliament by Sir Robert Peel. The economy collapsed utterly, with prices falling 30 percent on average. However, Ricardo, Alexander Baring, and the House of Rothschild obtained precisely the result they

The Fraud of Free Enterprise 135

wanted. As the managers of the national debt of Britain and later of the rest of Europe, the Baring-Rothschild nexus made up the difference by looting the national economies of Europe through a rentier system of national debt. How different this was from Hamilton's concept of national debt as the foundation for productive credit was shown by their first great swindle—the French war indemnity loan of 1819. The victorious Holy Alliance powers demanded a 700,000,000 franc reparation from defeated France. A Rothschild-led consortium financed this through a European bond issue that sucked England dry of capital. The plan followed precisely Ricardo's argument before the Bullion Committee: "An exportation of this sum" of excess money supply "would restore the value of Britain's currency to the value of the currencies of other countries."[60]

Identical to the evil Versailles Treaty reparations precisely a century later, the war-debt system created a self-perpetuating fund for rentier looting. Since the debts of war were contracted at sharply inflated prices, payments after the 1819 Great Deflation were much greater in real, deflated terms. The same was true of the World War I reparations, valued in inflated 1918 currency, after the Federal Reserve Bank of New York and the Bank of England rigged a similar deflation in 1921.

Baring followed the spate of war financing with a South American loan bubble. The new Latin American countries had broken from Spain with the support of British Foreign Minister George Canning, and boasted constitutions drafted by Jeremy Bentham in London. The Monroe Doctrine had been issued to prevent the direct expansion of the British Empire in the Western Hemisphere.[61] Now the City of London opened the floodgates of lending, and between 1823 and 1825, £17,500,000 were paid for securities of the Latin American countries, the first big "Third World" lending scheme. The bubble, based on a "Ponzi" system by which the proceeds of new loan issues paid interest on earlier ones, collapsed in 1826, creating the second general British financial crisis within the decade and the bankruptcies of a half-dozen Latin American and other debtor countries.[62]

Sir Robert Peel, who had effected the devastating Ricardo deflation in 1819, put the Ricardo "quantity theory of money" into finished form with his 1844 Reform of the Bank of England. Historically, this represents a landmark in rentier finance equaled, perhaps, only by the 1980 banking legislation adopted by U.S. House Banking and Currency Committee Chairman Henry Reuss. To the extent that a plethora of "country banks" and other institutions were still able in Malthus's time to finance important improvements in agriculture, transportation, and industry, the Peel Reform eliminated these. It followed Ricardo's prescription word for word. The Bank Charter Act of 1844 fixed the total money supply of Britain at the prevailing level, backed by £14 million of government debt and other securities, plus part of the Bank of England's gold reserve.

Except by increasing its gold hoard, the Bank of England could not by law expand the currency, no matter what domestic credit conditions prevailed! If England suffered an unfavorable trade balance and exported gold, the Bank of England, by law, "might have no alternative but to stop payment," as John Stuart Mill noted.[63]

England already had a balance of trade deficit, which reached £35 million annually in 1854 and £55 million by 1865. Ricardo had insisted that an unfavorable trade balance must be dealt with through deflation, as Hume had argued forty years before.

How did Britain avoid financial collapse? The Ricardian Bank of England Reform of 1844 was premised on the growth of the opium trade.

Two years before its passage, British guns had blasted open the gates of Canton, eliminating the imperial edicts that had interfered with the rapid growth of opium shipments to China. Between 1830 and 1840, the number of chests of opium imported into China rose from 10,000 to 40,000, or fourfold. By 1860, the volume had risen to 60,000, and by 1880 to 100,000, at a price, on average, of £1,500 a case. *The profits of the opium traffic were higher than the trade deficit.* Taking into account also the flow of debt service into London from virtually the entire world, what British financiers now call "invisible exports," or financial rake-off from other countries, made it possible for Britain to get by with its own decaying internal industry until the turn of the twentieth century.

Economist John Stuart Mill, who followed in his father's footsteps as Chief Examiner of Indian Correspondence for the East India Company, praised the new system. In particular, Mill approved the almost total elimination of credit to industry, "as advances to manufacturers and others, who pay wages . . . may get into the hands of others who expend them for consumption, and in that case the notes do constitute in themselves a demand for commodities and may for some time tend to promote a rise in prices."[64] The "quantity theory of money" eliminates "inflationary" credit to industry very efficiently.

Manchester cotton merchant and philosophical radical Frederick Engels, Karl Marx's patron, wrote a sophisticated apology for the Ricardians that found its way into most modern historical treatments. The Peel Reform of the Bank of England "deprived its management of the possibility of freely utilizing its entire available means at critical times," Engels wrote, "so that situations could arise in which the banking department might be on the verge of bankruptcy while the issue department still had intact several millions of gold and, in addition, its entire 14 million in securities," which were "frozen" as backing for the circulating currency.[65] Engels argued, in other words, that the Bank of England was now more vulnerable to financial crisis, because the major part of its resources was locked up behind the currency issue.

Considering how much business Engels's Manchester Cotton Exchange did with Indian opium producers, this account is disingenuous, to say the least. The Bank of England, of course, happily put the market through regular financial "crises" to redistribute the shares of loot among participating pirates, particularly when such events as the American Civil War and the emancipation of Southern slaves crimped the City of London's operations. However, the market was fixed by Chinese opium imports, and the Bank of England blithely suspended the Peel Reform in "crisis" periods throughout the remainder of the century.

Engels's dishonesty is more important in another regard. The Peel "opium standard" subjected not London but America to repeated financial crises. After Rothschild agent Andrew Jackson broke the Hamiltonian Second National Bank of the United States, the domestic banking reserve of the United States became dependent on the vagaries of the international credit and gold markets, that is, dependent on London.[66] Every British financial "panic" from 1835 to 1907 led to the calling in of loans to New York, and a resulting financial collapse in the United States. America's susceptibility to British-ignited financial crises became a major threat to national security during the Civil War, and was corrected by the Lincoln administration's return to Hamiltonian national banking, under the direction of the great economist Henry Carey. But the 1879 Specie Resumption Act undermined the gains of the Lincoln period and returned the United States to dependency on London.[67]

However evil were Ricardo and his policies, it is still unfair to Ricardo to compare him directly to Milton Friedman. Like Friedman, Ricardo thought the opium traffic being run through Hong Kong was the epitome of free enterprise; he put into their final form the zero-growth credit policies Friedman later reinvented; he apologized for a parasitical, rentier form of finance and fought bitterly against Hamiltonian industrial finance. But, to give Ricardo his due, the East India Company board member acknowledged the existence of real economic categories, if only to take inventory for looting purposes. He acknowledged his predecessors' use of the terms "constant capital," "variable capital," and "surplus" to describe the flow of tangible economic wealth. He proposed that rent, a category of nonproductive income, was particularly suited to taxation, on the premise that the less taken out of the productive process, the more there would be available to loot later on.

Friedman adopted Ricardo's "quantity theory of money" through the intermediation of the band of occultists, theosophists, and homosexuals who ran Oxford University in the second half of the nineteenth century. We have several rings of a Dantean hell yet to traverse before we find Milton Friedman, now that we have made acquaintance with his ancestors.

Milton Friedman and his wife, Rose Director Friedman, leaving 10 Downing Street in London after a visit to Prime Minister Margaret Thatcher.

The British School

John Stuart Mill, the employee of and apologist for the British East India Company.

Jeremy Bentham, whose "felicific calculus" became the basis for all modern monetarism.

Parson Thomas Malthus   David Ricardo

John Maynard Keynes (r.) with the New Deal's Harry Dexter White.

The Vienna School

Friedrich von Hayek, whose book *Road to Serfdom* belies monetarism's ultimate aim.

Nicholai Bukharin, student of the Vienna School, who would later argue against the industrialization of the Soviet Union.

Otto von Hapsburg, the heir to the throne of the defunct Austro-Hungarian Empire.

Richard Coudenhove-Kalergi, the founder of the Pan-European Union who brought the Vienna School to the United States.

The Chicago School

Beatrice and Sydney Webb, whose London School of Economics and settlement houses combined to become the model for the University of Chicago in the United States.

Thorstein Veblen, the author of the *Theory of the Leisure Class* who ended his days as a hermit in the hills of California.

The Great Crash

Winston Churchill, who had much to be happy about on Black Thursday.

John Kenneth Galbraith, whose book *The Great Crash* covered up London's role in bringing down the American stock market.

Black Thursday on Wall Street, 1929.

Hjalmar Schacht, Hitler's Economics Minister and colleague of the Bank of England's Montagu Norman.

Jacques Rueff, de Gaulle's economics adviser who analyzed Schacht's fascist regime as "inflation turned inward against the economy."

Oxford Monetarism and Hitler's Vienna

4

> *There is a destiny now possible to us—the highest ever set before a nation, to be accepted or refused. We are still undegenerate in race; a race mingled of the best northern blood.... We are rich in an inheritance of honor, which it should be our daily thirst to increase with splendid avarice. England must found colonies as fast and as far as she is able, seizing every piece of fruitful ground she can set her foot on, and teaching these her colonists that their first aim is to advance the power of England by land and sea.*
>
> —John Ruskin to the Oxford University student body, 1870

Monetarism runs like a red thread from John Ruskin's band of Oxford occultists—the future leaders of the British Roundtable—to the Hoover Institution office of Milton Friedman. It entwines an initially bewildering series of individuals and institutions, from the economists of the decayed Viennese court through the University of Chicago, from the Fabian Society to the Pan-

European Union, to the hard core of Hitler backers that has survived to the present day. Following this thread, we cross and recross the line between outwardly respectable academic institutions and the human garbage of the brownshirt mobs, the narcotics traffic, and political assassination. We shall discover that the conventional labels of "right" and "left" economics are a blind. The trail is made up of hard-packed evidence and will give us the solution to the question we have so far left unanswered: Why is Nazi economist Milton Friedman in a position of great public influence in the United States today?

Both *The New Dark Ages* and *Dope, Inc.* have shown in immense detail that the Ruskin-Jowett cult at Oxford created the Odin and Thule secret societies of Germany, the inner organization of Nazi fascism, and that the "geopolitics" of *Mein Kampf* was a plagiarism of British Roundtable strategist Halford Mackinder, through the Wittelsbach monarchy's Colonel Karl Haushofer, Hitler's political tutor. The notorious backing for Hitler until 1938 among members of the British ruling elite, the "Cliveden Set," merely continued what had been going on for much longer than Hitler had been on the scene. We heard earlier Jacques Rueff testify that British and New York financiers put Hitler and Schacht in power, during 1931 negotiations that Rueff attended as a junior French official. That Hitler was the vaunted "marcher lord" of the British aristocracy and the Bavarian Wittelsbach dynasty, and that their financial support of Hitler was no error on their part, is now documented in print.

Every element of Hitler's program had been devised

seventy years earlier in Oxford by John Ruskin's back-to-the-Middle-Ages ideologues, known as the Pre-Raphaelite Brotherhood. Initially formed as a group of "artists" who proposed to reverse the Golden Renaissance's advance of civilization epitomized by the artist Raphael, the Pre-Raphaelites branched out into political economy, "English" and later "Fabian" socialism, and a bizarre set of cult practices that ranged from Oscar Wilde's well-known sodomy to Madame Blavatsky's theosophy.

The brand of economics that English-speaking countries now suffer from emerged in undiluted form from the teachings of Ruskin and his sponsor, Benjamin Jowett, the Master of Balliol College and its professor of political economy. Jowett is otherwise well known as the mistranslator of Plato who propagated the lie that Plato favored homosexuality, in keeping with Ruskin and Oscar Wilde's personal habits.[1] Specifically, the economics of "marginal utility" emerged as the fruit of a thirty-year Oxford project to finally make Bentham's "felicific calculus" operational. Jowett and Ruskin trained the entire generation of British leaders who ran England until after World War I—including Cecil Rhodes, future Prime Minister Albert Grey, future Prime Minister Lord Arthur Balfour, sometime British intelligence research chief Arnold Toynbee, British Roundtable founder Lord Alfred Milner, and others—in the pre-Hitlerian brand of race theory cited at the beginning of this chapter.

"Austrian economics" emerged simultaneously as a Continental branch of the same cult. Interwoven, the Oxford and Vienna strands of pre-Hitlerian economics defined the orientation of the University of Chicago through Milton Friedman's appointment as Distinguished Service Professor there in the 1960s.

The ideologue for race imperialism

Ruskin drew around him an intellectual hit squad whose intended victim was industrial capitalism. One of his students in economics, George Bernard Shaw, founded the anticapitalist Fabian Society with Sidney and Beatrice Webb. Under the patronage of Opium War Prime Minister Lord Palmerston, Ruskin began a Workingman's College at Oxford in 1854, staffed by Dante Gabriel Rossetti and other Pre-Raphaelites. These were the counterpart in England of their collaborator Richard Wagner, Hitler's favorite composer, and the great propagandist of the Teutonic race myth. The Ruskin project first issued the slogan "Back to the Land!" This cry was later adopted by the Hitler youth movement and today's environmentalists.

Because of the countercultural socialism of Ruskin protégés William Morris and Oscar Wilde, and the association of Ruskin's Workingman's College with the Fabian Society, Ruskin is viewed as a "left-winger" by conservative American writers.[2] The characterization is misleading. Ruskin's anticapitalism was, at root, profeudalist oligarchism.

Ruskin drew his inspiration from his teacher, mystic writer Edward Bulwer-Lytton, the author of the novel *Rienzi,* which formed the libretto for Richard Wagner's first opera. A leader of the Order of St. John of Jerusalem and colonial minister during the Opium

Wars, Bulwer-Lytton comes down to us as the most hidebound of British reactionaries. His son became viceroy of India during the height of opium production during the 1880s, and gave the young Rudyard Kipling his start in life.

The Pre-Raphaelite Brotherhood itself declared its goal to be the extension of "medieval romanticism," and looked to the official court painters of Metternich's Holy Alliance for inspiration. Formed by the English members of a group of Metternich student artists who in 1810 made their home at the Villa Malta, the Rome headquarters of the Order of St. John of Jerusalem, the Pre-Raphaelites had an "inclination toward the Middle Ages . . . the fantastic often interwoven with the real," according to the Viennese artist Franz Pforr.[3] To this group of English painters were added such poets as Alfred, Lord Tennyson. They proceeded to saturate English-language culture with the same medievalism created a generation earlier by the Vienna Jesuits as a weapon against the humanism of Friedrich Schiller. This interplay between the Jesuitry of the Bavarian Wittelsbach dynasty and the British Empire produced nearly everything that is rotten in modern culture. The Pre-Raphaelite Brotherhood itself, ensconced at Oxford with John Ruskin from the 1850s onward, became the rallying point for a projected final assault on the fruits of the Renaissance: industrial capitalism and the republican nation-state.

It would be a mistake to view Ruskin as an aberration of Victorian England. On the contrary, his chair at Oxford University in fine arts was created in 1870 by the Royal Colonial Institute. The Royal Colonial Institute had been established only two years earlier by the major clearing banks, including Barclay's, Lloyd's, the old Baring house, the opium trading giant Jardine Matheson, and the Sassoon bank. In 1864, the same group of families had founded the Hongkong and Shanghai Bank as a central bank for the opium trade, opening a new era in British overseas finance. The rise in narcotics revenues was to replace the loss of income from the American slave system, which had been financed and backed politically by London until the end of the American Civil War.

The first staff economists of the Royal Colonial Institute were Ruskin and Jowett's prize students—W. S. Jevons and Alfred Marshall—renowned as the "founders of modern economics."

The principal weapon of Ruskin and his colleagues was exactly what it had been during the early 1790s, when Jeremy Bentham's agents Danton and Marat led the Jacobin mob against French science. Whether this mob wore the red shirts of Lord Palmerston agent and Young Italy leader Garibaldi, or the black shirts of Mussolini, has been immaterial to the apostles of unreason at Oxford. There is no more difference between these colorations of the Jacobin mob than there is between the brand of "medieval socialism" propagated by Ruskin and Bernard Shaw and the "medieval socialism" of the German National Socialists.

Accordingly, Ruskin's entry into politics came in 1871 under Benjamin Jowett's sponsorship, with the "Letters to the Working Men of England." Ruskin proposed to eliminate the industrial centralization and division of labor brought about by the industrial revolution, in favor of an "aesthetic movement."

Nothing that American college students suffered during the 1960s compares with the training Ruskin gave to the sons of the British elite at Oxford. "All education must be moral first, intellectual secondary," he wrote. "Intellectual before moral education is . . . a calamity." That meant ordering Oxford art students to spend a semester building a road, on the model of Mao's Cultural Revolution education programs. Ruskin's colleague William Morris, "the Father of English Socialism," "reconciled the medieval alliance of nobles and peasants," in Morris's own words, "and used it against the factory owners and capitalists." After graduating from Ruskin's Workingman's College at Oxford, Morris set out to revive the tradition of medieval guild craftsmanship, what he called "the work of the ancient handy craftsmen."

"The leading passion of my life is hatred of modern civilization. . . . The only healthy civilization was that of the Middle Ages before the decline set in with the Renaissance and the Industrial Revolution," he wrote.[4]

Morris created in 1884 the Socialist League, with Marx's daughter Eleanor and her husband Edward Aveling; he later established the Hammersmith Socialist Society, which became implicated in several anarchist bombings.

Another Ruskin product was Oscar Wilde, whose trial for homosexuality was the great scandal of the 1890s. In his essay "The Soul of Man Under Socialism," Wilde wrote that socialism is "romantic individualism and an improvement of the lot of workers, the latter to be achieved not through money but through the arts. . . . Pleasure is nature's test, her sign of approval. When a man is happy he is in harmony with himself and the environment." Morris and Wilde's assault on industrial capitalism found its great apostle in the United States in the person of Thorstein Veblen, the University of Chicago economist who trained Milton Friedman's teachers.

But the economic theory of the medieval reaction was not yet invented. Benjamin Jowett set an entire generation of Oxford graduate students to the task of completing Bentham's attempt to base economics solely on the pleasure-pain principle. Among these were W. J. Jevons, F. X. Edgeworth, and Alfred Marshall—names found in any standard textbook history of "modern economics." The first two were, as the profession sadly admits, among the most deplorable kooks in the history of economics. The last, Alfred Marshall, is revered as the founder of modern monetarism.

From Oxford to Chicago

Let us look at Oxford kookenomics through the eyes of Wesley Clair Mitchell, Milton Friedman's teacher and the founder of the National Bureau of Economic Research that sponsored him. Adopted by the Oxford group as an undergraduate at the University of Chicago, Mitchell is known as the American founder of business cycle theory and is something of a saint among the economics profession. He was, as we shall discover, one of the biggest kooks of them all, starting his career at the feet of Thorstein Veblen and the Austrian School feudal throwbacks, and concluding it as part of the American connection to the pro-Nazi Pan-European Union. His is an excellent introduction to the company we must keep in this chapter.

Bentham's fault, wrote Mitchell, lay in his great achievement: "In his *Principles of Morals and Legislation,* indeed, he ... discussed thirty-two 'circumstances influencing sensibility' to pleasure and pain. Since these thirty-two circumstances exist in an indefinite number of combinations, it would seem that the felicific calculus can scarcely be applied except individual by individual—a serious limitation."[5] The mathematical difficulties sprang also from a perverse sort of diminishing returns on additional increments of pleasure, for, as Mitchell quotes Bentham, "by high doses of the exciting matter applied to the organ, its sensibility is in a manner worn out."[6] Bentham devoted great effort to classifying the principle of utility, of which he said modestly, "I took it from Hume":

"To a person considered by himself, the value of a pleasure or pain considered by itself, will be greater or less, according to the four following circumstances: 1. Its intensity. 2. Its duration. 3. Its certainty ... 4. Its propinquity.... But when the value of any pleasure or pain is considered for the purpose of estimating the tendency of any act by which it is produced, there are two other circumstances to be taken into account; these are, 5. Its fecundity ... 6. Its purity.... [When a community is considered, it is also necessary to take account of] 7. Its extent; that is, the number of persons to whom it extends."[7]

As such, the "felicific calculus" becomes messy. Thirty-two sources of pleasure and pain with seven degrees of intensity produce more than 10^{62} possible combinations for the single individual. Undaunted, Bentham, with visions of becoming the Newton of the Moral World, proposed to put the "calculus" into practice. His *Panopticon* proposal for "prison reform" envisioned a combination concentration camp and Skinner Box, and became the adopted model for all modern forms of brainwashing torture.[8] However, unpublished manuscripts obtained and released by his twentieth-century adherents point a way out of the morass of complications. As Mitchell wrote:

"If then, speaking of the respective quantities of various pains and pleasures and agreeing in the same propositions concerning them, we would annex the same ideas to those propositions, that is, if we would understand one another, we must make use of some common measure. *The only common measure the nature of things affords is money.* . . . I speak and prompt mankind to speak a mercenary language. . . . Money is the instrument for measuring the quantity of pain or pleasure. Those who are not satisfied with the accuracy of this instrument must find out some other that shall be more accurate, or bid adieu to Politics and Morals."[9]

Unfortunately, Mitchell commented, "Bentham did not follow up this promising lead,"[10] and economics "remained substantially where Ricardo had left it in 1817."[11] Bentham died a recluse, madder than a hatter, willing his body to be mummified and placed at the University of London. Upon tipping the janitor, it may still be viewed there in a closet.

Various economists, including Menger, Walras, and Clark, attempted to replace Ricardo's "value" with the new principle, "utility," but "what they had found turned out to be merely a new variety of the Ricardian species," Mitchell continued. "Less noticed but more important in the long run was the issue Jevons raised by making his doctrine of utility rest explicitly upon Bentham's psychology of pleasure and pain."[12]

William Stanley Jevons, best remembered today as the "sunspot" economist, graduated from Bentham's University College in 1855 and published his *Theory of Political Economy* in 1871. "The ultimate quantities which we treat in Economics," said Jevons, "are Pleasures and Pains. But it is convenient to transfer our attention as soon as possible to the physical objects or actions which are the sources of pleasures and pains."[13]

However, Mitchell says disapprovingly, Jevons "pushed the use of money farther into the background" in his unsuccessful attempt to arrange productive relations according to the pleasure-pain principle. "Value depends solely on the final degree of utility. How can we vary this degree of utility?—By having more or less of the commodity to consume. And how shall we get more or less of it?—By spending more or less labour in obtaining a supply."[14] Labor was a pain submitted to for the pleasure of consuming. Capital investment was another pain—of postponed consumption—measured by intensity (the amount of capital) and duration (the maturity period of the investment). "The first modern book on economics," said John Maynard Keynes of Jevons's *Theory of Political Economy*.[15] But it did not yet solve the schizophrenic paradoxes left by Jeremy Bentham.

Jevons, predictably, was a raving Malthusian. In 1865, during a period of national pessimism brought on by the end of Britain's kept plantation system in the American South, he published *The Coal Question: An Inquiry Concerning the Progress of the Nation and the*

Probable Exhaustion of our Coal Mines. He argued, following Malthus, that continued industrial expansion demanded "geometrical growth" of coal mining, which, of course, was limited by nature. He propounded a "Natural Law of Social Growth," whose conclusion was: "So far, then, as our wealth and progress depend upon the superior command of coal, we must not only stop—we must go back."[16] Since the time of the great Malthus, argued Jevons, importation of grain had eliminated Britain's subsistence dependency on agriculture, but that merely "throws us from corn upon coal."[17] Short of Malthus's own dishonest prediction of a food shortage because of increased population, no more stupid prediction has ever been made by any economist.

In later years, Jevons's occult efforts to penetrate the secrets of the "trade cycle" drove him to insanity. An 1878 paper presented before the British Association for the Advancement of Science argued that the eleven-year cycle of sunspots caused a similar cycle of price fluctuations. Batty as the argument sounds, it was debated until well into the twentieth century by British economists. As late as 1911, Jevons's son wrote a paper defending the hypothesis. John Maynard Keynes later argued that Jevons's method was correct, although his data were unfortunately proven inaccurate![18] "By using these methods," Keynes said, "Jevons carried economics a long stride from the *a priori* moral sciences towards the natural sciences built on a firm foundation of experience." Jevons drowned while bathing in 1882.

Meanwhile, Jowett's prize pupil from Balliol College, Oxford, was busy writing index numbers and mathematical formulas to make Bentham's felicific calculus practicable. Francis X. Edgeworth was Britain's most famous economist during his lifetime, editing the *Economic Journal* from its founding in 1891 to 1926. In an 1881 volume entitled *Mathematical Psychics,* on the "calculus of *Feeling,* of Pleasure and Pain," Edgeworth "attempted to illustrate the possibility of Mathematical reasoning without numerical data.... We cannot *count* the golden sands of life; we cannot number the 'innumerable smiles of seas of love'; but we seem to be capable of observing that there is here a greater, there a less, multitude of pleasure-units, mass of happiness; and that is enough."[19]

Cambridge's Alfred Marshall, Wesley Clair Mitchell reports at length, solved the problem of following through on Bentham's original suggestion. Marshall declared that "money is the center around which economic science clusters ... it is the one convenient means of measuring human motive on a large scale." Marshall added: "If we then wish to compare even physical gratifications, we must do it not directly, but indirectly by the incentives which they afford to action.... The force of a person's motives—not the motives themselves—can be approximately measured by the sum of money which he will just give up in order to secure a desired satisfaction; or again by the sum which is just required to induce him to undergo a certain fatigue."[20]

In conclusion, Mitchell wrote in 1916: "Among recent tendencies in economic theory none seems to me more promising than the tendency to make the use of money the central feature of economic analysis ... (it) is a tendency to be fostered."[21] Thus, Mitchell announced an evil project which eventually found a name: Milton Friedman.

With Marshall, Benthamism splits into what have remained "right-wing" Vienna and "left-wing" Fabian branches.

According to Bernard Shaw, the Fabian Society had the object of "solving the social problem by a combination of peasant proprietorship with neo-Malthusianism,"[22] on the model of William Morris's "English Socialism." Fabian Society founder Sidney Webb, later patron of both the University of Chicago and the London School of Economics, began as a follower of John Stuart Mill.[23] But Bernard Shaw "became a convinced Jevonian, fascinated by the subtlety of Jevons's theory and the exquisiteness with which it adapted itself to all the cases that had driven previous economists, including Marx, to take refuge in clumsy distinctions between use value, exchange value, labor value, supply and demand value, and the rest of the muddlements of that time." Accordingly, Shaw reported, "the abstract economics of the Fabian Essays are, as regards value, the economics of Jevons."[24]

The only Fabians who really understood economics, Shaw complained, were "Sidney Webb and myself." "Ruskin's name was hardly mentioned in the Fabian Society," he charged. "My explanation is that . . . the Fabians were inveterate Philistines. My efforts to induce them to publish Richard Wagner's *Art and Revolution,* and later on, Oscar Wilde's *The Soul of Man under Socialism,* or even to do justice to William Morris . . . fell so flat that I doubt whether my colleagues were even conscious of them."[25]

Nonetheless, the Fabian *leaders* harkened to the Oxford kooks. Shaw beat the drum for the master race in *Man and Superman* (1901) and other Wagnerian sallies before anyone had heard of Hitler. Webb built the British Labour Party out of this foul stuff. One of his last actions was to move the Austrian School of "conservative" economics—von Hayek and all—to the "Fabian" London School of Economics.

The Viennese disease

The British economists, finally ensconced at Cambridge under Alfred Marshall, felt constrained to at least talk in polite terms of industrial capitalism. Not so their Viennese first cousins, the excrescence of the most decayed state in Europe, the Austro-Hungarian Empire. What the British economists fashioned out of a hedonistic, environmentalist assault upon industrial society, the Austrian School made into an attack on natural science itself. Nazism bred in this swamp, where Hitler spent his youth. The union of the British and the Austrian schools, to which Wesley Clair Mitchell committed his life, produced the University of Chicago and Milton Friedman.

Since Metternich's Holy Alliance—the great reaction enforced by the political police and the Jesuits—Vienna had been the continental capital for British influence. Its ruling family, the Hapsburgs, intermingled with the Bavarian House of Wittelsbach, the center of Jesuit evil in Europe since the sixteenth century. What later became known as Nazi ideology was the official Vienna court doctrine. Hapsburg Empress Elizabeth, a Wittelsbach and a cousin of Queen Victoria, was a friend and admirer of the British founder of "German race science," Houston Stewart Chamberlain. A ferocious pagan, Chamberlain married the daughter of Richard Wagner, the proto-Nazi composer who had been lifted out of poverty by Wittelsbach King Ludwig I. The Wittelsbachs had built Wagner his shrine at Bayreuth, the festival opera house that later became the cult center of Nazism.

The entire military apparatus of the Wittelsbach family, later to become the core of the Hitler SS, was tutored in the "geopolitical" theories of Sir Halford Mackinder, leader of John Ruskin's two successor organizations, the Roundtable and the Fabian Society.[26]

Financially, Vienna was the territory of the Austrian branch of the House of Rothschild, then at the acme of its power in England and abroad. From its London headquarters, the Rothschild family bankrolled the British Roundtable and Cecil Rhodes's designs in Africa. In Austria, the family controlled the Austrian national debt (starting from the Congress of Vienna in 1815), the Rothschild-built national railroads, and the Tyrolean silver mines. Its power was not broken until the collapse of the Austrian currency and the dismemberment of the empire after the First World War. Wittelsbach Empress Elizabeth's closest personal friend was Julie de Rothschild, the sister of the head of the Austrian branch of the family, Baron Albert de Rothschild.

The same year that Jevons's *Theory of Political Economy* appeared in London, an obscure Galician nobleman, Karl von Menger, brought out a virtually identical work, *Principles of Economics (Gründsätze der Volkswirtschaftslehre)*. But for Rothschild scribbler Karl Kraus, the most famous journalist in Vienna and the lion of the salons, Menger might have passed into oblivion. Kraus reviewed the work favorably, and Menger won a professorship at the University of Vienna. Although, as Ludwig von Mises later complained, "none of his teachers, friends, or colleagues took any interest" in von Menger's work, the Empress Elizabeth appointed him tutor to Crown Prince Rudolf in 1876. Rudolf and von Menger toured Europe for the next three years. Imperial approval or no, "until the end of the seventies there was no 'Austrian School.' There was only Karl Menger," wrote von Mises.[27]

Two books appeared in 1883, whose publication marks the formal birth of the Austrian School. One was Menger's tract, *Investigations on Method,* an assault on the Prussian economics that still ruled German-speaking academia. More important was Ernst Mach's *Science of Mechanics,* the first cannonade of radical positivism in the sciences. Mach attacked the foundations of science itself. Undoubtedly the leading intellectual power in Vienna, Mach proclaimed the principle of irrationality that, years later and in cruder form, appeared in Milton Friedman's *The Methodology of Positive Economics.*

Human thought "has nothing to do with the physical world itself," Mach wrote. Newtonian science, he argued with a sort of perverse accuracy, had never properly defined its terms. The Newtonian universe was still filled with metaphysical mysteries, such as "action at a distance" and the law of inertia. Newton's particles moving in a fixed time and space by fixed laws were an epistemological absurdity.[28]

At Göttingen University, physicists and mathematicians like Gauss, Weierstrass, and Bernard Riemann had already identified the solution to the Newtonian

158 The Ugly Truth About Milton Friedman

disaster along lines proposed two generations earlier by Lazare Carnot. Instead of the entropic Newtonian world, which runs down if it is not "wound up like a clock," the Göttingen scientists described the "nested manifolds" of increasingly complex geometries that correspond to increasingly higher orders of self-organization of energy. LaRouche demonstrated in 1951 that the mathematics of Riemann and Georg Cantor provides the solution to the problem of deterministic models of economic expanded reproduction through the introduction of advanced technology.

Mach, however, took Newton's failure as the starting point for the extreme form of know-nothingism that came to be known as "radical positivism." Mach dismissed Riemann's conception of ascending orders of physical space—subsequently rigorously proven in both physics and economics—as "merely conceivable." All that science could inspect were "the properties of actual space ... directly exhibited as objects of experience. As mathematical helps of this kind, spaces of more than three dimensions may be used. But it is not necessary to regard these ... as anything more than mental artifices."[29]

The history of science proves Mach to be a scoundrel. Half a century before experimental physics produced them, Riemann projected the existence of "shock waves," that is, the higher-energy organization of gases under pressure following the rapid addition of energy. Riemann's partial-differential equations for shock waves formed the basis of the construction of the hydrogen bomb a century after he wrote them, as Dr. Edward Teller has pointed out.[30]

Mach's counterproposal to Riemann was to revert to

nominalism. "The world consists *only* of our sensations," Mach wrote, "in which case we have knowledge *only* of sensations."[31] In this case, Mach continued, our perceptions of the physical universe have no direct connection whatsoever to the actual physical universe. If we perceive a force such as gravity acting at a distance, we merely name it "gravity," and leave matters there. Ten years after his first book appeared, Mach was awarded a new University Chair of Experimental Philosophy by Empress Elizabeth. Vienna's salons lionized him, and a generation of scientists, philosophers, and musicians learned at his feet. A close friend was Empress Elizabeth's appointee as Director of the Vienna State Opera, the neurotic composer Gustav Mahler. Mahler had earlier studied under fellow Wittelsbach favorite Richard Wagner, on a stipend from Baron Albert de Rothschild.

Mach held court with journalist Karl Kraus at the salon of Karl Wittgenstein, a Jewish steel magnate who had grown wealthy supplying Albert de Rothschild's railroads. To these sessions Mahler brought his leading student Arnold Schönberg who later wrote to Karl Kraus, "I have learned more from you, perhaps, than a man should learn."[32] Schönberg referred to the Machian inspiration for his abandonment of tonality in music in favor of the atonal, so-called twelve-tone system. Schönberg was correct; his music was the equivalent of Mach's antiscience. Tonality, the system of equal tempering that prevailed for at least 3,000 years before Schönberg, is the link between the physics of vibrating strings and the science of poetic irony.[33] Schönberg's "discovery" marked the termination of the tradition of classical composers.

Out of this degenerate climate came von Menger's statement of economic method, the primal Austrian School denunciation of state intervention into economic life. The target of von Menger's work was the now-obscure German Gustav von Schmöller, chairman of the economics department at the University of Berlin and the reigning defender of the German system of protectionism. The German protection policy was the legacy of the great economic scientist Friedrich List, the heir of the Carnot tradition and the collaborator of the forces around the Marquis de Lafayette in France and in the United States. List's Customs Union inside Germany, combined with protection against British dumping, ensured that German industry would not suffer the catastrophic consequences of Britain's "free trade" policy. Like Carey's policies during the Lincoln administration, List's success enabled Germany to share with America the highest rates of individual growth recorded in human history.

At the time von Menger published his denunciation of protection and his call for "free trade," Germany was registering 20 percent annual growth rates in steel, chemicals, and other basic industry. During this period of maximum growth, German industrialists were devoting upward of one fifth of their net profits to research and development, a policy that resulted in an explosion of new technological advances. Germany's economic power overtook Britain's during the 1890s. The "Grand Design" program of French Minister Gabriel Hanotaux, in potential combination with the great Russian industrializer Count Witte and the McKinley Republicans in the United States, represented a force powerful enough to sweep away the British Empire. Ruskin's students formed the British Roundtable under the chairmanship of Lord Milner in response to the industrial threat from America and continental Europe.[34]

However inferior von Schmöller and the German economists of the time were to their great teacher Friedrich List, they had one merit: "If nothing else roused the suspicions of the German scholars," wrote Ludwig von Mises bitterly, "they would have condemned economics for the sole reason that Bentham and Mill contributed to it."[35] Schmöller and von Menger exchanged vitriol, and what became known as the *Methodenstreit* began. Various Austrian economists, including von Menger's students von Wieser and his brother-in-law Böhm-Bawerk, held cabinet offices intermittently, presiding over the moribund Austrian economy. They eventually won the *Methodenstreit* by default, after the German 1918 defeat and the imposition of the Versailles Treaty and the rule of Hjalmar Schacht at the Reichsbank.

In the domain of method, the Austrians took the vantage point of Bentham and Mach to extremes that appear lunatic to the modern reader. Outdoing the most Chinese of the old physiocrats, Ludwig von Mises wrote in 1912:

"There is a naive view of production that regards it as the bringing into being of matter that did not previously exist, as creation in the true sense of the word. From this it is easy to derive a contrast between the creative work of production and the mere transportation of goods. This way of regarding the matter is entirely inadequate. In fact, the role played by man in production always consists solely in combining his personal forces with the forces of nature in such a way that the cooperation leads to some particular desired arrangement of material. No human act of production amounts to more than altering the position of things in space and leaving the rest to nature."[36]

According to von Mises, not only is industrial production undesirable, as the Oxford kooks say; it is impossible. Von Mises was such an extreme know-nothing that he looked with contempt at the statistics-gathering efforts of the Vienna School's own trainee, Wesley Mitchell, at the National Bureau of Economic Research:

"Today, all over the world, but first of all in the United States, hosts of statisticians are busy in institutes devoted to what people believe is 'economic research.' They collect figures provided by governments and various business units, rearrange, readjust, and reprint them, compute averages and draw charts. They surmise that they are thereby 'measuring' mankind's 'behavior' and there is no difference worth mentioning between their methods of investigation and those applied in the laboratories of physical, chemical, and biological research. They look with pity and contempt upon those economists who, as they say, rely on 'much speculative thinking' instead of 'experiments.' And they are fully convinced that out of their restless exertion there will one day emerge final and complete knowledge that will enable the planning authority of the future to make all people perfectly happy."[37]

To Vienna goes the dubious credit for the invention of the weird Stoic cult, the study of "trade cycles." Jevons, as we saw, went off the deep end in the attempt to account for the boom-bust cycles of City of London speculation. Earlier, Malthus and Ricardo had projected a crisis of capitalism, but as a distant Armageddon caused by a permanent scarcity of resources—an Armageddon that, of course, never arrived. But the Austrian School, which in the 1920s became the Austrian Institute for the Study of Trade Cycles, portrayed these developments as the unfortunate consequence of man's misguided attempt to change the natural order, and the inevitability of nature's revenge. Original sin, in the Austrian scheme of things, is the existence of credit itself—that requirement for the introduction of new technologies and hence economic survival. Friedrich von Hayek issued the "classic" statement of the Vienna position in his 1928 *Monetary Theory of the Trade Cycle,* revised in 1932 to defend the "inevitability" of the 1929 crash:

"The condition thus ... assumed ... is the *existence of credit* which, within reasonable limits, is always at the entrepreneur's disposal at an unchanged price. This, however, assumes the absence of the most important controls which, in the barter economy, keep the extension of the productive apparatus within economically permissible limits. Once we assume that even at a single point, the pricing process fails to equilibrate supply and demand, so that over a more or less long period demand may be satisfied at prices at which the available supply is inadequate to meet total demand, then the march of economic events loses its determinateness and a range of indeterminateness appears, within which events can originate leading away from equilibrium."[38]

What von Hayek is saying in the pseudoscientific language of Mach is that credit extension increases demand above the level of supply, leading to a disequilibrium in which a crisis will shut off demand until it again falls to the level of supply. The possibility of mere extension of the economy in scale, or of the introduction of new technologies, whereby new supply would equal or exceed credit extension, never seems to have occurred to von Hayek. Von Hayek's little world never changes. Indeed, he criticizes von Mises for suggesting that expansionary central bank policies provoke excessive credit expansion.[39] He argues instead that the mere existence of the credit-extension powers of commercial banks is the cause of crises.[40] He concludes:

"So long as we make use of bank credit as a means of furthering economic development we shall have to put up with the resulting trade cycles. They are, in a sense, the price we pay for a speed of development exceeding that which people would voluntarily make possible through their savings. . . . If it were possible . . . to keep the total amount of bank deposits entirely stable, that would constitute the only means of getting rid of cyclical fluctuations."[41]

As propounded by University of Chicago economist Henry Simons to his student Milton Friedman during the 1930s, that is the famous Friedman proposal for 100 percent reserve banking. Normally, banks hold in reserve only a portion of their deposits; the reserve ratio in the United States is 15 percent of demand deposits and 4 percent of less volatile savings deposits. As banks lend the portion of deposits not held in reserve, the loans are redeposited with the banks, creating new deposits and thus the basis for new loans. If banks were compelled to put up all their deposits as reserves, they could extend no loans; their business would consist, as

Friedman has suggested, of charging depositors for the privilege of depositing money.[42]

This would bring down the economy. Von Hayek, an octogenarian and still active, wrote the *Times* of London on February 21, 1980, to argue that governments had best be done with it and induce mass unemployment through immediate deflation. Since nature's revenge will occur in any event, the sooner the better; and besides, government will never have the political will to impose a slow, gradual deflation. Friedman's only point of disagreement with von Hayek is on the subject of timing; Friedman proposes slow strangulation, as opposed to von Hayek's beheading of the economy.

One hundred percent reserve banking as promulgated by von Mises and Friedman may seem absurd, but Friedman's friends in the banking community have already begun preparations to make it happen. New York's Citibank, whose economists are devout monetarists, has developed plans to eliminate commercial bank lending as a main feature of the bank's business. The bank believes that the United States is headed for a period of economic decline, and that the developing countries, into which the American banks poured funds during the past ten years, will not make it as creditworthy customers. Therefore, consumers and industrial enterprises, let alone nations like Zaire or the Philippines, will not make it as clients of Citibank over the years ahead.

But Citibank believes that it can still increase its profits by taking a fraction of a cent off the top of a gigantic flow of funds through the bank! For example:

166   The Ugly Truth About Milton Friedman

it currently plans to phase out "credit cards" and replace them with "debit cards." Instead of lending a customer money when he uses the card, the bank will deduct the amount instantaneously from his checking account—at a small service cost, of course. Citibank internal reports target $1.2 trillion in potential deposits now held by savings banks and smaller commercial banks, which Citibank thinks are fair game. The entire strategy is mad, but it is madness with a method: It is the only type of commercial banking that could survive in a zero-growth world.

Friedman has nothing whatsoever to add to von Hayek's final statement of Vienna irrationalism. Unlike the Viennese fanatics, he occasionally uses the rhetoric of capital formation and productivity, an attitude those throwbacks had no use for. We have seen that the Austrian School acted as the house retainers of the same Wittelsbach dynasty that created Hitler, and as the Austrian branch of the British Roundtable economics of Halford Mackinder and Houston Stewart Chamberlain. However, von Mises and von Hayek developed a convenient alibi for their behavior when Hitler kicked them out of Austria into the waiting arms of the London School of Economics. Von Hayek set out to prove, as in his 1944 *The Road to Serfdom,* that British economics meant "freedom" and that German economics, including that of Friedrich List, and any economics favoring state intervention into the economy represented Nazism:

"For over two hundred years English ideas had been spreading eastward. The rule of freedom which had been achieved in England seemed destined to spread throughout the world. By about 1870 the reign of these ideas had probably reached its easternmost expansion. From then onward it began to retreat, and a different set of ideas ... began to advance from the East. England lost her intellectual leadership in the political and social sphere and became an importer of ideas. For the next sixty years, Germany became the center from which the ideas destined to govern the world in the twentieth century spread east and west. Whether it was Hegel or Marx, List or Schmöller ... whether it was socialism in its more radical form or German 'organization' or planning of a less radical kind, German ideas were everywhere readily imported, and German institutions imitated."[43]

To this day, von Hayek remains loyal to the remnants of the Nazi machine, gathered together in the Pan-European Union around the last heir of the Hapsburg throne, Otto von Hapsburg. How he and von Mises ended up in London, rather than Berlin, explains much about the British-sponsored fascist machine. But the answer to this question takes us first through Chicago.

Monetarism Invades America

5

> *Economic analysis assumes men's acts are ruled by conscious motives [but] it is only to a limited extent of this character. Much of it is more or less impulsive and capricious. This limitation is far more sweeping than imagined [and] raises the fundamental question, how far human behavior is inherently subject to scientific treatments. In his views on this point the writer is very much of an irrationalist. . . . Interpretation of life as actively directed toward securing anything is highly artificial and unreal. It appears that a relatively small fraction of the activities of civilized man are devoted to the gratification of needs or desires having any foundation beyond the mere fact that impulse exists at the moment in the mind of the subject.*
> —Milton Friedman's teacher, University of Chicago economist Frank H. Knight

Although British economics has been entrenched to a greater or lesser extent in America since the friendship of Thomas Jefferson and Dugald Stewart, this country

170 The Ugly Truth About Milton Friedman

did not abandon the American System of Henry Carey and Friedrich List by slow erosion. Oxford's kook economists mounted an assault on America with all the subtlety of the landing of the Normandy invasion on the shores of Lake Michigan. Oxford built the University of Chicago up from bare ground as a center of British intellectual subversion against the fundamental tenet of the American System—the necessity of industrial progress.

Not until the 1929 crash did the British formula of limited growth gain credence among the American public. But the financial disaster that shattered the lives of a generation of Americans was not the revenge of nature against America's reckless optimism. As we will prove in detail, it was planned and executed by Britain's financial agents in this country, the men who gave Milton Friedman his start in life.

Contrary to its present conservative reputation, the University of Chicago began in 1892 as the chief American project of the Fabian Society. The fact that it incorporated both the "right-wing" economics of the Cobden Clubs and Thorstein Veblen's imitation of Ruskin-Morris socialism at the outset should not be surprising. The new university, launched with funds from the Rockefeller, Schiff, and Field families, transferred the entire package of Oxford kookery to the shores of Lake Michigan intact. Beatrice Webb, the Fabian Society stringpuller, is the real founder of the University of Chicago.

The University of Chicago began its existence in 1889 as the education program of Hull House, Jane Addams's social work project modeled after that of the Fabians. For five years prior, Addams had lived in

Britain studying with Beatrice Webb and working out of Toynbee Hall in London, the flagship for Jane Addams's "settlement house" movement. Toynbee Hall was a workshop for the Jacobin "guild socialism" cooked up in the 1850s at Oxford by John Ruskin and his friends and transmitted into the Fabian Society via Sidney Webb and Bernard Shaw. Ruskin's Oxford undergraduates, working out of Toynbee Hall, the Hammersmith Socialist Society, and similar institutions, trooped into the London slums to recruit the cadre of future Jacobin mobs, offering food, shelter, and education. Most of the anarchist followers of British agent Michael Bakunin passed through Toynbee Hall at some point.[1] Morris's little group in Hammersmith went over entirely to terrorist activities. With the settlement house movement, Jane Addams brought terrorism to the United States; President McKinley's assassin was sheltered at New York's Henry Street Settlement House by anarchist Emma Goldman.

When Hull House was founded in 1889, London *Times* editor-in-chief William Stead accompanied Jane Addams back to Chicago from London for the great event. Stead was a frank apologist for Cecil Rhodes's plan for a British Empire based on white race superiority, and a persistent advocate of the "reunification" of Britain and America on the basis of Ruskin's imperial program. Funding for Hull House came from the core of British supporters in the United States. Future Chief Justice Louis Brandeis, of the Anglo-Zionist "Our Crowd" Manhattan financial circuit, fundraised for Hull House in New York, while John D. Rockefeller and Marshall Field made heavy contributions. The founding documents of the University of Chicago state

172 The Ugly Truth About Milton Friedman

its purpose to be the center of "ideas and theories" for the settlements, which would provide the "practical endeavors . . . providing a broad field for testing ideas and theories." This was the first great exercise in the social control techniques that now come under the general heading "Fascism with a Democratic Face."

Hull House encompassed the entire group of future department heads of the University of Chicago.

John Dewey began the new Department of Philosophy after a career at Hull House, returning to the stockyards in 1894 with his own "University of Chicago Settlement House" jointly sponsored by Hull House. Economics Department Head J. Laurence Laughlin and his deputy, Thorstein Veblen, were Hull House professors. So was Charles Tufts, head of the Sociology Department. Tufts had come to Hull House from a job as labor negotiator for the Kuhn Loeb dry goods firm Hart, Schaeffner, and Marx. In overall charge was Yale Professor William Rainey Harper, brought in upon Jacob Schiff's recommendation.

Economist Laughlin came to Chicago as a national figure: He was chief spokesman for the Cobden Clubs, the "free trade" organization of British bankers and American opium traders that opposed the Carey-List policy of protecting American industry against British dumping. McKinley Republicans of the 1890s had not yet succumbed to the "free trade virus," a disease that subdued the Grand Old Party only with the accession of Calvin Coolidge, Andrew Mellon, and Herbert Hoover some thirty years later. During the 1896 election, McKinley had denounced the Cobden Clubs and defended a protective tariff because it "would increase the demand for American labor." The purpose of a new tariff bill, the future President said, "is to increase production here, diversify productive enterprise . . . and increase the demand for American workmen."[2]

Laughlin had already joined the fight on the British side with a slanderous attack on Alexander Hamilton published in the University of Chicago *Journal of Political Economy* in 1894. The article, "Hamilton as a Political Economist," argued that Hamilton's "inference was hasty" that America should develop manufactures instead of remaining a rural market for Britain.[3] Laughlin defended the spurious Ricardian theory of rent against Hamilton's attack and concluded that Hamilton's "rank as an economist is not high" compared with the "great names in the science—Adam Smith, Ricardo, Mill."[4]

Nearly every university lecturer today will tell the same lies. But in 1894 it was still a matter of controversy, at least in the American Midwest. An assassin's bullet, not Professor Laughlin, defeated McKinley protectionism.

Laughlin's reputation grew. In 1897 he prepared for banker Paul Warburg the Report of the National Monetary Commission. The report formed the content of the Federal Reserve Act of 1913, the formal introduction of English central banking methods into the United States.

But John Dewey and Thorstein Veblen, as Wesley Clair Mitchell remembers it, were "our two philosophers" and made the University of Chicago what it was.[5]

"There was Thorstein Veblen," Mitchell wrote, "that visitor from another world, who dissected the current commonplaces that the student had unconsciously acquired, as if the most familiar of his daily thoughts were curious products wrought in him by outside forces. . . . From Veblen's philosophic view of social institutions and social theories a straight path led to John Dewey's lectures. There the student interested in any phase of human behavior heard a master of philosophy and psychology analyze the processes involved in activities, from dealing with a broken shoestring to constructing a system of metaphysics. Not less effectively than Veblen, though with a different emphasis, Dewey helped an economist to drag out the psychological preconceptions lurking behind theories of value and distribution into consciousness."[6]

Thorstein Veblen was a half-mad Norwegian who terrorized undergraduates and had adopted William Morris's Dionysian variant of Oxford kookenomics. He corresponded with Bernard Shaw, Sidney and Beatrice Webb, Karl von Menger, and Eugen Böhm-Bawerk, and presented their version of Ruskin economics in his 1899 volume, *The Theory of the Leisure Class*. Emulating the Oxford medievalists, Veblen praised the preindustrial age, when "the master craftsman, embodying the instinct of workmanship," prevailed. "As the industrial system developed, he was separated from his tools [and] workmanship gave way to pecuniary drives." Now, Veblen expounded, instead of the worker in his primal state, former craftsmen "were made subservient to the profit-making requirements ... of the leisure class. . . . [who] sought to divert the social surplus to their own private purposes."[7]

Bentham had argued that man was bestial, but at least able to calculate how much pleasure or pain an action would bring. Veblen, immersed in studies of

American Indians, the Ainus of Japan, Australian bushmen, and Polynesian islanders, attempted to take the human species down a rung from Bentham! "The discipline of savage life has been by far the most protracted and probably the most exacting of any phase of culture in all the life-history of the human race; so that by heredity human nature still is, and must indefinitely continue to be, savage human nature."[8]

From a "left-wing" critique of industrial capitalism on the grounds thrown up by the Pre-Raphaelite Brotherhood half a century earlier, Veblen moved full circle to the ultraright position of von Mises and von Hayek, whose teachers had been Veblen's correspondents during the 1890s. In his last book, Veblen denounced the institution of credit as the source of all the industrial evils he deplored. The modern industrial corporation, he wrote in his 1924 work *Absentee Ownership and Business Enterprise,* "could never have arisen without corporate credit, [through which] the values of physical assets could be inflated." Credit meant to Veblen "the right of the corporation to debauch the national wealth."[9]

Veblen was hated at the University of Chicago, contrary to the impression given by his devoted student Wesley Clair Mitchell. By the time he left Chicago in 1906, Veblen's lecture audiences had almost disappeared; one class ended up with only one student.[10] Like Bentham and Jevons, he went mad at the end of his life, becoming a hermit in the California hills. One anecdote of these last years reported by economic historian Joseph Dorfman tells how Veblen was seized by the paranoid delusion that someone had stolen his plot of land: "He took a hatchet and methodically broke the windows, going at the matter with a dull intensity that was like madness, the intensity of a physically lazy person roused into sudden activity by anger."[11] This arch-hater of industry's despoilment of the "natural world" ended up as an environmentalist, "disturbing nothing of nature, not even a weed, and allowing the rats and skunks to brush by his legs and explore his cabin as he sat immobile, wrapped in unhappy distant thoughts."[12]

Such was the quality of inspiration at the University of Chicago. More important than Veblen, who merely burned hatred of industrial capitalism into such students as Wesley Clair Mitchell, was John Dewey.

Dewey's motto—"There is no psychology but social psychology"—proceeded from the American pragmatists' work in the Chicago slums at Hull House. The mind, according to Dewey, was a fixed set of inborn reflexes, instincts, and capacities, "inherited generation after generation with numberless differences as between individuals, but with slight changes as regards the species." Dewey admitted of no creative faculty. Certainly it is true, he said, that individuals manifest new behavior patterns. But learning is merely "the capacity to form innumerable *combinations* among the innumerable original propensities. . . . It is these changing combinations among substantially unchanging elements that differentiate the behavior of the civilized man from that of the savage."[13]

Scratch the surface of Dewey's benevolent "social psychology," and you find Jeremy Bentham's hideous *Panopticon*. Through social institutions, Dewey maintained, "behavioral habits" determine how these various inborn propensities combine into what ultimately is called "intelligence." Control the social institutions that form an individual, and you have controlled his mind.

To Wesley Clair Mitchell, this was gospel revelation. It solved the paradoxes of "economic science" that had plagued the monetarists since the time of Bentham. Mitchell wrote excitedly: "To find the basis of rationality, then, we must not look inside the individual at his capacity to abstract from the totality of experience the feeling elements, and to compare their magnitudes" as Bentham proposed. "Rather we must look outside the individual to the habits of behavior slowly evolved by society and painfully learned by himself. Of course, the use of money is one of these great rationalizing habits. It gives society the technical machinery of exchange. . . . It is the foundation of that complex system of prices to which the individual must adjust his behavior in getting a living. . . . Since it molds his objective behavior, it becomes part of his subjective life. . . . Because it thus rationalizes economic life itself, the use of money lays the foundation for a rational theory of that life. Money may not be the root of all evil, but it is the root of economic science."[14]

It is not that monetarism "fits the facts of economic life"; *the point is that men can be made to fit into monetarism.* Mitchell finally abandoned the silly fiction promoted by Ricardo and even Alfred Marshall that the money decisions of countless individuals determine economic life. Why should this be the case, Mitchell wanted to know. The individual consumer is the most irrational creature on earth, he argued in an essay entitled "The

Backward Art of Spending Money." If that were true, there could be no economic theory of his type. But since the necessity for money is "one of these great rationalizing habits," the individual can be made to accept the consequences that money dictates, even if it provokes a great deal of pain on the Jeremy Bentham scale.

"The psychological type of theory [engendered by John Dewey's work at the University of Chicago] has brought money back into the very center of economics," Mitchell concluded. "From the use of money is derived not only the whole set of pecuniary concepts which the theorists and his subjects employ, but also the whole counting-house attitude toward economic activities. In its use are found the molds of economic rationality."[15]

How can society operate under the monetarist regime proposed successively by Hume, Ricardo, Marshall, and the Austrians, since the "quantity theory of money" violates the physical laws on which human society is based? By excluding the introduction of new technologies, monetarism dooms society to Malthusian extinction through failure to attain the "reducing power" that calls new "natural resources" into being. Long before the point of physical exhaustion of resources, monetarist-run economies undergo financial crisis.

The solution, according to the quantity theory of money preached by Ricardo, Marshall, and Friedman, is to loot the real resources of the economy to meet accumulated demands for debt service payment. If individual citizens are forced into what the monetarists dictate to be "the molds of economic rationality," they can be made to undergo looting of the type imposed by the Hitler regime. John Dewey, who later became an enthusiastic defender of Italian fascist Benito Mussolini, called this "social psychology." Today's fascists, who style themselves "the Aquarian Conspiracy," call it "operant conditioning." How to impose fascist economic measures without the "inefficiencies" of the Hitler and Mussolini regimes has been the major concern of the monetarists *as a matter of public record* since 1974, when the Initiatives Committee for National Economic Planning published its manifesto entitled "The Coming Corporativism: Fascism with a Democratic Face." On American soil, this project has its origins in 1892, when the students of Beatrice Webb formed the University of Chicago.

We can now stop discussing what it is that Milton Friedman thinks, a line of investigation that earlier produced unimpressive results. We are concerned, instead, with what Milton Friedman *is*. He is the dream of Wesley Clair Mitchell come true on the television screens and bookshelves of American homes. From his place among the Falsifiers in Malebolge, we can see Mitchell nod in agreement with us.

Economic behavior is what concerns us, Mitchell would say, not "objective" theories. The content of Milton Friedman's "theories" is what he persuades people to do. If he provokes his listeners to act in the manner required for the success of a fascist social order, that is the University of Chicago tradition. Mitchell once likened his beloved teacher Thorstein Veblen to David Hume.[16] Like Hume, and like Milton Friedman later, Veblen did not concern himself with the truth-content of his own statements, but with the "molds of rationality" he could impose on his listeners. Mitchell and his pupil Friedman are *right-wing Fabians.*

As an undergraduate, Mitchell proved his usefulness to the University of Chicago with a journal article, later published as his doctoral dissertation, entitled *A History of the Greenbacks.*[17] Mitchell denounced the Lincoln administration's "greenback" policy, which was actually a financial warfare device adopted by Lincoln's economists as a defense against London, and praised the 1879 Specie Resumption Act, which brought London back into financial control over America and provoked the great 1879 depression. In 1897 Dewey and Laughlin sent him for a year's study with Karl von Menger and Eugen Böhm-Bawerk in Vienna. In 1898 Mitchell spent a year at Oxford and took his master's degree, only eight years after John Ruskin's death. In 1912, Mitchell went to Vienna for additional graduate studies and shared Böhm-Bawerk's classroom with future Soviet official Nikolai Bukharin.

Bukharin's name on the class roll is not as surprising as it would seem. Already a British intelligence agent in training at the University of Vienna, he published in 1914 *The Economic Theory of the Leisure Class,* an almost verbatim copy of Veblen's 1899 work, of which he probably learned from Veblen's famous student Mitchell.[18] Later, as a Soviet planner, the Vienna graduate fought unsuccessfully for the economic policies that Veblen had promoted in the capitalist countries: nonindustrial, rural development, or what is now called the Chinese Maoist model.

Mitchell paid visits to Fabian Society leaders Sidney and Beatrice Webb and Bernard Shaw at the London

School of Economics, and to Alfred Marshall at Cambridge. John Dewey, who moved from Chicago to Columbia University in 1913, called on Mitchell in that year to join him, and Mitchell finished his long career there.

The fruits of Mitchell's work in Vienna appeared in 1913, in the form of his first book, entitled *Business Cycles*. Based on the frog-pond monetary cycles theory of the Austrians, Mitchell's volume sought to prove that inflation and depression are "not disruptions . . . but fluctuations systematically generated by economic organization itself," as Mitchell's leading student and successor, Arthur F. Burns, commented. Mitchell piled up statistics covering the previous 100 years of American "economic indicators." Not once did he mention that every American depression through the recently concluded Panic of 1907 was the direct and immediate result of contractions in loans available on the London market.

The 1879 Specie Resumption Act had placed America in the same vulnerable position that followed the scuttling of Nicholas Biddle's Second Bank of the United States in the 1830s. England still maintained the control over international trade financing that Ricardo and Sir Robert Peel had carved out during the first half of the nineteenth century. Even though America ran a surplus of exports to foreign countries over imports during every year since 1875, America's net liabilities to foreign countries—almost all to Britain—grew from $2.7 billion in 1897 to $3.9 billion in 1908. This sum, equal to three years' worth of imports at the time, was stupendous. The weak American money markets were dominated by the London-centered Morgan Bank, which pulled out

182   The Ugly Truth About Milton Friedman

liquid capital at every adverse turn of speculation in London. No single American economic crisis during the century analyzed by Mitchell was domestic in origin.

The entire subject of "business cycle theory" is so replete with unabashed dishonesty that Mitchell's "statistical work" recalls Jacques Rueff's warning about Hitler: "he turned a lie into a system of government."

If Mitchell did not honestly analyze a single "trade cycle" in American history, he instigated plenty of them, including the 1929 crash. Mitchell's set of "statistical indices" became the ruling economic theory at the just-created central bank, the Federal Reserve System. By Mitchell's methods, once the Federal Reserve determined that a downtrend in trade was in store, the Fed tightened credit and forced a downturn in trade. The Aquarian Conspiracy calls this a "feedback mechanism."

As a graduate research assistant to Chicago Professor J. Laurence Laughlin, known as the detractor of Alexander Hamilton's central banking policies, Mitchell helped to draft the Report of the National Monetary Commission that subsequently became the Federal Reserve Act of 1913. In 1909, Mitchell and Harvard Economics Professor Edwin Gay drew up plans for a national economic research institute as a counterpart to the proposed Fed System. Mitchell and Gay jumped into national prominence, however, only with the August 1917 American entry into World War I. On the advice of banker Paul Warburg, the "Father of the Federal Reserve," President Woodrow Wilson named Bernard Baruch to create a War Industries Board, with economic powers like those of the present Federal Emergency Management Agency. Baruch, a grandson of B'nai B'rith founder Kuntner Baruch, was attorney for the Anglo-American financial firm of Guggenheim and a personal friend of Winston Churchill. The War Industries Board became the central planning agency for the wartime economy, allocating raw materials, machinery, and labor, and making or breaking great fortunes at will.

Baruch appointed Gay the chief and Mitchell the deputy head of the War Industries Board's Division of Planning and Statistics. Within a short twenty years, the men of the University of Chicago had risen from the settlement houses of the Chicago stockyards to become the directors of national economic policy. The agents of the British Roundtable, which had first convened in 1890 to protect the British Empire from the advancing industrial nations, were now in official control of American economic policy.

Mitchell's "new" statistical methods entered the government, whence they have never left. Three days after the armistice, Baruch assigned Gay and Mitchell to continue their operation as the Central Bureau of Planning and Statistics. Mitchell prepared all American statistics for the Versailles Treaty, including estimates for the reparations bill.

In February 1920, Edwin Gay, Wesley Mitchell, and their entire wartime staff met in New York with partners of the Roundtable investment banks Lazard Frères and Kuhn Loeb.[19] The meeting produced the National Bureau of Economic Research, the privately controlled but quasi-official arbiter of economic statistics. Two Nobel Prize-winning economists have been prominently associated with the National Bureau. One is Milton Friedman, who joined its staff in 1946 while Wesley

184   The Ugly Truth About Milton Friedman

Mitchell was still research director. The other is Wassily Leontief. Mitchell and Gay personally brought Leontief from the University of Berlin to New York in 1931 to conduct the research on Gross National Product and input-output models, for which Leontief won the Swedish prize in 1973.

Two features of this transaction are revealing. The first is Leontief's career itself. From the National Bureau, Leontief made his reputation as the chief statistician of the Strategic Bombing Survey and provided the "evidence" that led Milton Friedman, Burton C. Klein, and other defenders of the Nazi system to conclude that Schacht was "too cautious." This scholarly atrocity heavily implicates chief economist Leontief. If that were not sufficient damnation, Leontief showed up on the podium of the inaugural press conference of the Initiatives Committee on National Economic Planning, the proponent organization for "Fascism with a Democratic Face."

More interesting is the close relationship between Leontief's sponsor in New York, Wesley Mitchell, and his protector at Berlin, Werner Sombart. A close friend of Mitchell's, Sombart had virtually adopted Leontief when the young Russian was nineteen and persuaded him not to return to the Soviet Union. At Mitchell's request, Sombart dispatched Leontief to New York. Two years earlier, in 1929, Mitchell had published a glowing review of Sombart's treatise *High Capitalism:* "Sombart's work promises to stimulate further enquiry. That is the greatest service a scientific investigation can perform."[20] Mitchell won him honorary membership that year in the American Economic Association.

Sombart had spent most of his career as a "Marxist"

opponent of the Austrian School. "Then," writes Ludwig von Mises maliciously, "when the Nazis seized power, he crowned a literary career of forty-five years by a book on German Socialism [*Deutscher Sozialismus*, translated into English in 1937 as *A New Social Philosophy*]. The guiding idea of this work was that the *Führer* gets his orders from God, the supreme *Führer* of the Universe, and that *Führertum* is a permanent revelation."[21]

The relationship of the National Bureau of Economic Research to Nazi fascism is, however, more tangible than a general agreement on so-called economic theory or mere personal associations.

How Britain caused the crash

The Mitchell "theory of business cycles" provided the Federal Reserve—Paul Warburg's institution—with the pretext for provoking such "cycles" through monetary action. The 1929 crash and the subsequent Great Depression were brought on by the Federal Reserve and the Bank of England's stated intent to create such a crash.

The lobby for an American depression had been active for years before 1929. It opened for business in 1923 when the National Bureau of Economic Research, under a commission from Secretary of Commerce Herbert Hoover, issued Mitchell's *Business Cycles and Unemployment*. The report proposed the Viennese quack cure for "cycles": "To lessen the excesses of booms and the sufferings of depressions," wrote Mitchell, the Federal Reserve must take "effective action . . . when industrial activity is approaching the elastic limit set by full use of existing plant, and when further expansion will be primarily a speculative boom ... it is desirable to raise discount rates in periods of sustained expansion."[22]

The type of long-term sustained growth the American economy had achieved could no longer take place under the regime the National Bureau prescribed for the Federal Reserve and Hoover. Noteworthy is that the main Wall Street proponent of Mitchell's understandably unpopular program was Paul Warburg, brother of Hjalmar Schacht's right-hand man Max Warburg, whose plans for the Federal Reserve had put J. Laurence Laughlin and Wesley Mitchell in business in the first place.[23] Almost alone among leading bankers, Warburg called for the Federal Reserve to crush the economy's expansion, claiming that it would "bring about a general depression involving the entire country."[24]

In Chicago, Economics Professor Henry Simons restyled the Viennese proposal to eliminate credit expansion from the economy, in the form of "100 percent reserve banking." Simons "was my teacher and my friend," Milton Friedman told a 1967 memorial gathering for Simons at the University of Chicago, "and above all, a shaper of my ideas. . . . Mine would be very different than they are if I had not the good fortune to be exposed to Henry Simons."[25] Simons, like Mitchell, had done his graduate studies at the University of Vienna.

The results of Mitchell-Warburg-Simons agitation for a money crunch are a matter of record: We recall the floor of the New York Stock Exchange, October 24, 1929. Clerks in shirtsleeves chalk up, rub out, and frantically chalk up again prices that show that the market value of American industry has collapsed by 10 percent over the morning. The ticker has fallen hopelessly behind, as sell orders from across the country swamp the trading floor. Big blocks of equity find no buyers. A crowd has gathered outside the marble pillars of the Exchange. At the Morgan Bank on 23 Wall Street, New York's leading bankers devise secret, fruitless plans to quench the panic. The Great Depression has begun.[26]

Overlooking the scene of chaos, in the visitors' gallery, stands a short, dog-faced man, who watches with a grim feeling of accomplishment. The enemy has been put to rout, he must have thought to himself. He wrote later: "The whole wealth so swiftly gathered in the proper values of previous years vanished. The prosperity of millions of Americans had grown upon a gigantic structure of inflated credit, now suddenly proved phantom."

The name of the watcher in the visitors' gallery was Winston Churchill. He had reason to gloat.

Documents that prove that London had conspired to bring on the crash are in the public domain. An official Federal Reserve memo dated February 7, 1929, noted that the Bank of England demanded that American interest rates "be raised, at some unspecified time by a full one percent with a view to breaking the spirit of speculation, and then subsequently if necessary by another one percent, in order to provoke liquidation, and then after a fall in the stock market similar rate action at the first sign of the next revival. By thus prostrating the stock market . . . we should be cutting at the root of the current situation."

In a February 4, 1929, cable the Governor of the Bank of England, Montagu Norman, wrote: "A scramble for gold is threatened. This threat arises from credit position in the United States as shown particularly by abnormal Call and Time rates [short-term money rates] which appear to be due to Stock Exchange speculation. Therefore expectation is that Boston and/or Philadelphia [Federal Reserve Banks] will recommend one percent increase in Bank Rate on 6th or 13th. . . . Further increases may follow if needed to adjust credit position."

That cable informed the Bank of England of Montagu Norman's agreement with the New York Federal Reserve Bank to provoke a stock market crash.

On Black Thursday, October 24, Montagu Norman cabled the New York Federal Reserve with congratulations—before the panic had actually occurred! "Recent liquidation in your stock market and reduction in call money rates have been satisfactory and have helped to reestablish international position."

As the cited cables state, the Bank of England and the New York Federal Reserve conspired to put up interest rates and take related measures to choke off the flow of funds into the stock market. In September, the Bank of England raised its discount rate from 5.5 percent to 6.5 percent in order to draw funds off from the New York market, while the Federal Bank of New York did as much as it dared to tighten credit at the source. Seventeen days before the crash, New York Fed President George L. Harrison bragged about the success of the credit squeeze: "The policy which we adopted early in August, of putting out funds through the bill market under the protection of an effective six percent rate, has thus far worked much better than I had even dared hope. Bills [trade-related paper] have gone up, discounts [Fed issuance of direct credits to banks] have gone down, and the total volume of Federal Reserve credit has expanded only in proportion to the historic seasonal line.... We can continue this program so that the total volume of discounts in the system will gradually decline to a figure much less than we have averaged during the past year."

But as the crash demonstrated, further action was superfluous. The New York Fed, staffed by British collaborators from the Morgan bank and the Bank of England, had brought the roof down.

These facts are well known and widely available. Also well known is that British banks began withdrawing immense amounts of funds from the New York money market, which had supported purchases of stocks on margin. Britain's pound sterling, bled white by the drain of international money into the New York stock market boom, had undergone a spectacular recovery on the markets in October 1929, *before* Black Thursday, as the City of London sucked in money in preparation for the crash!

No one at the time of the crash doubted that the British had done it. As another vulture who descended on New York City to watch Black Thursday, London *Economist* editor Josiah Hirst, wrote later: "I recollect at a London gathering of economists early in 1929 a discussion of the Stock Exchange boom in New York.... We all agreed, I think, that a slump or crash was then probable. The rise of the London Bank [of England] Rate to 6.5 percent on September 26 precipitated the Stock Exchange crisis and slump of October. Whether the action of the Bank [of England] in raising its rate was right or wrong need not be discussed here.... The mob of small speculators held on till the last moment, whereas many of the big speculators, being better informed and impressed by the selling movements from London and the Continent, began to liquidate in September and unloaded their holdings on the market, which was consequently weakened."

In New York City, the financial page of the *New York Times* had been egging on the crash for months. In fact, by the time the panic struck, the Roundtable's *New York Times* had declared a half-dozen previous breaks in the market to be the Last Day for the hordes of sinning speculators.

The United States did not have a depression because it had a stock market crash. It had a stock market crash because British control of the international markets created a depression. Above all, the financial policies of British Treasury Minister Winston Churchill wrecked the postwar prospect of an American-led boom in world trade. Churchill's tenure as Britain's Chancellor of the Exchequer from 1924 to 1929 shut American industry out of world markets. In a close parallel to the London Eurodollar cancer during the 1970s, London bled American capital to revive the bankrupt financial empire of the pound sterling, at the direct expense of American industry. American acquiescence in Winston Churchill's world looting plan passed a death sentence on the American economy, marked by the 1929 crash.

From the disastrous 1919 Treaty of Versailles to the 1931 collapse of the pound sterling itself, the bankrupt British provoked a series of economic disasters and extricated themselves from each by provoking a worse one. The irony of 1929 is that the great stock market boom was the runaway consequence of Winston Churchill's 1925 attempt to repeg world currencies to a valueless pound backed only by borrowed American gold reserves. Once the City of London had transformed the world economy into a speculative madhouse, the world's free capital flooded into shares in American industry, the one viable sector of the international economy. When the flight into the New York stock market threatened to bring down the valueless pound, London decided to collapse the market.

But the stock market crash set in motion the chain of events that led to the great chain-reaction bankruptcy of 1931 and brought down sterling. The City of London then played its last card: to place their agent Adolf Hitler at the head of Germany as a marcher-lord against the Soviet Union. London had already dug the 50 million graves of the next war.

That unspeakable string of British crimes is the hidden subject of the lies about the Great Crash. Canadian-born Professor John Kenneth Galbraith, an intimate of the Warburg banking family that played a key "insider" role in the crash itself, assembled the most widely read package of lies in his book *The Great Crash.* An outspoken apologist for Hitler's Economics Minister Hjalmar Schacht, Galbraith denies that the credit policies of the Bank of England and their collaborators at the New York Fed created the mess: "Far more important than rate of interest and the supply of credit is the mood. Speculation on a large scale requires a pervasive sense of confidence and optimism that ordinary people were meant to be rich. . . . Sometime, sooner or later, confidence in the short-run reality of increasing common stock values would weaken. When this happened, some people would sell, and this would destroy the reality of increasing values."

That is, a burst of madness created the speculative wave, and the "ten good years of the Twenties had to be paid for by the ten bad ones of the Thirties."

The other side of Galbraith's clipped coin is the lie that the American economy was already "naturally" slipping into depression and that the stock market crash only hastened the inevitable. The centerpiece of this lie, which is a favorite of British writers, is the claim that capital investment rose too fast:

"Throughout the Twenties, production and productivity per worker grew steadily: Between 1919 and 1929, output per worker in manufacturing industries increased by about 43 percent ... costs fell, and with prices the same, profit increased. ... A large and increasing investment in capital goods was a principal device by which the profits were being spent."

Therefore, "anything that interrupted the investment outlays—anything, indeed, which kept them from showing the necessary rate of increase—could cause trouble." In other words, the American economy collapsed because it was successful, because it did not follow the contemporary British model of deindustrialization! The New Deal myth of the "Mature Society," the granddaddy of all zero-growth, income redistribution programs, found rationalization in this lie.

But there is one significant kernel of truth to sustain the "over-investment" propaganda line. Between 1926 and 1929, capital investment in American industry rose at a compound annual rate of 11 percent—several times higher than during the last decade to the present. After the crash and subsequent financial disasters, capital investment fell to virtually zero. The entire workforce of the capital goods industries found itself on the pavement. These workers ceased buying consumer goods, which shut down production in much of the consumer goods industry. At the depth of the slump, industrial production had fallen a crushing 40 percent, total output of goods and services had halved, and unemployment was over 30 percent.

An American System economy based on high rates of technological progress must either grow at an accelerating rate or dissipate its energies into collapse. There is no in-between. For this reason, the strongest economy of the 1920s had the farthest to fall during the 1930s.

The supercilious Galbraith and his fellow liars demonstrate the opposite of what they intend: An American economy based on American System principles cannot exist in a world market ruled by Britain. There was not during the 1920s, nor can there ever be, a reconciliation between the American System and the British System. Once London chained the world economy to a system of war-debt repayment at Versailles, American industry was shut out from the world market. The decline of the world market ultimately prevented America from achieving the accelerating growth rate it had geared up for. London's domination of world financial policy created the theater for the sequence of British covert manipulation and haywire effects.

In the economic data of the 1920s, all this is immediately evident. Between 1921 and 1929, output of all industrial commodities for domestic consumption rose from $26 billion to $38 billion. As noted, capital investment rose at rates that dwarf anything since 1958. A good pointer is auto production. At 5,358,000 in 1929, new-car registration had almost reached the level of the height of the post-World War II boom in 1953, when registration totaled 5,700,000.

In complete variance, exports hardly rose at all. Foreign shipments stood at $3.3 billion in 1921, $3.7 billion in 1926, and a marginally increased $3.9 billion in the year of the crash. As a percentage of output, exports actually *fell* from 12 percent to 10 percent. In lockstep, the *rate of rise* of production began falling in 1926, from a 1921-1926 compound growth rate of over 11 percent a year, to a 1926-1929 rate of only 1 percent a year! By the summer of 1929, a few months before the crash, all major categories of production and transportation had already begun shrinking, a circumstance reported out of context by the lying proponents of "inevitable depression."

What makes the stagnation of exports, which brought down the entire economy, especially shocking is that America was lending to foreign customers throughout the period at a rate greater than at the apex of the 1970s Eurodollar boom. In the six years from 1924 to 1930, America lent over $3 billion to foreign countries. Foreign lending reached the incredible rate of $1 billion a year during 1928—at the precise point that exports started to fall. In the smaller scale of the 1920s, these numbers are indeed huge; total plant and equipment purchases during the period were only $17.3 billion.

How could this have happened?

The great betrayal

American foreign lending did the American economy no good because nearly all foreign lending was either to the City of London or to investment sinkholes created by the City of London. It happened that way because Thomas Lamont of Morgan and Benjamin Strong of the New York Federal Reserve conspired with Winston Churchill and Montagu Norman of the Bank of England to make sure it happened. Billions in American capital were put to the service of the bankrupt pound sterling, in order to restore its status as the top international lending currency—which Winston Churchill attempted in 1925.

In a nutshell, the City of London blackmailed the world for the costs of servicing the monstrous war debt perpetuated by the British Roundtable's Versailles "peace" treaty in 1919. A single fact about the monetary system of the 1920s makes all the later disintegration obvious: *Debt service payments on war obligations were roughly equal to all other loans extended to all foreign borrowers for all purposes!*

Of course, the relationship between the Versailles Treaty's war debts and the international lending during the 1920s was not direct in the sense that every dollar lent immediately went to service war debts. Nor could it have been: International trade would have ceased to exist. Instead, the debts contracted through the end of 1919 were "restructured" into an even greater mass of longer-term obligations whose payment schedules stretched out through the next half-century, as shown by the table below (in billions of dollars).

The bloated mass of debts cost almost $400 million a year to maintain, against a tough average of $600 million a year in new loans. No wonder, then, that American exports stagnated.

These numbers represent only the Allied interwar debt. Under British Roundtable progeny Lloyd George's slogan, "Squeeze Them Till the Pips Squeak,"

	War debts as of 1919	War debts after refinancing
Britain	4.604	11.0
France	4.625	7.547
Italy	0.631	2.685
Belgium	0.418	0.728

the Roundtable's Versailles Treaty imposed $33 billion in reparations on defeated Germany. That was equivalent to Germany's total production in a good year.

To nail the coffin lid shut, Montagu Norman and Benjamin Strong intentionally pricked the monetary bubble that had built up during the war years, throwing the United States into a brief but severe depression in 1921. A fulminating Norman wrote to Strong, his agent-of-influence at the New York Federal Reserve who had engineered a credit crunch on Norman's orders, on the subject of the U.S. postwar economic boom: "We are determined to stop this mad march of speculation and expansion, whether it be in securities, real estate, commodities or what not.... At last the first step has been taken towards freeing Federal Reserve rate policy" for a deflationary coup.

Norman's outburst was penned in January 1920. In December of that year, Benjamin Strong visited London and wrote back to his colleagues at the New York Fed that the Bank of England "considers that general rate policy has so far been wonderfully successful although the position here might be better today had they been more drastic six months earlier. The fact remains that world deflation had been started."

The conspirators had instigated a "wonderfully successful" act of economic sabotage against the American economy, which threatened to shove the bankrupt British out of world trade. The effect was shattering. Prices in world trade fell to half their 1920 levels by 1922. In cold cash, that meant that the real cost of international debt service, in terms of deflated prices for goods, had doubled.

With the United States in temporary decline, the British made their grand play at a meeting of world central bankers at Genoa in 1922. Previously, Norman said, central banks had held their reserves in gold. That would no longer do. Henceforward, only Britain and the United States will hold reserves in gold. Everyone else will hold their reserves in pound sterling, or perhaps dollars—but principally sterling. Norman was asking for the world. London had consciously and deliberately destroyed what might have remained of Britain's industrial markets after the war. America's emergence as the one sound postwar economy prevented London from skimming world trade off the top through financial control, as it had done since 1782. So Montagu Norman wanted the world's foreign exchange reserves!

The Genoa meeting itself broke up without results, partly because President Harding's Treasury Secretary, Andrew Mellon, did not want to bail the British out, and put the anglophile Strong on a short leash. But two years later, Norman got precisely what he demanded on a silver platter, courtesy of the New York Federal Reserve and its backers at the Morgan Bank.

By 1925, the Bank of England, the New York Fed,

and the Morgan Bank had ridden over Europe like the Apocalyptic horsemen. German reparations were refinanced through a 900 million gold mark loan organized by the Morgan Bank, under the control of future U.S. ambassador to Britain Charles Dawes. The New York Federal Reserve's official historian wrote, "The vacuum left by the United States authorities was filled by J. P. Morgan and Co." Placed in charge, Hitler's future economic czar Hjalmar Schacht vigorously enforced the Dawes Loan provision that capital investment in the German economy cease. All of continental Europe, excepting France, was a protectorate of the Bank of England—directly in Central Europe, where Bank of England agents officially ran all central banking, and indirectly in Italy, where Winston Churchill's protégé Mussolini had seized power in 1922.

It fell to Chancellor of the Exchequer Churchill to announce the culmination of London's struggle to the top of the rubble heap. On April 1925, the dog-faced Churchill told the British Parliament that Britain had returned to the prewar gold standard, at the prewar parity of 4.85 pounds to the dollar. In fact, the rotten shell of the British currency was reinforced by hundreds of millions of dollars cheerfully provided by British agents-of-influence at the New York Fed and the Morgan Bank.

The betrayal of the dollar to the bankrupt pound was comprehensive. For six months prior to Churchill's gleeful announcement, Strong at the New York Fed dropped the bank's discount rate from 4.5 to 3 percent, and increased the money supply in the New York Federal Reserve District at an annual rate that, in present-day terms, would be the equivalent of 40 percent a year! With the dollar weakened by this hyperinflationary burst, sterling was sufficiently "strong" to repeg to gold.

Together, Morgan and the New York Fed jointly bankrolled the "gold pound." The Federal Reserve became a virtual branch of the Bank of England in a $200 million credit line for support of sterling. In turn, the Bank of England pledged an equivalent amount, two fifths of its own assets, to the New York Fed, and the two central banks agreed to subordinate all American credit policy to the grand design of keeping the bankrupt pound afloat. Two weeks after the deed had been done, Churchill assured Parliament of a glorious pecuniary future for the Empire.

On the contrary, the financial system immediately went haywire.

Churchill's action was one of the most onerous in world financial history. Even the British Roundtable saw how shaky their position was. Their agent, John Maynard Keynes, immediately opened a new flank, denounced Churchill in a pamphlet, and joined Sir Oswald Mosley, protégé of the Fabian Webbs and the future führer of the British Union of Fascists. Working with Mosley, Keynes wrote the prototype fascist economic program in 1926, the forerunner of Schacht's "autarky"—which Keynes would also enthusiastically support.

From the psychotic vantage point of a Churchill or Norman, there was one great monkey-wrench in the works: the still-prosperous United States economy. The City of London had almost no funds of its own. It depended on loans from New York, which it converted into sterling and re-lent to Germany, Central Europe, and Australia. After great bursts of lending in 1924 and 1925, American capital suddenly became obstinate. During 1926 it flooded into the New York stock market and ignored London. Sterling tottered. Churchill had fits of apoplexy.

In panic, Schacht and Norman arrived in New York in July 1927 to persuade Strong to shovel more money into the system and save sterling. Strong—despite vehement opposition from the Chicago Federal Reserve Bank and the threat of congressional investigation—cut his lending rate from 4 percent to 3.5 percent, and bought dollar and sterling securities alike to pump money into the system.

Strong's second great dose of monetary inflation had horrible side effects. Initially, it revived the outflow of funds—Britain's looting of American capital—to a then stupendous level of over $1 billion during 1928. But it also set off a modest bubble in the New York Stock Exchange, whose shares doubled in value between the beginning of 1928 and the crash of October 24, 1929. Relative to American industrial strength and the size of the American economy, the sudden takeoff in share values was less than a mortal problem. Britain had turned the world into a roulette table, and America was the only confidence-inspiring game in town. Funds pouring in from abroad buoyed the market, and the drain pushed sterling to the brink. As reported above, the City of London had resolved to kill the stock market by the beginning of 1929 at the very latest.

Norman's October 24, 1929 boast that the crash had "helped to reestablish Britain's international position" meant, specifically, that the American capital markets were Britain's for the picking once again. The American securities markets did not collapse immediately after Black Thursday. On the contrary, Morgan and its allies raised a then record $700 million in foreign loans during the first half of 1930.

What had collapsed was American industry's fighting spirit. Three years of stagnating production and exports had taken their toll on America's capacity to sustain the necessary rising rate of productive investment. The crash killed it. Britain's black operation created panic, which had its own self-feeding effects. Chief among these was the mammoth error of the Hawley-Smoot protective tariff, passed with the support of American industrialists and farmers who despaired of access to world markets.

In an act of supreme irresponsibility, the City of London had wrung the neck of the Golden Goose. The collapse of the American economy, the one pillar of world economic activity during the 1920s, brought world disaster. World trade closed down, prices fell by 1931 to half their 1929 levels, and the big borrowers of the 1920s defaulted in a chain reaction.

Britain itself was nonplussed, shifting the worst of the 30 percent collapse of sterling's international parity onto its colonies, the price of whose raw material shipments to Britain had dropped 60 percent. The Hitler policy was in the works as far back as 1928, when Norman spoke of Germany to a financial friend, "There will be no real settlement without a crisis—real and sufficiently real to frighten politicians and public."

The line of investigation opened in the first chapter citing Jacques Rueff's report that Anglo-American financiers had delivered Germany into Hjalmar Schacht's hands, now comes full circle. After the July 1931 collapse of the Austrian *Kreditanstalt,* a chain-reaction of banking collapses swept Europe. Germany, laboring under the immense burden of Allied reparations demands, faced national disaster after Paul Warburg, chairman of the International Acceptance Bank, vetoed the proposal among a syndicate of Germany's private creditors to provide an emergency short-term loan. Rueff, then financial attaché to the French embassy in London, was a witness to the set-up of Schacht's policy.

"The governments reacted as they always do in such cases; they called an international conference," Rueff reported, "which met in London during the holiday period."[27] Over French objections, the British and American delegations decided that "the threat hanging over the German currency is due to the flight of short-term capital invested in Germany in the face of a potential new inflation. Since it is the outflow of such capital that endangers German currency, there is only one solution, which is to tie it up in Germany, or, in other words, to prevent it from leaving the mark area."[28] As we noted earlier, the London conference imposed the Schachtian controls system on Germany. "When Hitler assumed power he found already established the system that would enable his regime to function and endure," Rueff concluded.[29]

The Viennese economists were filled with ghoulish glee over the collapse of the world's financial system. Friedrich von Hayek lied: "There is no reason to assume that the crisis was started by a deliberate deflationary action on the part of the monetary authorities, or that the deflation itself is anything but a process induced by the maladjustments of industry left over from the boom."[30]

Unlike von Hayek, Friedman—perversely—admits that "the severity of each of the major contractions—1920-21, 1929-33, and 1937-38—is directly attributable to acts of commission and omission by the Reserve authorities."[31] Friedman says this in order to promote his own variant of the old von Mises-Henry Simons plan to eliminate the extension of credit in the national economy. Friedman's famous proposal is to "drastically curtail the discretionary power of the monetary authorities," in favor of "a legislated rule instructing the monetary authority to achieve a specified rate of growth in the stock of money.... I would specify that the Reserve System shall see to it that the total stock of money so defined rises month by month, and indeed, so far as possible, day by day, at an annual rate of X percent, where X is some number between 3 and 5."[32]

The choice Friedman presents is between a central bank that deliberately undercuts economic growth, and a "legislated rule" that would prevent economic growth altogether. This idea is to be taken no more seriously than his suggestion to cut the federal budget outright by $100 billion. It is a form of Deweyan operant conditioning aimed at hardening the "molds of economic rationality" discussed by Friedman's teacher Wesley Mitchell.

Friedman's "analysis" of the post-1929 misery of the American economy is a laughingstock, even at the National Bureau of Economic Research. Friedman's contention is the following: "All told, from July 1929 to March 1933, the money stock in the United States fell by one-third, and over two-thirds of the decline came from England's departure [in 1931] from the gold standard. Had the money stock been kept from declining, as it clearly could and should have been, the contraction would have been both shorter and far milder. It might have still been relatively severe by historical standards. But it is literally inconceivable that money income could have declined by over one-half and prices by over one-third in the course of four years if there had been no decline in the stock of money."[33]

The directors of the National Bureau of Economic Research felt constrained to write an appendix to Friedman's *Monetary History of the United States,* which the Bureau itself published, explaining the idiocy of Friedman's "underlying assumption."[34] Written by National Bureau director and Lazard Frères partner Albert J. Hettinger, Jr., the appendix points out that the Federal Reserve cannot simply increase the money supply in a general banking panic. "This is not a controlled experiment," Hettinger admonished Friedman, "with high-powered money held constant. Depositors were watching their banks. . . . With respect to the final statement that the [1931] collapse of the monetary system was unnecessary, this I cannot feel has been proved."[35]

Hettinger's argument is that once a worldwide panic was in full tilt, it was not the Federal Reserve's prerogative to prevent a decline in the money supply. Black Thursday unleashed a series of uncontrollable consequences, uncontrollable even from the vantage point of the men who touched off the 1929 collapse. Albert Hettinger quotes Lord Keynes in 1931: "Nothing is more suicidal than a rational investment policy in an irrational world."[36] Milton Friedman's own worm's-eye view of the matter was incompetent in the opinion of the National Bureau directors.

We know with hindsight that the least manageable of the consequences of the 1929 crash was Adolf Hitler. The Austrian corporal took his race theory from John Ruskin and Houston Stewart Chamberlain, his geopolitical theories from Sir Halford Mackinder and Colonel Haushofer, his exotic mysticism from the Oxford cultists, and his economics from Hjalmar Schacht. Even the swastika symbol was a favorite of the British kooks before Hitler was born; a hooked cross is carved into the stone of Ruskin's tomb at Oxford, and Rudyard Kipling had it engraved on the frontispieces of his first books.[37] The historian is at a loss to discover any innovations beyond the quirks of nineteenth-century Oxford and Vienna in later Nazi activities. Carol White has shown why Hitler, British product though he was, did not fulfill the British geopolitical aim of marching east against the "heartland" instead of west.[38] Although British sympathies for Hitler persisted almost until the fall of Prime Minister Neville Chamberlain (a relative of Houston Stewart Chamberlain), the split between Dr. Frankenstein—London—and his monster—Nazi Germany—is dated more or less officially from Schacht's 1938 break with Hitler.

In understanding the relationship between Nazi fascism and its creators, it is important to understand that fascism did not begin with Hitler or Mussolini, and did not end with them. The afterbirth of Nazism has never been cleaned up. The central European and British nobility who sponsored Adolf Hitler from his Vienna days onward reorganized themselves during the 1930s into a new international body, perpetuating the cult and policy features of Nazism into another generation. It is certain that in a better-ordered world, some of the Allied victors would have been in the Nuremberg dock with Göring and Speer.

One of the unsettling ironies in the entire business is that the child of impoverished Jewish emigrants to the United States, Milton Friedman, turned up like a foundling on the doorstep of the Nazi economists.

The Undead of Economics

6

> *It is science and not men of science we want to enlighten and animate our politics and rule the world.*
> —H. G. Wells

Without exception, the history of ideas drags up more skulduggery, plots, cloak-and-dagger operations, and so forth than comparatively tame subjects like espionage. As we proceed to uncover the more recent history of the Vienna cult of irrationalism, and in particular, the activities of the semisecret organization known as the Mont Pelerin Society, some well-known occult novels will seem more biographical than fictional. Central are the figures of Count Coudenhove-Kalergi and his successor as chairman of the Pan-European Union, Otto von Hapsburg, the pretender to the defunct crown of Austria. Hapsburg, whose shadowy existence has taken him from the Madrid terror networks of the old SS commando Otto von Skorzeny to the side of West Germany's Franz-Josef Strauss, deserves more recognition among American conservatives than he currently enjoys: it is his web of regrouped aristocrats that controls Milton Friedman, vice-president of the Mont Pelerin Society.

Coudenhove-Kalergi and his protégé von Hapsburg are the tangible, living connection between the Vienna of Hitler's painter days under the reign of Wittelsbach Empress Elizabeth, and the "free enterprise" phalanx of idea factories that employs Milton Friedman as chief publications man. The pseudopods of Nazi economics at the University of Chicago, Columbia, and elsewhere ensured the direct continuity of the strain: John Dewey and his friends brought von Mises and von Hayek to the United States. After World War II, the members of the old Vienna web reconvened at Mont Pelerin in Switzerland, where they launched the campaign to take America, a campaign that may now be on the verge of final victory.

Never mentioned in the newspapers, and cited only in hushed tones by its own members, the Mont Pelerin Society wields sovereign power over the right wing of American politics. Every loudspeaker through which Milton Friedman's voice filters is wired back into the Society's European headquarters, directed by its secretary, Max von Thurn und Taxis of the centuries-old Hapsburg-related family, and by its president, Friedrich von Hayek. Along with von Hayek, Archduke Otto von Hapsburg directs the Society's German-speaking branch.

At any given political function in the United States on behalf of "free market" economics or "sound money" principles, one of the hundred or so American members of the Society is usually featured as a speaker. When asked about the Mont Pelerin Society, the individual concerned will say that he is indeed a member of an innocuous organization of that name, whose only function is to serve as a forum for the discussion of liberal economics—the way Murder, Inc. was a florist's delivery service. Pressed, the individual will invariably back off, saying that he cannot discuss the Society's activities with nonmembers. How does one join the Society? "Membership is by invitation only."

The Mont Pelerin Society's American operatives infiltrate every institution that professes conservative ideology. They include Milton Friedman and George Stigler of the University of Chicago, vice-president and president, respectively, of the Society; Hoover Institution director Glenn Campbell and Hoover economist Martin Anderson, both advisers to Ronald Reagan; *Barron's Magazine* editor Robert M. Bleiberg; *National Review* editor William F. Buckley, Jr.; National Committee on Monetary Reform president Donald Kemmerer and board member John Exter; former U.S. attorney general and Chicago professor Edward H. Levi; *Wall Street Journal* columnist Edwin McDowell; Heritage Foundation director Edwin J. Feulner, Jr.; and American Enterprise Institute president William J. Baroody, Sr.[1]

That these ideological ghouls are walking around in leading positions in American political life is like something out of a cheap horror movie. Whatever was most rotten in the irrationalist, zero-growth, racist circles in Vienna at the turn of the century re-formed itself in exile as the Mont Pelerin Society in 1947.

Count Richard Coudenhove-Kalergi, named after family friend Richard Wagner, is the subject of thick dossiers at every police headquarters in Europe. He was the son of an Austrian diplomat who was an intimate

210   The Ugly Truth About Milton Friedman

friend of such Vienna luminaries as Richard Wagner, Theodore Herzl, and race ideologue Houston Stewart Chamberlain, whom the Count described in his memoirs as "a friendly old intellectual."[2]

Particularly after the Second World War, his name and organization, the Pan-European Union, have been linked to the terrorist network known as "Die Spinne" (the Spider), or the "Black International." One facet of the Black International is the international assassination bureau called Permindex, which was cited for involvement in the assassination of John Kennedy.

To the extent that the Vienna kooks and their allies in Germany maintained an open political front-organization, it was the Pan-European Union, which Coudenhove-Kalergi founded in 1924. The objectives of this organization had nothing to do with what is now the European Community, the organization of European unity that flowered under French President de Gaulle and West German Chancellor Adenauer, and that flourishes now under President Valéry Giscard d'Estaing and Chancellor Helmut Schmidt. The objectives of the Pan-European Union were, simply, to revive the Austro-Hungarian Empire and restore feudal Europe. Otto von Hapsburg was barred from West German parliamentary elections in 1979 because he holds these views, deemed correctly by the West German government as "anti-constitutional."

Coudenhove-Kalergi reports the founding of the Pan-European Union straightforwardly in his memoirs:

"At the beginning of 1924, we received a call from Baron Louis Rothschild: one of his friends, Max Warburg from Hamburg, had read my book and wanted to get to know us. To my great surprise, Warburg spontaneously offered us 60,000 gold marks, to tide the movement over for its first three years. I suggested to him that we spend half of it in Austria, and half in Germany ... Max Warburg, who was one of the most distinguished and wisest men that I have ever come into contact with, had a principle of financing these movements. ... He remained a convinced Pan European for his entire life, and we were bound by a warm friendship up until his death in 1946."

Later that year, Coudenhove-Kalergi went to Berlin, where "Hjalmar Schacht was the main speaker at the first German Pan-European meeting in the Reichstag building." Schacht and Max Warburg were president and vice-president of the Hitler Reichsbank together until 1938.

Touring Europe, Coudenhove-Kalergi enunciated the viewpoint that has since borne the label "One-Worldism." He argued that the League of Nations should rule and secure British interests against *both* fledgling superpowers, the United States and the Soviet Union.

"The rapprochement of the British Empire," he wrote, "as a section of the League of Nations, would strengthen its firm ties, and a united continent, in closest association with England ... could prevent a world hegemonic Russia or America, [and] would set up a world balance of powers under the control of the League of Nations." The League was then run by Sir Robert Cecil, whose own man, Winston Churchill, became a fervent supporter of the Pan-European Union.[3]

Max Warburg, Coudenhove-Kalergi reports, arranged his 1925 trip to the United States. There to receive him in America were Max's brother Paul Warburg and financier Bernard Baruch, the patrons of Wesley Clair Mitchell's National Bureau of Economic Research. Coudenhove-Kalergi was introduced to the entire anglophile banking elite, including Owen Young, author of the Young plan to refinance World War I reparations; Commerce Secretary Herbert Hoover; and Woodrow Wilson's *eminense grise,* Colonel House. At the conclusion of his trip, Coudenhove-Kalergi founded the American Cooperative Committee of the Pan-European Union, under the chairmanship of Columbia University President Nicholas Murray Butler, also president of the Carnegie Foundation. Butler is the man who had told his students that totalitarian regimes brought forth "men of far greater intelligence, far stronger character, and far more courage than the system of elections." Earlier he had brought Chicago's John Dewey and Wesley Mitchell to Columbia.

Throughout the 1920s, Coudenhove-Kalergi resided in Switzerland to savor "the eternal Europe of the peasantry as a great cultural entity along the side of the thin and transient veneer of urban art." In effect, the Pan-European Union operated at the behest of the British Empire, as Coudenhove-Kalergi had told Churchill and other British leaders in 1925.

The Pan-European Union, more than any other organization, legitimized the Hitler coup d'état in 1933. With the British leaders, the Pan-European Union believed that "Hitler will bring about Pan-Europa—Hitler alone can create Pan-Europa, because he alone does not have to fear any right-wing opposition," as Coudenhove-Kalergi quoted Hjalmar Schacht's briefing to him in January 1933. Schacht added: "Hitler alone doesn't have to have any consideration for this opposition; therefore he, and he alone, will succeed in finally guaranteeing Europe's peace and cooperation."

A few days later, Coudenhove-Kalergi met in Vienna with Colonel Karl Haushofer, the Bavarian student of British geopolitician Halford Mackinder and the man who had ghostwritten *Mein Kampf* ten years earlier. Haushofer, whose *Zeitschrift für Geopolitik* "always had a friendly word for Pan-Europa," the Count recalled, "described Hitler, whom he personally knew, as a typically half-educated person. But on the other hand, Haushofer spoke in a very friendly fashion about Rudolf Hess."

The same March, Coudenhove-Kalergi met Mussolini. His interchange with the Italian fascist dictator is published in the Count's own memoirs: "The idea of fascism traced itself back to Nietzsche's anti-democratic philosophy, just as Hitler's dreams went back not in the least to the romanticism of Wagner's operas. I remarked that Nietzsche was a predecessor of the Pan-European Movement, and I gave him the publication *Paneuropa,* with a complete collection of Nietzsche's writings on the United States of Europe." The meeting with Mussolini lasted several days.

The Pan-European Union's mission, however, was not to join Hitler, but to maintain the international climate in which Hitler would be tolerated. Coudenhove-Kalergi settled on Austrian fascist Engelberg Dollfuss, then the honorary president of the Pan-European Union in Austria, and took up residence in Vienna. Hitler murdered Dollfuss after the 1938 *Anschluss* with Austria, and Coudenhove-Kalergi fled to England and to the open arms of Winston Churchill.

As the events of 1938 showed, Hjalmar Schacht had

erred in his original estimation of Hitler. A Frankenstein monster, Hitler—and his generals—could not be made to strike only east at Russia. To the British leadership, this was not obvious until Hitler and Göring threw Schacht and Max Warburg out of the Reichsbank. Even then Prime Minister Chamberlain backed Hitler at Munich. Quietly, however, the leading cadre of Pan-Europe packed their coffins and moved to the safety of England and America, their mission in German-speaking Europe complete.

The march west

The migration of the Vienna School was far more than a matter of convenience. Britain's elite was determined to realize Coudenhove-Kalergi's objectives in the war of ideas. Coudenhove-Kalergi's close friend in England, H. G. Wells, expostulated before an Oxford University audience in 1932, "I am asking for a liberal Fascisti, for enlightened Nazis. I am proposing that you consider the formation of a greater Communist Party, a Western response to Russia."[4]

Coudenhove-Kalergi, on the European side, and John Dewey, on the American side, proceeded to select which European scholars and scientists would survive the Nazi holocaust. Coudenhove-Kalergi's close associate, Hungarian physicist Leo Szilard, had already moved to Switzerland to be with Coudenhove-Kalergi in 1932, after a decade of organizing for the Pan-European Union in Budapest. In 1932, Szilard began to move the Pan-European Union's treasury into Switzerland, out of sensitive Germany. A few days after the Reichstag fire,

Szilard, an official of the Christian Social Party of Austria named Gottfried Kuhnwald, and British economist Sir William Beveridge—a classmate of von Mises and von Hayek—met in Vienna to plan the exodus.

Sir William Beveridge returned to England to form the Academic Assistance Council, and Szilard created the Society to Aid German Scientists Abroad in Zürich. At Columbia University, at the prompting of Columbia University President Nicholas Murray Butler, John Dewey and Wesley Clair Mitchell formed the Columbia Faculty Fellowship Fund, which later brought Szilard himself to Columbia. The center of the effort was the recruitment of German scientific personnel, in anticipation of the requirements of the Manhattan Project. In charge of scientific recruitment was Thorstein Veblen's brother Oswald Veblen, who wrote in May 1933: "The idea which seems to receive most favor is that of having a committee for the natural scientists, which should be composed in large part of what the Germans would call aryan scientists, together with a few men of affairs who would know how to raise funds. The idea would be to distribute the German scientists ... to allow them to continue their scientific work."[5]

As a matter of expedience, the Dewey-Veblen recruitment campaign brought to America some of the best of European scientists of the tradition of Bernhard Riemann and the Leibnizian Göttingen University. The success of the Manhattan Project and related Allied scientific ventures owes much to these Europeans. However, the migration of these gifted men took place under the political oversight of the Viennese irrationalists and their Oxford-Cambridge opposite numbers. In one of the more poignant ironies of the period, the great

Göttingen mathematician Richard Courant wound up at New York University—creating a powerful scientific faculty there for the first time—along with Count Richard Coudehove-Kalergi and his aide-de-camp, Vienna school economist Ludwig von Mises.

Von Mises, one of the house economists of the Hapsburg family before the First World War, rose in exile to membership on the Council of the Pan-European Union and, with Coudenhove-Kalergi, created the Research Seminar for European Federation at New York University. Again, Coudenhove-Kalergi's appearance at New York University was due to the financial support of John Dewey's U.S. Emergency Committee in Aid of Displaced Foreign Scholars, and the personal influence of Dewey's sponsor, Columbia president Butler. Von Mises's Viennese twin, Friedrich von Hayek, was meanwhile ensconced at the London School of Economics—writing justifications for letting the Great Depression ravage its course without interference.

Not the least benefit the British oligarchy had from Hitler was sudden, life-and-death rule over most of European continental science. Sixty years earlier, the mindless physics of Ernst Mach and the economic theories of Karl von Menger and W. S. Jevons had been an occult challenge to the achievements of American and German political economy, and to the scientific conquests of Bernhard Riemann and his Göttingen colleagues. Oxford and Vienna began the fight as raving medievalists, demanding the reversal of human progress since the Golden Renaissance. Now, anchored at the University of Chicago in America and at Oxford and Cambridge in England, the kooks were in position for the first time to dictate the terms of thought to the English-speaking world.

They made their official bid for world status in 1935 at the Seventh International Congress of Philosophy at Oxford, in the presence of Ludwig von Mises, Bertrand Russell, and the philosophical adherents of mad old Ernst Mach—future Mont Pelerin Society founder Karl Popper and Rudolf Carnap from Vienna. They heralded a "new era in philosophy," in fact, the superimposition of the old Vienna outrage against the *notion of causality* on reluctant Western minds. What became known as the "logical positivist movement," with early fortified positions at the University of Chicago and Columbia, was born there.

The various economists, physicists, mathematicians, and philosophers who made up the movement merely elaborated on what Mach and kook economist Karl von Menger had said half a century earlier: The human race must remain a spectator in nature, not the active shaper of nature. The Viennese and Oxford economists insisted that all wealth was fixed by nature, and that what man arrogantly calls production merely "alters the position in space" of this fixed wealth—a lie that dates back to Aristotle's *Politics*. Ernst Mach and the Viennese science mafia insisted that since there is no correspondence between the workings of the human mind and the laws of physical nature, man is condemned to stand forever bewildered and uncertain before the old pagan gods.

With the convening of the International Congress for Unity of Science in 1935, organized by Dewey and Russell, the Vienna ideologues acted like an amoeba, sucking in and nullifying opposing viewpoints. In 1938, at Dewey's University of Chicago, "boy wonder" president Robert Hutchins published the *International Encyclopedia of Unified Sciences,* under the direction of newly migrated Viennese Rudolf Carnap. The introductory article was written jointly by Russell, Dewey, and Carnap, restating a program of action set forth by Russell's collaborator H. G. Wells ten years earlier:

"I want to suggest that something, a new social organization, a new institution—which for a time I shall call *World Encyclopedia.* This World Encyclopedia would be the mental background of every intelligent man in the world. Such an Encyclopedia would play the role of an undogmatic Bible to world culture. It would do just what our scattered and disoriented intellectual organizations of today fall short of doing. It would hold the world together mentally. It would *compel* men to come to terms with one another. It is a super university I am thinking of, a World Brain, no less. Ultimately if our dream is realized it must exert a very great influence upon everyone who controls administrations, makes wars, directs mass behavior, feeds, moves, starves and kills populations. . . . You see how such an Encyclopedia organization could spread like a nervous network, a system of mental control, knitting a system of mental control about the globe, knitting all the intellectual workers of the world through a common interest and common medium of expression."[6]

That was in 1928. Russell, then preparing the 1935 Oxford conference mentioned above, wrote Wells, "I do not know anything with which I agree more entirely."[7] From his eyrie in Switzerland, Count Coudenhove-Kalergi dispatched Leo Szilard to London to obtain the Central European translation rights to Wells's work.[8]

Surveying the ruins of American intellectual life, it must be concluded that Wells's 1928 project, realized in the 1938 *International Encyclopedia of Unified Science* at the University of Chicago, was a devastating success. Published while Milton Friedman was a young Chicago graduate student, the *Encyclopedia* filled Wells's recommendation to the letter and "spread like a nervous network, a system of mental control about the globe."

There is no need at this point to review the conclusions of the project; we reviewed them in detail in the first chapter, citing Milton Friedman's call-to-arms, "The Methodology of Positive Economics." In that essay, Friedman insisted that "the relation between the significance of a theory and the 'realism' of its 'assumptions' is almost the opposite of that suggested by the view under criticism. Truly important and significant hypotheses will be found to have assumptions that are wildly inaccurate descriptive representations of reality, and, in general, the more significant the theory, the more unrealistic the assumptions."[9]

Friedman put in brash, blunt, American language the kernel of the Viennese method—which the Viennese themselves would have stated in less jarring and less comprehensible language. The great enemy of this theory of nonthinking is the principle of causality, the notion that the human mind can know the workings of the physical universe and act upon them. The conclusions of the Viennese assault are obvious: Man cannot intervene in nature to build industrial republics because wealth is fixed by nature and the workings of the economy are unknowable; science cannot penetrate further than it already has in the physical sciences because of the "uncertainty principle"; the human race is fixed in declining circumstances and subject to "limits to growth." That is what Milton Friedman says. All his blather about "free markets," "limited government," and "individual liberty" is by way of convincing the unwary reader to accept these limits.

Between Wells's 1928 proclamation for "universal mind control" and the first publication of the Chicago-based *Encyclopedia,* the Anglo-Viennese kooks carried out—among other things—the objectives for "economic science" set forth by Wesley Clair Mitchell and John Dewey at the turn of the century. As we reported, Mitchell complained that a mass of individuals acting on the motivations of Jeremy Bentham's pleasure-pain principle would be an irrational, incoherent, jarring mass. The solution to this problem Mitchell found in Dewey's "social psychology" or what Wells more bluntly called "mind control": *imposing* what Mitchell said was a "rational theory of economic life." As we quoted Mitchell earlier, "Because it thus rationalizes economic life itself, the use of money lays the foundation for a rational theory of that life."[10]

Friedman's monetary theory and the Machian *Encyclopedia* project were spawned as twins at the University of Chicago, from the intermingling of John Dewey's "social psychologists" and the Austrian mental stormtroopers shipped to the United States by Coudenhove-Kalergi. Of course, between Wells's initial statement of objectives and the appearance of the *Encyclopedia*'s first volume and Friedman's first essays, the talk of "mind control" attenuated, and Wells himself remained in the background. Wells wanted it that way. His "system of mental control" was to act subtly, "informing without pressure or propaganda, directing without tyranny."[11]

Today Wells's 1928 call is praised by the avant-garde of America's would-be mind controllers as their founding document. In *The Aquarian Conspiracy*, which presents the blueprint for reducing America to a gigantic drug commune, author Marilyn Ferguson hails Wells's 1928 document as the origin of the "conspiracy":

"In *The Open Conspiracy: Blueprints for a World Revolution*, novelist-historian H. G. Wells proposed that the time was nearly ripe for the coalescence of small groups into a flexible network that could spawn global change."[12]

To trace through every rivulet of irrationality proceeding from the "Unified Sciences" conspiracy would require a book in itself. Here, we center attention on one of them: the Mont Pelerin Society, founded by Friedrich von Hayek and Ludwig von Mises in 1947.

Mont Pelerin and the road to fascism

Von Hayek wrote the Mont Pelerin Society's founding document, *The Road to Serfdom*, in London in 1943. The title contains an inside joke: On the surface, von Hayek oozed the same concern for "individual liberty" against the "tyranny of the state" that Friedman bores us with in *Capitalism and Freedom*. However, his conclusions and policy recommendations evoke the serfdom of feudal Europe, the "eternal Europe of the peasantry" that his friend Coudenhove-Kalergi had extolled from his Swiss manor.

"We shall not rebuild civilization on the large scale," wrote von Hayek of postwar objectives. "It is no accident that on the whole there was more beauty and decency to be found in the life of the small peoples, and that among the large ones there was more happiness and content in proportion as they had avoided the deadly blight of centralization."[13]

What must be avoided, von Hayek said, is the form of the nation-state republic. "It is worth recalling that the idea of the world at last finding peace through the absorption of the separate states in large federated groups and ultimately in one single federation, far from being new, was indeed the ideal of almost all the liberal thinkers of the nineteenth century—that is, of the British enemies of the American Republic.[14]

"An international authority which effectively limits the powers of the state over the individual will be one of the best safeguards of peace. The International Rule of Law must become a safeguard as much against the tyranny of the state over the individual as against the tyranny of the new superstate [Hayek means the United States] over the national communities [Hayek means the bankrupt British Empire]."[15]

A year later from Yale University, Mont Pelerin's co-founder Ludwig von Mises wrote an identical tract, *Omnipotent Government*. What a belly-laugh the two of them must have had, watching American conservatives tout their One-Worldism as if it were an appendix to the New Testament! What supreme hypocrisy for the lieutenants of the fascist Count Coudenhove-Kalergi to represent themselves as the "libertarian" alternative to Adolf Hitler!

In 1939, von Hayek, then at the London School of Economics, had already brought together the initiating core for the Mont Pelerin Society under the name,

"Society for the Renovation of Liberalism." Among the members were Frank Knight and Henry Simons, Milton Friedman's teachers at the University of Chicago; Coudenhove-Kalergi's close friend Walter Lippmann from New York; Viennese philosopher and president of the Aristotelian Society, Karl Popper; and Sir John Clapham from the Bank of England, along with von Mises. Mises had just moved to New York University, after a stint at the National Bureau of Economic Research with Wesley Clair Mitchell.

Minus "uncertainty theorist" Frank Knight, who died in the interim, the same group reconvened after the war at the small resort of Mont Pelerin, on the far side of Lake Geneva in Switzerland, in April 1947. In attendance were the troops of H. G. Wells's "Open Conspiracy." Austrian Karl Popper had just succeeded Bertrand Russell to the presidency of the ultra-elite Aristotelian Society, the inner core of British positivists. Clapham, the official historian of the Bank of England, had just finished six years in office as president of Britain's Royal Society. Walter Lippmann and Chicago's Henry Simons represented the Americans, and Simons brought with him his prize graduate student, the author of a set of essays denouncing "realism" in economics, Milton Friedman.

With the Viennese von Hayek and von Mises, the Mont Pelerin founding conference represented not the "unity of science" but the operational union of the Oxford-Cambridge, Chicago, and old University of Vienna networks. Coudenhove-Kalergi's feudal patron, Baron Max von Thurn und Taxis, whose family had controlled the intelligence service of the Holy Roman Empire for 400 years, supervised the proceedings on behalf of the European high aristocracy.

Count Coudenhove-Kalergi, the man to whom von Mises and von Hayek owed their safe passage out of war-torn Europe, did not attend. He was busy elsewhere; almost simultaneously, he had reconstituted the old Pan-European Union as the European Parliamentary Union at Gstaad, Switzerland, culminating the work that he and von Mises had started at New York University seminars six years earlier. Formally, the old Pan-European Union was not re-formed until 1954, with Coudenhove-Kalergi as president, and his protégé, Archduke Otto von Hapsburg, as a Central Council member. General de Gaulle ensured that the organization's influence in European public life would not go far, snubbing its offer of the honorary presidency.

The Mont Pelerin Society is merely the economic arm of the "political" Pan-European Union, and the controlling members of the two organizations overlap. One of von Hapsburg's closest friends in the Mont Pelerin Society, for instance, is William F. Buckley, Friedman's close collaborator and publisher throughout the 1960s. In *The Buckleys—A Family Examined,* author Charles Markmann writes:

"Buckley's friendship with Otto von Hapsburg, the pretender to the non-existent Austro-Hungarian throne, is anything but a secret of course: Buckley neither hides it nor flaunts it, and has himself disclosed that they are both members of a very secret group that meets in Europe two or three times a year, without any fanfare [the Mont Pelerin Society] to discuss world problems from a Right-Wing point of view and to weigh possible courses of action. But [Murray] Rothbard recalls discussions among his friends at *National Review* in which the theme was simply which monarchy ought to be restored—some favored the recalls of the Hapsburgs to Austria-Hungary and of the Stuarts to the United Kingdom. Others wanted a Hapsburg monarch for America."[16]

In such endeavors, the public face of the Pan-European Union is less important than its covert role.

Quietly, Otto von Hapsburg moved the field headquarters of the old Pan-European Union, the Center for Documentation and Information created by Coudenhove-Kalergi and von Mises at New York University, to Spain. Von Hapsburg took up residence in Madrid, along with various remnants of the Hitler regime, including Hjalmar Schacht's son-in-law, SS Commando Otto von Skorzeny. Hapsburg's Madrid Center was the "safehouse" for visiting ex-Nazis and their Latin American friends.

Otto von Hapsburg and his friends are not merely intellectual terrorists, but terrorists in fact—something that will become more relevant when we discuss Milton Friedman's relationship to the Chilean dictatorship. Apart from Skorzeny, whose association with his father-in-law Schacht persisted through their escapades in Egypt during the early 1950s, Hapsburg's Center for Documentation and Information housed some of the most despised ex-Nazis in Europe throughout the 1950s. One was Leon DeGrelle, the Belgian Quisling who joined the Waffen SS in 1943, an action that forced him to seek asylum in Franco Spain in 1945. While DeGrelle was associated with Hapsburg in Madrid—according to reports published in the West German weekly *Der*

Spiegel in 1959—he collaborated with a putschist movement in Germany centered around Joseph Goebbels's old propaganda chief Werner Naumann.

Another Hapsburg contact was the Nazis' puppet prime minister in wartime Hungary, Ferenc Nagy, who later founded the terrorist organization Permindex.

Permindex was booted out of Europe by de Gaulle after the French discovery that the supposed trading company had conduited the funds to de Gaulle's would-be assassins. Nagy personally handled the money transfers through White Russian sub-agents based out of New Orleans. In New Orleans District Attorney James Garrison's investigation of the assassination of John Kennedy, Nagy figures as a principal suspect; he had been in Dallas immediately before Kennedy was killed and was in close touch with all the principal suspects in the Garrison investigation, including Clay Shaw, Permindex's New Orleans representative. When Nagy conduited funds to the French Secret Army Organization generals for a projected hit against de Gaulle, Skorzeny was in collaboration with the coup plotters. This fact emerged after French counterintelligence kidnapped the OAS chief of intelligence, Colonel Argoud, in Munich in 1961.

Leader of the Latin American contingent in Hapsburg's Center for Documentation and Information in Madrid is the chief of Colombia's drug lobby, Alvaro Gomez Hurtado, who wrote in his daily newspaper *El Siglo* in August 1977: "Colombians must think very seriously about legalizing marijuana immediately, first, because it will yield us foreign exchange. And second, because we have proven that to prohibit it, to help a country that is not interested in its promotion, is damaging to the morals of those charged with enforcing the law."[17]

Buckley and Friedman's endorsement of marijuana legalization dates from the same year.

Gomez's paper *El Siglo* was founded in 1936 by his father, Laureano Gomez, who had just returned from Germany after a stint as Colombia's ambassador. In a founding editorial, Laureano echoed what could pass as the credo of the Mont Pelerin Society:

"Hitler has proven that it is possible to wage a long, difficult and immensely costly war without money. The Jews thought they could boycott Germany by removing all the gold and transferring it to the U.S. They were mistaken. The Führer has made a truly miraculous discovery: he has found that he and his people can get along on the work standard."[18]

Laureano Gomez used the Nazi salute in public. He became Colombia's president in 1950, and launched the series of massacres known as *La Violencia*, in which 300,000 Colombian men, women, children, and infants were systematically murdered in an attempted "purge" of "heretics" and "liberals." His son Alvaro took over the paper's editorship in 1952—at the height of his father's massacres—the same year that he became a member of Hapsburg's Center in Madrid.

Another Latin American member of the Center for Documentation and Information is Andres Marcelo Sada, a former graduate student of Ludwig von Mises. As head of the Mexican Employers Confederation in 1977, Sada attempted to bring down the Echeverria government in response to the Mexican president's aggressive land reform program. Documents introduced as evidence in the Mexican Congress on September 7, 1978, indicate that Sada had tried to persuade the Central Intelligence Agency to join in a plan to overthrow the Mexican government, along with Spanish right-wing terrorists and agents of the fascist Chilean secret police.[19]

Otto von Hapsburg's operation is a barely cleaned-up version of Count Coudenhove-Kalergi's Nazi support organization, integrating sections of the old Nazi machine itself. The Mont Pelerin Society is Hapsburg's economic think tank. The monarchist terror network affiliated with Otto von Hapsburg in Madrid is composed of men trained personally by Ludwig von Mises and Count Coudenhove-Kalergi at their New York University seminar in the 1940s. One of these is Andres Marcelo Sada. Another is Gustavo R. Velasco, professor and founder of the Free School of Law in Mexico City. Velasco, head of the Mont Pelerin Society in Latin America, dates back to the Hitler sympathizers in the Mexican National Action Party who funded his "Free School" in 1944.

Velasco's student at the Free School, Luis Pasos, is Milton Friedman's closest personal contact in Mexico. The author of several books praising Friedman, Pasos was a founder of what Mexican intelligence sources call "a right-wing shock troop and terrorist unit," the Spanish-American Unification Guard, or *Guía*— "Führer"—in its Spanish acronym. Pasos, who arranges Friedman's speaking engagements in Mexico, is also director of the Institute of Interamerican Integration.

When Milton Friedman's former University of Chicago students in the junta that seized Chile in 1973 proceeded to butcher the Chilean population, Friedman's personal role in the affair drew attention internationally. To the detriment of clear thinking, the furor over Friedman's support for Chilean fascism became an endless back-and-forth over what Friedman's actual relationship to the Pinochet junta was. Friedman denounced as "hysterical" allegations that he was a collaborator of a regime comparable to that of Hitler or Mussolini.

This debate is all wasted breath. The point is not *merely* that Friedman got his hands and possibly his elbows dipped in blood in Chile, but that he has been part of a neo-Nazi movement since 1947. Worse, he is an officer of a Nazi organization—vice-president of the Mont Pelerin Society. Milton Friedman is not sullied by contact with the Chilean Nazis. He, Pinochet, Alvaro Gomez Hurtado, and the rest are part of a fascist machine that has been in place for thirty-five years.

All this helps to clarify why a mediocrity like Friedman won an international reputation, and why he is so fond of the economic policies of Adolf Hitler.

The Worst Economist in the World

7

> *My only concern is that they push it long and hard enough.*
> —Milton Friedman on the Chile dictatorship's "shock treatment" economic program

This year's 20 percent inflation rate has made it fashionable to blame inflation on big-government spending programs and to yearn for a "Friedmanesque" regime of monetary stability. Even more amazing than the public's failure to see through Friedman's policy is its short memory. Americans voted the Republican Party out of office, and defeated its bid for office three times in postwar presidential elections as punishment for listening to Milton Friedman and his cothinkers. On the record, they are the worst economists in the world.

Milton Friedman's claim that his theory has never been put into practice for a sufficiently long period of time is akin to the complaint of a doctor who advises his patients to hold their heads under water to cure influenza. Before long, the sputtering patient will pull his head out of the tub and gasp for air, still suffering from influenza. "You didn't follow my instructions!" the doctor explodes. "You didn't continue the treatment long enough!"

In the United States, Friedman shares the blame for the recessions of 1953, 1957, and 1960, bears principal responsibility for the 1969 recession, and was instrumental in starting the 1979 collapse. In Israel, Friedman's advice to the newly elected Begin government was largely responsible for that country's 20 percent *per month* inflation, which has destroyed the Israeli currency. In Chile, Friedman devised an economic policy that reduced average caloric intake to less than 1200 calories a day and condemned large sections of the population to malnutrition, disease, child prostitution, and other miseries.

However, from the standpoint of economic science, these atrocities pale beside Friedman's performance during the past year as economic adviser to the Conservative government of Margaret Thatcher in Great Britain. Granted that the Keynesian program of deliberate unproductive investment is responsible for much of the world's inflation problem, Friedman has achieved an experimental result that no Keynesian ever dreamed of. When Friedman was invited publicly by the newly elected Tory government to prescribe his monetary medicine to the world's most decrepit economy, the British inflation rate stood at 6 percent. As of April 1980, British inflation had nearly *quadrupled* to 22 percent per year, the worst in the entire industrial sector, while industrial production had fallen off sharply by more than 4 percent! All this occurred while Chancellor of the Exchequer Geoffrey Howe faithfully reduced money supply to an average growth rate of just over 10 percent per year.

Never once in postwar history has anyone managed to increase the inflation rate of an industrial country fourfold in a mere twelve months, not even after the price of the world's most essential commodity, petroleum, rose fourfold at the end of 1973. Friedman at least deserves a sort of congratulation for producing a laboratory result where his Keynesian competitors failed.

It may be argued that Great Britain, so depleted that its industrial production per capita is now lower than that of Spain, is not a fair experimental subject. However, according to Heritage Foundation economist and *Daily Telegraph* correspondent John O'Sullivan, "This is the most important test that monetarist economics has ever had."[1] Recent gurglings from Chancellor of the Exchequer Howe make clear that the British government will, indeed, keep its head under the water until the experiment succeeds or fails. If the Tory government stays in power long enough, the inflation rate will doubtless fall, once a sufficient number of Britons have emigrated to prosperous neighboring countries like Ireland.

Where Ike went wrong

Americans remember the Eisenhower years as the good old days. Relative to the last decade, that is sensible. Yet, the Eisenhower years began this nation's postwar economic misery. It is not merely that the country suffered three recessions during the General's two terms in office. America failed to build its productive capital, or, more accurately, was prevented from doing so by a combination of Friedmanite economic policies at home, and International Monetary Fund policies abroad.

This was not Ike's intention. He did not know economics and depended on the Wesley Clair Mitchell mafia at Columbia University, including future Federal Reserve Chairman Arthur Burns, for advice. That advice was terrible. It was no different in principle, or in consequence, than the advice that Wesley Clair Mitchell and the National Bureau of Economic Research gave Herbert Hoover.

To Eisenhower's credit, he did manage to reverse gears after the Soviet launching of Sputnik, and laid the foundation for the scientific and economic successes of the National Aeronautics and Space Administration during the 1960s. Prior to the "big-government" approach to fostering research and development under NASA, the American economy ran on the momentum of the wartime economic build-up, when rates of real capital formation in industry exceeded 20 percent per year. While consumer income rose slowly, the growth of labor productivity inched along at an average of less than 2 percent per year during the period from 1950 to 1958. Eisenhower's action with regard to space research—the outcome of a successful brawl with Gen. John B. Medaris and the kooks who wanted to go into space for military purposes only—was by and large responsible for the one brief burst of real productive growth the American economy had during the postwar period, from 1959 to 1967.

In matters of basic economic policy, Eisenhower never had a chance. After the war, he moved to the presidency of Columbia University—where John Dewey and a hit squad of Viennese emigrés ran the social sciences and Wesley Clair Mitchell's students ran economics—as a steppingstone to the White House, under the sponsorship of the Thomas E. Dewey wing of the Republican Party. Wesley Clair Mitchell's prize graduate student, Arthur F. Burns, then ruled the Economics Department in a condominium with the future president of the Mont Pelerin Society and Milton Friedman's closest academic ally, Professor George Stigler. When Ike replaced the deceased Nicholas Murray Butler as president of Columbia in 1949, Arthur Burns became Eisenhower's fawning, omnipresent personal aide. Eisenhower had displayed considerable resourcefulness in dealing with the armed forces of Nazi fascism. Columbia was a more subtle and dangerous enemy; it was the Eastern fortress of the men who had sponsored Count Coudenhove-Kalergi, Hjalmar Schacht, and Hitler's controllers.

It was not, of course, possible to say the same things in the late 1940s to an American population that had fought against Hitler that the same men had said in the 1930s. By weight of sheer popular reaction, the hardcore kooks like von Hayek and von Mises became an academic fringe, predicting the doom of capitalist society and the end of industrial progress; they were despised for their open apologies for the Great Depression. George Stigler found himself hated by the generation of GI Bill graduate students who came to Columbia fresh out of the armed forces, and soon decamped to the University of Chicago with Milton Friedman.

Arthur F. Burns, who played the "pragmatist" to Stigler's ideologue image, remained at Columbia.

The differences between Burns and Stigler were

strictly on the surface. Beginning in 1921 when he entered Columbia as a seventeen-year-old freshman, Burns was Wesley Mitchell's lifetime protégé. He joined the National Bureau of Economic Research staff in 1930 and later replaced Mitchell as the Bureau's director when Mitchell died. It was also in 1930 that he picked up Milton Friedman, an accounting student at Rutgers University in New Jersey.

Milton Friedman was an Arthur F. Burns project. Born in Brooklyn, New York, in 1912, Friedman was the son of poor Jewish emigrants from the Ruthenia region of the Austrian empire. His family moved to Rahway, New Jersey, after his father's death when Milton was fifteen years old. The boy was good at numbers, not sufficiently gifted for the sciences, but clever at accounting. At age sixteen he received a state scholarship to train as an actuary at Rutgers. There he caught the eye of Arthur Burns, who was doing an instructorship at Rutgers and conducting a seminar on Wesley Mitchell's theory of the business cycle. It was one year before the biggest business cycle of them all—1928. Burns knew the kind of talent he was looking for, and took young Friedman to meet Mitchell at Columbia; Mitchell and Burns arranged a graduate scholarship at the University of Chicago for the impecunious young Friedman. After graduating from Rutgers, Friedman wound up in Professor Frank Knight's seminar at Chicago.

Knight represented the outer fringe of monetarism, the closest thing to a Viennese without a German accent. Although Friedman felt personally closer to monetarist Henry Simons, he did his master's thesis for Knight. Knight's view was that since human beings do

The Worst Economist in the World 237

not act rationally, profit merely represents the fortuitous income a corporation obtains when it lucks out in the marketplace. According to Knight, who is lauded as "the founder of the modern theory of the firm," whether a corporation invests in more productive capital goods and attracts more skilled labor is irrelevant, since profit is in all cases a matter of "uncertainty." He tried to translate into the language of business school courses the Viennese view that production did not create wealth, but that "the human act of production amounts to no more than altering the position of things in space and leaving the rest to nature."[2] So much for Milton Friedman's basic training.

Friedman returned to Columbia, now working directly for Wesley Mitchell in a doctoral program. In 1935, Mitchell sent him to Washington to work as a staff researcher at the Natural Resources Committee of Roosevelt's New Deal, one of the National Bureau's tentacles in government. In 1937 he returned to New York as a staffer for the National Bureau. The next year he married Rose Director—the sister of Chicago economics professor and future Mont Pelerin Society cofounder Aaron Director. Rose Director Friedman is the coauthor of Friedman's 1979 retread of *Capitalism and Freedom, Free to Choose*.

Back in those days, the hard-and-fast distinction between "liberal" and "conservative" economics that later became stock in the theater of post-World War II economics was unknown. After all, the University of Chicago had been a project from the start of the British Fabians, Toynbee Hall, and Jane Addams's Hull House. Even the Chicago mafia sent telegrams to Roosevelt in those days urging more government spending to lift the economy out of the Depression trough. Friedman learned the just-published Keynes theory at Columbia, and, as we saw in the first chapter, used enough of Keynes's bag-of-tricks to make it difficult for him to tell the Keynesians where, exactly, he disagreed with them.

At the National Bureau and later at the wartime Treasury, Friedman was hard to separate from the other products of the Chicago, Columbia, Yale, and Harvard economics departments. His young assistant at the National Bureau was Walter W. Heller, later the arch-Keynesian chairman of John F. Kennedy's Council of Economic Advisors. "His technical work was brilliant," Heller said of his old teacher.[3] Possibly, by Heller's standards. At the National Bureau with Friedman was another Keynesian, Joseph Pechman, now the director of economic studies at that liberal citadel, the Brookings Institution.

To a contemporary observer, Friedman appeared on the fast track to a senior position in the New Deal bureaucracy. In 1941 he became chief economist at the United States Treasury Division of Tax Research. Planning wartime tax collections, he drew on the British Treasury's tax program, devised by John Maynard Keynes and F. W. Paish, as Friedman reported in a 1943 book, *Taxing to Prevent Inflation.* This first work is what Friedman would now shun as Keynesian fiscalism. It is less concerned with financing the war effort as such than with reducing consumption. The book's thesis is that the federal government should compensate for deficit spending by increasing taxes to prevent consumption. (The Roosevelt administration adopted the superior alternative of locking up consumer income in savings bonds and rationing instead.)

The high point of Friedman's wartime career was a 1943 switch to the statistical section of the Division of War Research. He was now working for another Wesley Mitchell pickup, Wassily Leontief, later the founder of the Initiatives Committee for National Economic Planning. Friedman's department prepared the statistical tables for Leontief's top-secret "Project Scoop," a plan to put the entire American economy on the same input-output matrix that Leontief was preparing for the Strategic Bombing Survey. Air Force intelligence put up $1.5 million for the plan, a furtive (and unsuccessful) attempt to put America under the total "National Planning" regime that Leontief and his Initiatives Committee were still boosting thirty years later. Friedman's apprenticeship under the fascist economists of the Strategic Bombing Survey should be no shocker at this point in the story; Friedman later endorsed the Survey's warm recommendation of Hitler's economic management in his 1956 book *Studies in the Quantity Theory of Money*.

America had emerged from World War II as a world superpower, the nightmare that Friedrich von Hayek railed against in his 1943 *The Road to Serfdom*. Even the American leaders who had cut their teeth on British principles of policy and had backed Britain through the worst no longer felt like junior partners. Roosevelt informed an apoplectic Winston Churchill bluntly at the Casablanca conference that America would no longer cooperate with the colonialism of the British

Empire. Roosevelt wanted American industry to export its know-how and industrialize the developing sector economies. Because of Harry Truman's bungling of the Marshall Plan, that was never to happen. The International Monetary Fund and its tentacles in the planning organs of the Marshall Plan shut off America's export markets, in repetition of Churchill's financial warfare strategy of the 1920s. We are going to look at the same business again, from the inside.

Republican America reacted to the conspiracy that Milton Friedman, Leontief, and others were up to their ears in. This was not government-sponsored economic growth, as with the National Aeronautics and Space Administration, but an antigrowth conspiracy inside the federal government.[4]

Richard Nixon—who emblematized how stupid the reaction was—describes the mood when he first attained public office as a congressman:

"People were tired of the privations and shortages of four years of war, and in the burst of postwar prosperity they were beginning to bridle against the governmental regulations and interference that were written into so much of the New Deal legislation. . . . Returning veterans could not find homes at prices or rents they could afford; many could not find housing at all. The shortage of consumer goods was exacerbated by the many long strikes in 1946, and prices skyrocketed as a result. Some butcher shops in the district put signs in the window: 'No meat today? Ask your congressman.'"[5]

Unfortunately for this nation, Nixon's description was accurate. A generation that had gone out to remake the world in wartime came home to find an economy mismanaged by Harry Truman and his advisers; the beginnings of Cold War instead of the promised postwar entente with the Soviet Union; the start of an anticommunist witchhunt that made a disgusting farce out of American political morality; and the absence of the qualities of national leadership that Roosevelt had, during the war years, provided. The postwar resolve collapsed into the suburban banality that Richard Nixon represented so well. As LaRouche described it in his 1979 autobiography *Power of Reason,* "The United States was plunging downhill morally."

"Mass insanity, moral imbecility are not inappropriate terms, not exaggerations, no matter how much you wish to reject the truth of such terms. Your behavior during what is usually termed 'the McCarthyism period' is comparable as an historical sociopsychological phenomenon to the spread of flagellantism during the fourteenth century, and to the phenomenon usually cited as comparable during the turn of the 1950s: 'witchhunt.' You were, speaking on the average, *insane*."[6] The generation of suckers that put Friedman's *Capitalism and Freedom* on the bestseller lists in 1962 was in incubation.

Friedman, who heretofore had been the epitome of the New Deal bureaucrat the Republicans ran against in 1946, changed horses fast. In 1946, he coauthored with George Stigler the first of his free-market tracts, on the housing market: "Roofs or Ceilings." Stigler and Friedman attacked rent control at a time of extreme inflation in housing prices, arguing that a free market in house prices would ultimately provide builders the incentive to build more. In the meantime, they recommended "doubling up."

The tract was unpopular and largely ignored, but it

represented something of an initiation rite for Milton Friedman. He had earned his passage to the exclusive Mont Pelerin conclave in Switzerland the following year.

When Friedrich von Hayek rose to deliver the inaugural address of the Mont Pelerin Society in 1947, he surveyed an audience that included most of Wesley Mitchell's boys: George Stigler, Henry Simons, Chicago professor Aaron Director, and Director's young brother-in-law, Milton Friedman. Von Hayek, Viennese aristocrat right down to his pince-nez, told them: "The old liberal is not of much use for our purpose. What we need are people who have faced the arguments from the other side, who have struggled with them, and fought themselves through to a position from which they can justify their views."[7] Milton Friedman was reborn a free enterpriser.

These are the men who lay in wait for the unsuspecting Dwight Eisenhower when he walked into his office at Columbia's Low Library in 1949. Stigler, Burns, and Raymond Saulnier ran the Columbia Economics Department, and attached themselves to Eisenhower with sufficient tenacity to gain control of economic policy during Eisenhower's first administration. Burns became chairman of the Council of Economic Advisors, Saulnier his deputy. Stigler joined Milton Friedman and Aaron Director, who had chaired the panel on free enterprise at the University of Chicago. Stigler and Friedman, the future leaders of the Mont Pelerin Society, did what von Hayek wanted them to do: stake out the extreme ideological position of monetarist economics no matter who listened to them. "Twenty years ago, when I was at Yale, Milton Friedman was considered a crackpot," one of Friedman's Chicago colleagues reminisced in 1976. "If he had applied for a job, he would have been turned down."[8]

Eisenhower did, unfortunately, listen to Arthur Burns, who threw the economy into recession the month Ike took office. In January 1953, for no particular reason, the Federal Reserve raised the discount rate, and told banks to cut back their loans. The Reserve formally withdrew support for the Treasury's own financing operations in March, producing what was then the worst postwar bond market crisis. The economy had done no more than expand at a moderate rate, with a significant rise in stock prices in late 1952, to which Milton Friedman attributed the Fed's "concern about inflation."[9] With remarkable candor, Arthur Burns later wrote that the ensuing recession "reflected the bewilderment of a financial community that had become accustomed to stable interest rates and had forgotten how a restrictive credit policy works. Government officials could overlook the criticism that 'tight money' brought on the recession which became visible around mid-1953. They knew better, as did many others."[10]

Arthur Burns and Federal Reserve Chairman William McChesney Martin began tightening the monetary thumbscrew again in April 1955, gradually raising the discount rate from 1 percent to 3 percent in August 1957—by which time the big 1957-1958 recession was already well in progress. The Republican Party was butchered at the polls during the 1958 congressional elections; for the first time the old McKinley Republican base in Ohio lost out to the Democrats. Unemployment had risen to 4.7 million from 2.8 million, while capital investment, at $37 billion in 1957, dropped to $30 billion in 1958.

Although the Gross National Product rose during the 1950s, the health of the American economy, from the standpoint of Alexander Hamilton or Claude Chaptal, declined. Under the Arthur Burns regime of stop-and-go monetary policies, American industry, barred de facto from export markets by the International Monetary Fund, suffered from the lowest rate of industrial capital formation and productivity growth among the major industrial powers. The booms and contractions of the 1950s represented, against a base of inadequate industrial development, mere expansion and contraction of consumer credit.

Figures 1 and 2 provide us with two basic measurements of America's economic performance. The first looks at the productivity of the American economy in real terms, measuring the *energy intensivity* of the American economy against the economy's *productivity growth*. Figure 1 shows that during the years 1954 to 1959, the economy expanded quantitatively without expanding qualitatively. The rate of productivity growth remained constant at a low level, while increased energy consumption in manufacturing showed an expansion in scale.

The picture changed dramatically in 1959. By that time Eisenhower had sent Arthur Burns back to Columbia, changed Treasury secretaries and, most important, inaugurated the NASA space program. For the next eight years—due to a research and development policy begun by the Eisenhower administration—the trend line in Figure 1 turns sharply upward. At this point, the economy grew both quantitatively *and* qualitatively. By the estimate of one private study, NASA

**Figure 1
Manufacturing output vs. energy flux density
1954-1977**

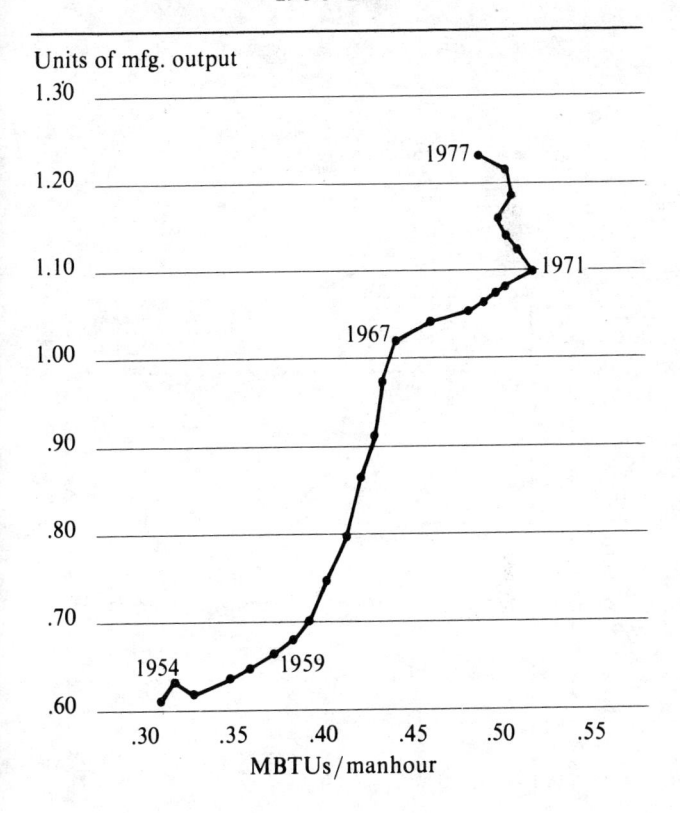

Figure 2
U.S. employment

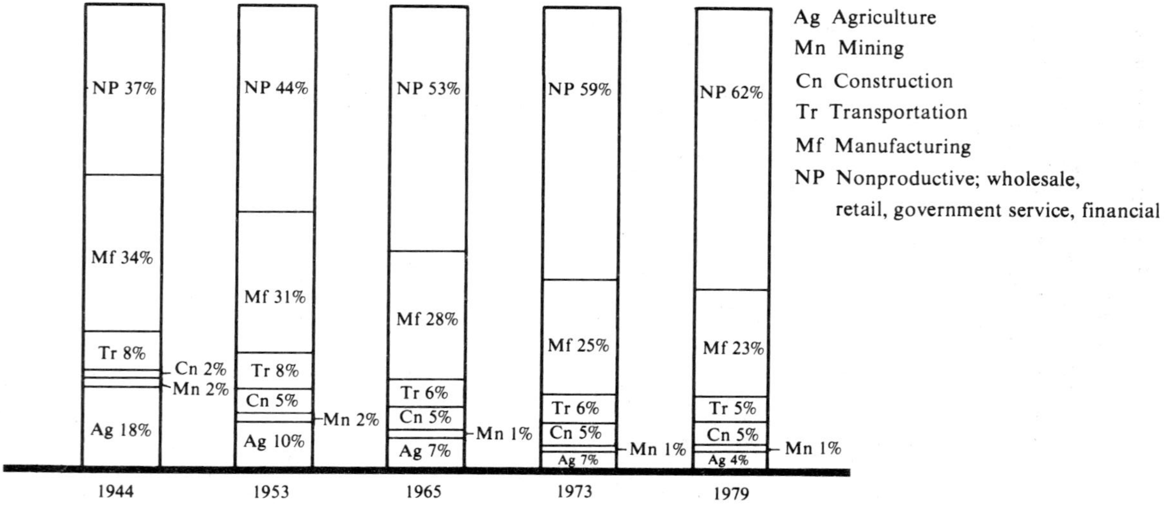

Ag Agriculture
Mn Mining
Cn Construction
Tr Transportation
Mf Manufacturing
NP Nonproductive: wholesale, retail, government service, financial

1944	1953	1965	1973	1979
NP 37%	NP 44%	NP 53%	NP 59%	NP 62%
Mf 34%	Mf 31%	Mf 28%	Mf 25%	Mf 23%
Tr 8%	Tr 8%	Tr 6%	Tr 6%	Tr 5%
Cn 2%	Cn 5%	Cn 5%	Cn 5%	Cn 5%
Mn 2%	Mn 2%	Mn 1%	Mn 1%	Mn 1%
Ag 18%	Ag 10%	Ag 7%	Ag 7%	Ag 4%

research contributed $4 to the economy for every $1 the agency spent. During these years, American productivity growth averaged better than 3 percent, due to the rapid incorporation into production of new scientific knowledge transmitted by NASA. The nation's stock of productive capital grew from $130 billion (in 1972 dollars) to $180 billion, the fastest rate of capital formation in postwar history.

The other adverse change, which persisted from the 1950s into the later period, was the decline in the percentage of Americans employed in goods-producing industries. This fell from roughly half at the end of World War II to barely a third by the early 1970s. Because of the low rates of capital formation under the dictatorship of the National Bureau of Economic Research in Washington, business oriented its investment away from basic industry into the so-called service economy. This and the related low rate of productivity growth define the basic weakness of the U.S. economy.

Eisenhower never got the credit he deserved for the policy shift he brought about quietly in 1958. Americans remembered only the recessions, and rejected—or at least made it possible for a margin of vote fraud to defeat—Richard Nixon at the polls in 1960.

What the Republican Party did afterwards is an unparalleled exercise in political masochism: It rejected Arthur Burns for Milton Friedman, William F. Buckley, and a crew of Viennese spooks. These included Robert Strauz-Hupe, now chairman of the Foreign Policy Research Institute at Philadelphia and an adviser to Ronald Reagan; Viennese economist Gottfried Haberler, now, with von Hayek, the last survivor of the old prewar group; and Karl Brandt of Stanford University.

248 The Ugly Truth About Milton Friedman

The political strategy that von Hayek set forth in 1947 had succeeded in capturing, if not the United States, at least the Republican Party. Milton Friedman was Goldwater's chief economic spokesman, his position secured by the cult bestseller status of *Capitalism and Freedom* in 1962. In speeches and position papers for the campaign, Friedman argued that Goldwater was not against labor unions; he merely wished to put them under antitrust laws, eliminating the rights that labor had won in the industrial organizing drives of the early 1930s. Goldwater did not want to eliminate Social Security, said Friedman; he merely wanted to make it voluntary. The *New York Times* quoted a liberal economist during the campaign saying that Friedman is "brilliant and articulate, but he is also utterly irresponsible and doesn't give advice that anyone would follow."[11]

Democratic Party economists had a field day with this. Paul Samuelson wrote in the *New York Times* two weeks before the November 1964 elections:

"Knowledgeable people who are themselves enthusiastic about trade unions and about the Social Security trends of our times will be astounded to read Milton Friedman's words that Senator Goldwater is *not against* Social Security or labor unions. To many of them, this will seem an odd interpretation. But actually, if you understand the vantage point from which Milton Friedman looks at Barry Goldwater, you will understand these statements: in his many scholarly writings, Dr. Friedman has expressed the views that trade unions, as they are *now* functioning, are not a good thing for the community or even for the workers as a whole. But that does not mean he is against trade unions as such. Stripped of their powers to interfere with competitive pricing of labor, unions may continue to exist as fraternal organizations to promote *Gemütlichkeit* and innocent merriment.

"Senator Goldwater's attitude in 1964 can be fairly described by what Finley Peter Dunne said about the attitude of employers toward unions:

"Mr. Hennessey: But these open-shop min say they're fir Unions.

"Mr. Dolley: Shure, if properly conducted. No strikes, no rules, no contracts, no scales, hardly iny wages and dam few members."[12]

Painful as it is to agree with Paul Samuelson about anything, it was all true. Americans defeated Goldwater by a landslide margin, which he richly deserved (more than the country deserved Lyndon Johnson). Friedman, whom any person in his right mind would recognize as "utterly irresponsible," led Goldwater all the way down the garden path.

This makes even more astonishing Richard Nixon's decision to make Friedman the administration's chief, if unofficial, economic adviser, after his election in 1969. Journalist Leonard Silk, who chronicled the tortuous route of Nixon's economic policy with partisan glee, suggested it was because Nixon and his colleagues were stupid: "Mr. Nixon's economists were by no means unaware of the complexities surrounding an application of Friedman's money-supply rule; they were, after all, 'Friedmanesque,' as [Council of Economic Advisors Chairman] Paul McCracken described himself, rather than 'Friedmanite.' Yet Professor Friedman's rule, if pragmatically applied, had overwhelming appeal to an Administration that did not want to increase taxes as a means of stopping inflation."[13]

Nixon, in any event, had been a wartime pal of

Friedman's at the Office of Price Stability at Treasury, and learned his economics at the White House at Arthur Burns's knee. Burns now moved back to the White House from Columbia as Counselor to the President. The next year, Burns replaced the aging William McChesney Martin as chairman of the Federal Reserve's Board of Governors.

During the first half of 1969, the Federal Reserve held the rate of money supply growth to 4.4 percent per year, right in the middle of Friedman's recommended range of 3 to 5 percent. Prices rose by an annual rate of 5.8 percent, faster than they had during what Nixon considered a period of monetary laxity under Lyndon Johnson, when they had risen by 4.6 percent per year. This did not upset Friedman, who believed that monetary policy operated with a six-month lag. He wrote, however, in August 1969, "If the rate of price rise has not begun to abate by the fourth quarter of this year, it will be time to ask us for an explanation."[14]

But the rate of price inflation did not abate. It continued at 5.8 percent per year through the second half of 1969, and showed no signs of improvement.

Friedman prescribed more of the same medicine, and the Federal Reserve, under Nixon's imprimatur, obeyed. Monetary growth stopped dead in the half-year from June 1969 to December 1969, and the economy collapsed. Starting in the summer, industrial production fell, and unemployment rose from 3.5 percent in 1969 to 5 percent in May 1970. Despite the deterioration of economic conditions, inflation did not fall. During the first half of 1970, inflation was *higher* than it had been the previous year. As Leonard Silk summed it up:

"The economy was slipping into recession, with no

tangible evidence that inflation was abating. Interest rates had climbed to levels not seen in a hundred years, with devastating effects on housing. The federal budget was dropping into deficit, aggravating pressures on money markets. The stock market went into the worst decline it had experienced since the Great Depression."[15]

Friedman nearly brought the American economy through a repetition of the 1929 crash, by identical methods. In May the Penn Central Railroad went bankrupt, leaving hundreds of millions of dollars in short-term commercial paper outstanding. The entire structure of American short-term credit, which depended on tens of billions of dollars in short-term promissory notes secured only by the faith of the borrower, was in danger. Bankers sat in their offices deciding whether or not to panic, and Arthur Burns made a series of frantic phone calls to New York and Chicago promising that the Fed would provide as much money as needed as soon as they needed it. From dead zero, the rate of money supply growth jumped to 13 percent.

Penn Central did not lead to a general panic in the American credit markets. However, the sudden lurch from monetary strangulation to a postwar extreme in monetary laxity sent the American dollar skidding down toward the great debacle of August 1971. The first big dollar crisis of the Nixon administration broke out almost as soon as Burns opened the floodgates in May 1970.

Richard Nixon was stupid, but not that stupid. On the next moonless night he buried Milton Friedman's reputation in the White House back lawn. Immediately after followed Nixon's great recantation, "We are all Keynesians now," meaning, "We are no longer Friedmanites"!

That didn't get either the White House or the United States out of the hole that a year of Friedman's medicine had put it in. By August 15, 1971, Nixon caved in to the demands of Rep. Henry Reuss and Treasury Undersecretary Paul Volcker, de-linked the dollar from gold, and placed wage-price controls on the American economy that would, within two years, lead to double-digit inflation.

Friedman's mugging-mate, William F. Buckley, Jr., had what turned out to be the most appropriate comment on Milton Friedman's brief career as oracle to the White House. In an August 16, 1971 editorial in *National Review* entitled "Goodbye Milton Friedman," Buckley wrote:

"Mr. Friedman can absolutely be counted upon to say that his theories were not given an adequate exercise. There is no doubting that he is correct. *But it is possible that his theories suffer from the overriding disqualification that they simply cannot get a sufficient exercise in democratic situations*—because it takes longer for them to produce results than the public is prepared to wait."[16]

Friedman in Chile

Buckley was one hundred percent correct, although tactless to admit that the Friedman program requires a dictatorship to operate. As it turned out, Friedman did not have long to cool his heels at the University of

Chicago. The overthrow of the Allende regime in September 1973 gave Friedman's students, known locally as "the Chicago boys," a semi-industrial country to experiment with.

Chile's rape at the hands of the Chicago mafia must have occasioned a cheery moment in hell among the Palmerston cabinet, who did the same to China during the Opium Wars. It is not merely that the Pinochet regime, staffed by Friedman's University of Chicago trainees, engaged in torture on a scale that disgusted the civilized world. They took a country that had the makings of industrial republicanism—with or without the help of overthrown President Salvador Allende—and broke its industry, turned it over to raw materials extraction, and bled it dry for debt service.

This is the unfortunate nation that, Milton Friedman told *Business Week* magazine November 26, 1979, "will be regarded as one of the economic miracles of the twentieth century." We will see what kind of miracle it is.

Friedman represents Chile as a nation of "free trade." This is an outrageous lie. Chile has become a creditors' dictatorship. Between the coup in 1973 and the beginning of 1979, Chile's annual payment of debt service to international banks rose from $200 million annually to $1.6 billion—an eightfold increase that is unparalleled in modern history. This stupendous increase in debt service payments occurred while the economy had collapsed to production levels barely half of what they were under the deposed Allende regime. At the time of the coup, debt service consumed about 10 percent of all export revenues. By 1979, two thirds of Chile's exports went to pay debt service. A century earlier, the East

India Company had done the Chinese the courtesy of providing a commodity—opium—in return for China's foreign exchange. This time the bankers simply grabbed.

A few fortuitous factors, such as an increase in the world market price of Chile's major export, copper, helped pay some of the debt burden. But the Pinochet regime did the bulk of it by eliminating food imports. To do this, it reduced average caloric consumption in 1975 to less than 1,200 calories per day. In a 1976 report to the Organization of American States, the French scientific institute *L'Evolution Psychiatrique* wrote of the government's economic policy:

"Its most dramatic consequences are observed in the psycho-motor development of children. The spirit saddens to see a two-year-old seated on the ground, scarcely able to keep its balance. It cannot smile, or play, or look at its hands; it cannot stand, much less walk or speak. It weighs only 20 pounds. . . . Why even talk of the lack of maternal attention, the increase in child prostitution, the deterioration of all forms of social aid? Why need one speak of mental health under a regime of terror, of systematic torture?"[17]

Such are the consequences of Friedman's policies when given enough time "to work." Friedman's reaction to being caught in the act was that of a four-year-old who has drowned his baby sister in the bathtub. For example, *Business Week,* whose economics department is composed of professed Friedmanites, reported as a bland matter of fact on May 11, 1976: "The Chilean coup that overthrew Salvadore Allende in late 1973 replaced one set of economic ideologues with another. The Marxists who strove for total regulation of the economy have been succeeded by a group of policymakers known as the 'Chicago Boys.' Reason: they ardently embrace the free-market teachings of University of Chicago economist Milton Friedman, who visited Chile for six days last year to counsel them." At the time, industrial production was only half the 1973 level if copper is taken out of account, unemployment stood at 20 percent, and inflation had *increased* from 270 percent a year under the Allende regime to 340 percent a year under the Chicago boys.

Business Week squeamishly reported that the Chicago boys had taken their toll: "Despite the fearful repression, people still cautiously complain. In Conchali, a northern district of Santiago, the families are decidedly lower middle class—taxi drivers, mechanics, seamstresses. Over the years they had hauled themselves out of poverty. Now unemployment and recession have pushed them back again. 'My husband drives a cab from curfew to curfew,' says one housewife, 'but still he does not make enough to feed us all.' "

Friedman blew up at the staid magazine that until then had usually supported his views. "I have no regrets except for the utter irresponsibility of American publications, including *Business Week,* in dealing with this," he said a few months later.[18] But he frantically tried to dissociate himself from the practices of the Pinochet government, the closest thing to the Hitler regime in the postwar period. "I did not then and do not now condone the regime in Chile," he said. "I had no contact with people in Chile prior to the visit, and have had none since."[19]

Considering that Chile's Economics Minister Sergio de Castro and Central Bank President Pablo Barahona were personally trained by Friedman at the University of Chicago, Friedman's disclaimer is astonishing. The truth is that Friedman took a more extreme stand on cutting consumption than any of the military junta. When he traveled to Chile in early 1975, when the country was at the absolute nadir of economic collapse, Friedman "chided the Chileans for not cutting their spending enough."[20]

He did more than make such demands in private; he issued them in the Spanish-language public press in Latin America. In one particularly egregious example, he warned the Chileans not to take any measures to relieve the genocidal conditions of mass impoverishment brought on by his economic policies:

"Whenever social programs either in the United States or in Chile have been initiated on the basis of 'helping the poor,' they have ended up hurting the poor and helping middle and upper income people. It is not possible to maintain healthy prosperity by this route. I challenge you to examine the experience of the history of other countries; there is no country in the world that has obtained wide-scale and sustained economic improvement, except through the mechanism of the private market economy.... We must not be equivocal: the end of inflation will not be achieved without costs."[21]

He continued in the same essay: "I have been informed that the government of Chile had adopted many measures which are in agreement with the orientation that I affirm and defend. It has been a force for the return of economic activity to the private sector. It has taken measures to reduce government expenditures and the government deficit.... All this is positive. I am

Industrial category	1972*	1977*
Consumer goods:		
Nondurable	116.6	101.6
Durable	128.3	82.5
Transport equipment	105.9	61.5
Construction materials	123.5	93.3
Other manufactures	120.5	96.4

* 1968 = 100 on index

confident that Chile will have the courage, the strength and the wisdom to accelerate this process and to get past this initial difficult period." So much for Friedman's hypocritical attempt to distance himself from the junta's malnutrition economics.

The statistics for Chile's economic performance tell a horror story. All categories of consumables produced domestically fell by drastic amounts. Food imports—on which Chile is still dependent—fell from $500 million in 1974 to $300 million in 1977, while domestic food production declined. The table above shows the state of the industrial production index in 1972 before the coup, and in 1977 after the junta had been in power for four years.

Unemployment, which in 1977 had reached 20 percent officially and more than 40 percent by unofficial calculations, was still 14 percent (officially) in 1978, and 22 percent by University of Chile estimates. Gross

Domestic Product never recovered from the 13 percent fall that occurred during the worst year, 1975. Real wages fell during 1974 to barely *half* their 1971 level, and are still a full third below the 1971 level. By the 1978 harvest, agricultural production was off by 27 percent.

The one "success" of the Chicago Boys was to reduce government expenditure from 15.8 percent of national consumption in 1972 to 12.1 percent of national consumption in 1977, a figure that understates the real decline, because total consumption fell sharply over the period. However, the decline in the budget deficit was achieved by laying off millions of state employees, nearly eliminating public health and education services, and by auctioning off 454 enterprises owned by the state at about 10 cents on the dollar.

By 1979, the New York financial magazine *Institutional Investor* reported that "Chile had firmly moved back into the good graces of the international bankers."[22] A consortium of New York banks provided the junta with a giant $370 million loan, the largest the country had ever received, strictly for stretching out the country's mammoth debt. All was well, the magazine said. "De Castro [Chile's minister of economics and a student of Friedman's], a polite, soft-spoken, tennis-playing 48-year old economics professor, is a cult figure in Santiago. Devotedly admired by his followers, he is at the same time widely regarded by his detractors as an extremist every bit as morally committed, and perhaps as dangerous, as his communist predecessors a few years ago. The de Castro economic policies have their spiritual roots in the so-called Chicago School of economic thought pioneered by Nobel Prize-winning economist Milton Friedman. In fact, one Chilean critic of those policies, successful banker and industrialist Orlando Saenz, cracks that 'what's happened here is as if Jimmy Carter had appointed Milton Friedman and then left him to get on with the economy just as he pleased.' "[23]

Institutional Investor published this encomium in March 1979, six months before Jimmy Carter and Paul Volcker did precisely that.

The magazine, which writes for a select audience of international bankers, was nonetheless cautious in its praise. It quoted a "prominent industrialist" warning: "It's not that Sergio de Castro is politically insensitive. It's just that he isn't a politician. He thinks that politics is irrelevant. But he and his friends wouldn't last a minute if you took away Pinochet's bayonets. These kids' schemes always last exactly as long as the dictators behind them."

Chile remains on the verge of both financial collapse—a wave of bankruptcies shook the Chilean financial sector during 1979—and political upheaval.

For the moment, however, the near-doubling of the price of copper on the international markets has enabled Chile to cover its $1 billion annual oil import bill. This has given the country at least some of the trappings of prosperity, the *New York Times* reported on February 24, 1980:

"After a major riot here at the overcrowded central jail, which embarrassed Chile's law-and-order regime, President Augusto Pinochet ordered the immediate construction of a new prison, the first since 1893. 'The work will begin tomorrow morning,' said the executive decree ordering construction of the $20 million jail. The sense of urgency reflects both sensitivity to social criticism by opponents of the regime and a new ability to pay for public investments."

That is the first fruit of Milton Friedman's Chilean "miracle."

Friedman in Israel

Unlike his proud attitude toward Chile, Friedman avoids talking about his role as chief economics adviser to Israel's now-failing Begin government, which began the week after Begin was elected in the spring of 1978. It is hard to say at this writing which will go first: Begin or the Israeli currency. Now suffering an annual rate of inflation of over 200 percent a year and devalued on the international markets by several percent per month, the Israeli currency of legal tender since independence is scheduled to be withdrawn from circulation in September 1980. At that time, the battered Israeli lira will be traded in for a new Israeli "shekel" at ten shekels for every lira.

The Israeli government, after two years of Milton Friedman's economic program, does not have much choice but to call in the old money and issue new. From 1978, when Begin invited Friedman to Jerusalem for consultations, to February 1980, inflation tripled. Begin's first finance minister, Simcha Ehrlich, took Friedman's advice and eliminated government subsidies and price controls on consumer goods, producing a 25 percent across-the-board price increase. In a country where a cheap two-bedroom apartment costs $50,000, and a small car costs $16,000, that was a brutal exercise. It provoked a short-lived general strike by the Israel

Labor Federation, which is controlled by Begin's Labor Party opponents.

Ehrlich lasted barely a year. In the fall of 1979, Begin dumped the unpopular minister for Yigal Hurvitz, because of "the finance minister's inability to make any dent in the inflation figure, and [because of] the gaping balance of payments deficit created by his own policy," the London *Financial Times*'s *World Business Weekly* reported April 14, 1980. Hurvitz's prescribed medicine was more of the same Friedman formula, according to *World Busines Weekly:* "tight credit restriction, savagely pruned subsidies on basic consumer items, warnings of unemployment, and a promise of a no-growth budget."

Hurvitz fared as badly as Ehrlich had before him. "The stagflation such policies produced made no one happy," *World Business Weekly* said. "But even worse was the Hurvitz failure to keep government spending down. Despite heroic efforts to cut government spending in the 1980-81 budget, a 6 percent reduction in the social ministries was wiped out by a 9 percent rise in local defense spending. Domestic government spending will rise by 4.5 percent this year."

With Friedman as his adviser, Begin has transformed Israel into a model Schachtian state, where military expenditures consume one third of all government expenditures. The nightmare of the Zionist movement is that Begin will adopt Goebbels's solution to the Schachtian economic paradox. Despite the savage cuts in social expenditures under his government, Begin has had to increase military expenditures even further, pushing Israel into hyperinflation. Since debt service already consumes one quarter of the Israeli budget, Begin's failure to find a peace settlement, or rather his

Figure 3
Israeli Exports and Imports

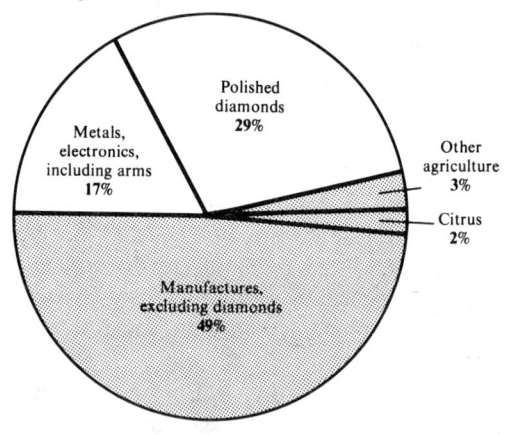

1977 Exports: $5.68 billion

- Polished diamonds 29%
- Metals, electronics, including arms 17%
- Other agriculture 3%
- Citrus 2%
- Manufactures, excluding diamonds 49%

1977 Imports: $8.37 billion

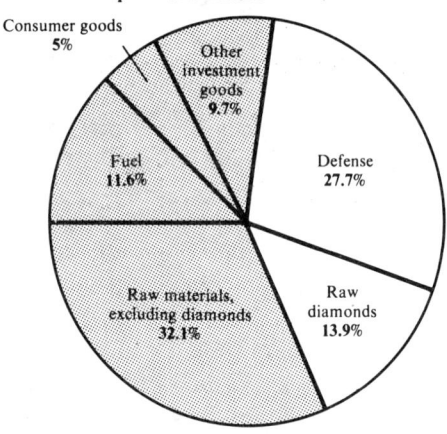

- Consumer goods 5%
- Other investment goods 9.7%
- Fuel 11.6%
- Defense 27.7%
- Raw materials, excluding diamonds 32.1%
- Raw diamonds 13.9%

Trade deficit
1977 ... $2.69 bil.
1976 .... 1.70 bil.
1975 .... 2.20 bil.
1974 .... 2.37 bil.

Source: Ampal-American Israel Corporation

Figure 4
Israel's inflation

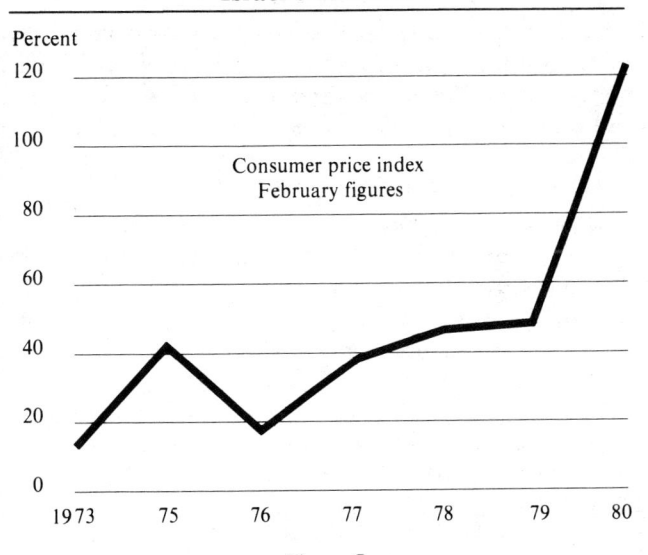

Percent

Consumer price index
February figures

1973   75   76   77   78   79   80

Figure 5
Israel's balance of payments

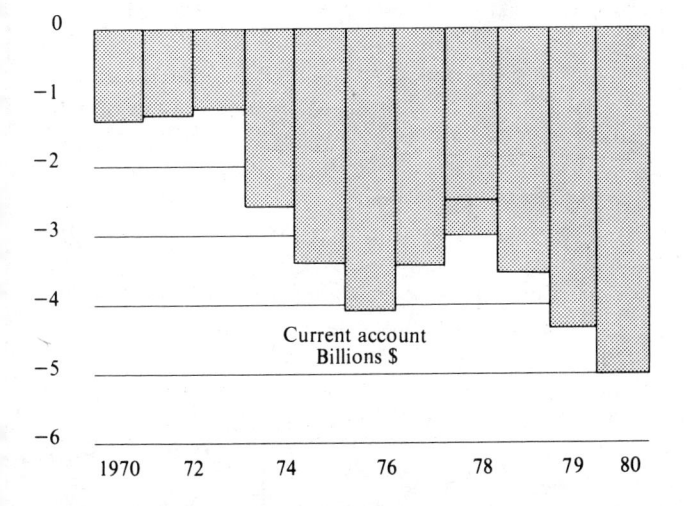

Current account
Billions $

1970   72   74   76   78   79   80

attempt to use the Camp David agreement with Egypt as flank-covering for an overt territorial expansion policy on the West Bank and possibly into Lebanon, has produced the same results that Schacht's policies did in the great 1938 crisis.

Friedman's role in the matter is somewhat ironic, because Israel's hidden source of export strength—the compensation for the greatest military and debt-service dependencies of any country in the world—is a special kind of old-fashioned "free trade." More than one third of total Israeli exports is polished diamonds, a business established by emigrés from South Africa and encouraged by De Beers, the Oppenheimer cartel that controls 85 percent of world diamond marketing. Marketed through Amsterdam, Antwerp, and New York, the diamond trade is not only the most secretive of any major commodity—all transactions in the diamond exchanges are verbal and unreported—but also the most untraceable. Next to pure, refined heroin, diamonds are the most easily concealed high-value medium of exchange, and about half the trade in diamonds runs into illegal channels, including those of the narcotics trade. That fact is surprising only out of context. Consolidated Gold Fields of South Africa estimates that half of world gold production as well flows into illegal operations.[24]

In addition, an estimated 15 percent of Israel's exports are armaments; the actual figure, possibly higher, is a well-kept secret. Apart from the Israeli-made Uzi submachine gun, used by Pinochet's troops in Chile and favored by many Latin American dictatorships for its high rapidity of fire, Israel also exports homemade imitations of American fighter aircraft, recoilless rifles, and surface-to-air missiles to those countries that find it uncomfortable to purchase weapons directly from either the United States or Western Europe, including South Africa and the Soviet Union. Until 1979 Israel's biggest customer in Latin American was dictator Anastasio Somoza, whose military forces were largely Israeli-equipped. For example, the Gabriel sea-to-sea missile, the Shafrir air-to-air missile, the Kfir jet fighter, and other weapons that Israel markets internationally are all spinoffs of American designs. Because some of the sales are made possible by Israeli pirating of designs, patents, and imported components from the United States—something that is forbidden under U.S. military aid agreements—the trade must be kept quiet.

In addition, some of the leading Israeli arms manufacturers, like Israel Aircraft Corporation founder Saul Eisenberg, who works out of Hong Kong with financing from Standard Chartered Bank, deal in other countries' arms as well.

The official Israeli estimate is that such sales amount to $320 million annually, but *Aviation Week and Space Technology* estimates that the figure is closer to $1 billion.[25] That is a substantial sum, particularly for a nation whose balance of payments deficit has risen from less than $1 billion in 1972 to an estimated $5 billion for 1980.

The British disease catches the Friedman cure

Early in 1980, Milton Friedman received a triumphal welcome in London from Margaret Thatcher's Conservative government, including a visit in February to 10

Downing Street and British public television screenings of his American-made series, "Free to Choose." A year previously, at the end of April 1979, Margaret Thatcher came to power with the promise that she would deal with Britain's chronic inflation by application of Friedman's methods of monetary control.

There is a great deal of theater in this discussion. After all, how can one blame poor Milton Friedman for anything the British do? They invented monetarism, both the Ricardo and Alfred Marshall varieties. For that matter, they invented the University of Chicago. Nonetheless, Milton Friedman has been adopted by the British government of Thatcher, Industry Minister Sir Keith Joseph, and Chancellor of the Exchequer Geoffrey Howe as its official adviser, and Friedman has acknowledged his role enthusiastically. Therefore, we are within our rights to enjoy Friedman's discomfiture at the disastrous turn economic events have taken in Britain since his policies were put into practice.

A year after Thatcher's election, the Bank of England had, indeed, brought money supply growth down from more than 15 percent per year to a mere 7 percent per year, at the direction of Mont Pelerin Society members Geoffrey Howe and his deputy, John Biffen. The result was not merely the opposite of what they and Milton Friedman had predicted, but the opposite by such a wide margin as to make British economic management the laughing stock of the industrial world—and it takes extraordinary events to get people to laugh at new jokes about the British economy.

In that year, the rate of inflation rose from 6 percent a year to 22 percent a year; the industrial production index fell by 10 percent, or from 108.2 to 98.1 (on a

Country	% Change in industrial output*	% Change in prices*
Britain	−8½	+22
United States	−4	+14½
West Germany	+5	+9
France	+3	+13½
Japan	+18½	+8

* Year to April 1979

scale 1975=100), down to the trough-level of the 1975 world recession; official unemployment rose from 5.6 percent to 6.1 percent of the employed workforce; and interest rates nearly doubled to over 20 percent.

The British disaster is not only devastating in its own terms, but utterly unique among industrial countries, none of whom, except the United States, has applied Friedman's methods. The performance of the leading industrial countries in the past year is given by the table above.

Even the United States, subject since October 1979 to Friedmanite monetary policy, has done better than Britain. When the American economy fell off a sharp edge in late March 1980 following Federal Reserve Chairman Paul Volcker's imposition of strict credit controls, at least interest rates fell with the production indices. Dollar interest rates have fallen between early April and July 1980 by about half on the short-term side, that is, from 20 percent for overnight interbank loans to less than 10 percent. British interest rates, despite a much sharper drop in credit demand with a much steeper falloff of production, have hardly fallen from the stratospheric range of 20 percent.

Even Milton Friedman's friends in London have begun to turn on him, which is somewhat unfair, since they put him and his school in business in the first place. The London *Economist,* the century-and-a-half-old British weekly now published by Evelyn de Rothschild, complained April 26, 1980, "Britain is not winning its fight against inflation."

"A year ago next week," wrote the *Economist,* "Mrs. Thatcher's government was elected with the firm belief that strict monetary control would be the long-run cure for Britain's endemic inflation. With wage and price inflation both around 20 percent, confidence has subsided to the point where honest and unremarkable reservations by a treasury minister have been uproariously greeted by open revolt.

"All that poor Mr. John Biffen admitted this week was that there is no God- or Friedman-given 18-month lag between a slowdown of money growth and a drop in inflation. Sir Geoffrey Howe said as much months ago. . . . But there has, just the same, been a change for the gloomier in ministers' view of how the fight against inflation is going to work out. . . .

"Nor will the medium-term plan for a monetary slowdown to 4 to 8 percent, unveiled with the [March] budget, cut much more ice. The economic forecast at the other end of the little red budget book is an open admission that the monetary restraint will bear harshly on output, and only sluggishly on inflation, this year."[26]

Britain's experience with Friedmanism is no accident, but a *repeatable experiment*. Money supply is not an interesting parameter. To understand inflation, we must look at two processes: the growth of total debt and equity capitalization in the economy, and the rate of growth of real tangible output. The economy's *real* rate of profit is not a mere aggregation of the profits of individual firms. If it were, the Chicago School's contentions would be true that real profit does not exist and that the profits of individual firms represent the mere chance distribution of income according to an uncertainty principle. The real rate of profit must be measured in terms of society's production of tangible wealth in excess of the requirements of maintaining the population at existing living standards, and maintaining existing productive plant and equipment at prevailing technological levels.

When the rate of growth of nominal claims on income, through debt service, dividends, and rents, exceeds the rate of growth of real profits in the economy, the result is inflation; the wholesale price of tangible goods must be increased to cover the additional income demands. The official rate of inflation, as measured, for example, by the consumer price index, will vary somewhat from this basic underlying inflation rate. Monetary inflation will produce speculative booms in the commodities markets, cartels may bid up the price of oil or other essentials, and the results will be transmitted through the economy's entire price structure. But the secondary forms of inflation only become a significant problem when the economy's credit process and production process are out of phase.

The "normal" condition of an industrial economy is a long-term trend toward lower prices, due to higher productivity through the introduction of new technologies. This is sectorally the case even in the American economy, where the cost of computer data-processing fell during the 1970s, on average, by 50 percent per year. We can say, in general, that prices will fall whenever the rate of increase of productivity is higher than the cost of credit or equity required to employ additional labor at the new, higher level of productivity.

In an industrial economy, the rate of increase in productivity and the cost of debt service are not independent variables, but mutually reinforcing conditions of the total economic process. We see in Figure 6 how sharp the divergence between the productivity growth rate of the American economy and the rate of increase of debt has been. The growth of the area between the two lines measures the underlying rate of inflation. Inflation leads to higher interest rates—because creditors demand the addition of the inflation rate to their yield on lent money. Higher interest rates penalize capital investment in industry more than any other form of economic activity, because of longer investment lead-times. Inflation itself reinforces the negative tendency toward investment in services rather than goods-producing industries, in a self-feeding cycle.

At the point of economic breakdown, the self-feeding rise in inflation accelerates toward *hyperinflation*. That is the substance of the past year's developments in Britain. The British economy is so depleted that the rise in interest rates authored by the Thatcher government not only wiped out capital investment but cut the profitability of a huge chunk of Britain's manufactur-

**Figure 6
Productivity and total debt**

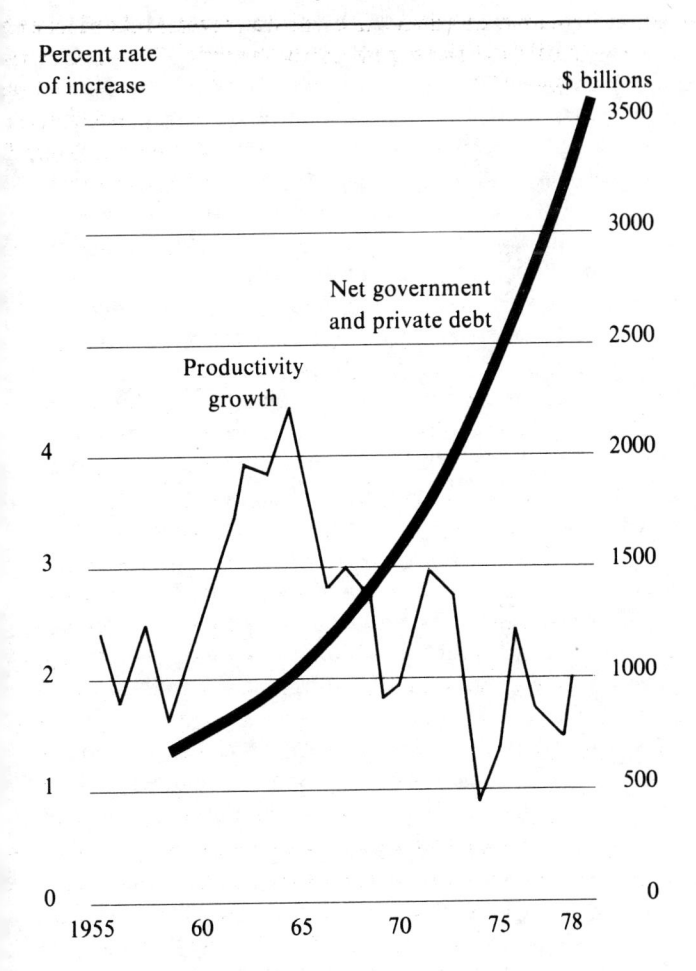

ing. British Steel was the first to go, for rather evident reasons; this is the national steel sector that in 1975 closed down the Bessemer furnace, first built by Dr. Bessemer a century ago! The Thatcher government laid off 60,000 workers from the nationalized steel sector, provoking an extended, bitter strike that lasted through the winter and into the early spring of 1980.

Overall, domestic costs in manufacturing in Britain rose by 20 percent in the past twelve months. The Bank of England predicted in September 1979 that "industrial companies may be faced with a financial squeeze as severe, if not as abrupt, as in 1974-75. Falling consumer sales have hurt them badly. In addition, the interest and exchange rate structure of the pound sterling have made it impossible for British companies to market abroad, producing a $7.3 billion trade deficit in the past year." The pound sterling is currently worth about $2.30 on the foreign exchange market. It is vastly overvalued, according to London *Times* editor-in-chief William Rees-Mogg. Rees-Mogg calculates that sterling, measured by how much productivity investment in Britain will buy, is worth only $1.60, or barely two thirds its market value.

Nonetheless, the Bank of England maintains artificially high interest rates in order to attract international "hot money" to London, where it can get the highest rate of return in the world on very short-term investments. It uses this short-term money to finance Britain's budget deficit, which Sir Geoffrey Howe has been trying frantically (and unsuccessfully) to cut. Without this artificial prop, the entire structure of British government debt would come crashing down, as surely as it did in 1798, when Prime Minister William Pitt hired Parson Malthus to justify the repeal of the Poor Laws.

British industrial companies are losing money. The London *Economist* estimates that the deficit of manufacturing companies will rise to £5.1 billion in 1980 from £2.2 billion in 1978 and £4.3 billion in 1979, and that the minimum the companies must borrow in 1980 will rise to £7 billion—almost as much as the government's own borrowing requirement—from £2.5 billion in 1978 and £5.9 billion in 1979.[27]

The result, predictably, is a scramble to raise prices. All that Milton Friedman's money crunch has accomplished is to drive up the cost structure of industry, including pay increases to workers (who are not keeping up with inflation in any case), and to force the inflation spiral ever upwards.

Of course, continued application of monetary austerity will *ultimately* produce a lower rate of inflation, as it did in Chile, in the same way that holding an influenza patient's head under water will ultimately cure influenza. General bankruptcy—Friedrich von Hayek's explicit proposal—will reduce the demands for income in the victim economy by wiping off the books masses of equity and debt capital. The assumption is that a chain-reaction will wipe out more paper than production, and therefore bring prices down. That is one way to do things. The consequences of this method, however, led not only to the Great Depression but to World War II. Von Hayek's proposal is death—on a mass scale.

In summary, it can be said that in the last ten years, between his tenure at the Nixon White House and his role as Britain's chief economic adviser, Milton Friedman has attached his name to more economic disasters than anyone since the East India Company gang around Jeremy Bentham. The Nobel Prize committee must have been drinking nitroglycerin when they gave him the award in 1976. If awards were given out for it, Friedman would be first choice for "World's Worst Economist."

The Basis of Real Economics

8

> *To cherish and stimulate the activity of the human mind, by multiplying the objects of enterprise, is not among the least considerable of the expedients by which the wealth of a nation may be promoted.*
> —**Alexander Hamilton**, *Report to Congress on the Subject of Manufactures,* **1791**

Now that we have dispensed with the hoax that Milton Friedman misrepresents as economics, the real work begins. Friedman has survived in the profession this long because the public and its leaders are ignorant of the ABCs of real economics. At this juncture, this ignorance is as dangerous to America's welfare and the world's as Friedman's deliberate misinformation. Nothing less than a renaissance of economic science will save this country from devolution into a futureless condition like that of Great Britain.

To start with, most of the theoretical baggage of Friedman's National Bureau of Economic Research has to go if we are to find a direction out of the present crisis. At the outset we emphasized that the single defining measure of economic performance was man's capacity to command nature. This can be expressed as the rate of increase of the productivity of labor, or more broadly as the rate of assimilation of new technology into the economic process. This criterion immediately tells us why such measures as "Gross National Product" are confusing absurdities.

Gross National Product is the sum of all goods and services sold over a given period of time. But what effect do these sales have? GNP registers a boom in building gambling casinos no differently than a boom in building steel mills. If, as Milton Friedman proposes, we legalized and taxed the narcotics traffic, GNP would immediately rise by $100 billion. If we legalized criminal activities such as prostitution and the numbers racket, which Friedman also approves, it would rise by another $100 billion.

The problems of GNP measurement include some less obvious, but much more dangerous, failings. It is a useful first step to consider the reasons a "zero technological growth" economy is impossible. In other words, any effort to impose neo-Malthusian limitations to technological growth on a modern economy must send that economy into a hyperinflationary sort of collapse.

In the final analysis, there is no limitation on the resources available to man on earth or in the universe. For example, fusion energy technologies lead us to virtually unlimited, cheap energy. With advanced fusion technologies, about a cubic mile of the earth's crust contains all of the mineral resources mankind presently requires in a year. The limitation on resources is strictly a matter of the level of productive technology mankind is currently using.

However, for any one fixed level of technology or production, certain kinds of all the available resources (minerals, for example) are economical resources. As we proceed to technologies at a higher average level of energy flux density, kinds of ore that are unusable to societies on a lower level of technology become cheap, and for a while abundant, new resources. This indicates that to maintain a society even at a constant level of productivity, a certain rate of progress in applied productive technology is required. Otherwise, the cost of marginal resources will increase, rising at an accelerating rate, as the depletion of presently economical kinds of resources proceeds.

That is why any economy that adopts a practice of relatively low rates of technological progress must collapse.

If there are still any competent high schools in existence in the United States, every qualified graduate is acquainted with the introductory physics and chemistry textbook discussion of "reducing power." Such a student can easily understand the next point.

The question of what grades of potential ore are economical for society is essentially a matter of the level of energy-intensity of the average productive technology in use by that society's economy. This rise in the "reducing power" of the society's productive technology means an increase in the amount of energy available per capita. It means something more. There must also be an increase in what is termed the "energy flux density" of basic modes of productive technology in general usage. We measure reducing power in terms of increases in the energy flux density of society's productive technology.

But from the standpoint of GNP accounting, there is no distinction between output at the existing technological level and output at improved technological levels. Yet, at the point where a given resource becomes scarce, all the technology associated with it becomes worthless, and will precipitously "fall out" of GNP when no use is found for it. Those technologies that have been defined into being new resources—for example, fission and fusion nuclear power, replacing the consumption of fossil fuels for power production—will retain value.

These considerations define our choice of economic paths for the future. A synthetic fuels plant, which demands an effective per barrel oil price of double the present world market level, may make the same contribution to GNP as a nuclear power plant, which can deliver electricity at a fraction of the cost. Because the synthetic fuels plant is several times less productive than the nuclear power plant, its construction is a net loss. We require an entirely different set of yardsticks capable of telling us whether different policy alternatives will get us where we must go.

We earlier divided the economy's product into the cost of labor, or V; the cost of maintaining existing capital stock, or C; gross surplus above these costs, or S; nonproductive economic overhead expenses, or d; and net investible surplus, or S'. As "scalar" quantities, that is, as fixed aggregates of goods, these terms are less absurd than Gross National Product, but they are still entirely inadequate. Under conditions of technological progress, the value of a week's productive labor by an average member of the labor force in one period is not comparable to a week's productive labor in either earlier or subsequent epochs of the ongoing economic process. The capital stock's value and current maintenance requirements are also entirely contingent on the rate of technological progress. What is the value of a buggy whip factory after mass production of automobiles takes off, or the value of a vacuum type factory after the mass production of the transistor?

The problem that has bedeviled the standard academic "production functions" is that *they attempt to measure technology in terms of parameters that are themselves changed by technology.* No matter how many bits and pieces of labor-input, hours worked, investments made, and other such measures the National Bureau of Economic Research collects, it would come no closer to a solution of this problem.

However, if we start from the *effect* of rising labor productivity on our initial categories, instead of taking fixed aggregations of goods or hours worked as our starting point, we have the beginning of a solution.

We know that rising labor productivity is associated with a rising ratio, $S'/(C + V)$, that is, a greater amount of investible surplus compared to the maintenance requirements of the capital stock and the labor pool. This ratio is the basic accounting measure of competent economics. It tells us whether the economy is producing sufficient "free energy" to meet the investment requirements in new technology and new labor skills that we require. Without the production of such investible surplus, the economy would function only at its existing technological level, and would ultimately collapse through a resource-scarcity crisis. If the ratio is negative, that is, if the economy is producing less tangible output than is required to meet its own maintenance requirements, the economy is in crisis.

The American economy is now undergoing that negative growth, as the two graphs generated by the LaRouche-Riemann computer model demonstrate (Figures 7 and 8).

In addition, we can specify the following further conditions for rising labor productivity:

1. The real content of the average wage, or V, must rise—a correlative of the increase in the education and cultural level of the productive labor force.

2. C/V must rise, that is, the average worker will command more capital in the production process.

3. $S/(C + V)$, or gross surplus compared to the economy's maintenance requirements, must also rise. That is to say, the economy's expenditures on such overhead functions as research and development, education, music, and other requirements for enhanced labor productivity must rise along with the surplus product invested in expanded production.

4. $S/(C + V)$ must rise more rapidly than $d/(C + V)$, so that the ratio $S'/(C + V)$ also rises.

The limitations of measuring S', C, V, and d in constant-dollar terms are obvious, since these values may reflect erroneous policy decisions. For example, in price terms, the agricultural sector is operating in net deficit; yet it is demonstrably one of the economy's most productive sectors. This apparent deficit is unrelated to the agriculture sector's performance in real terms. It stems from Carter administration policies that have held farm prices down, while letting the cost of farm

Figure 7
Reinvested profit since 1970

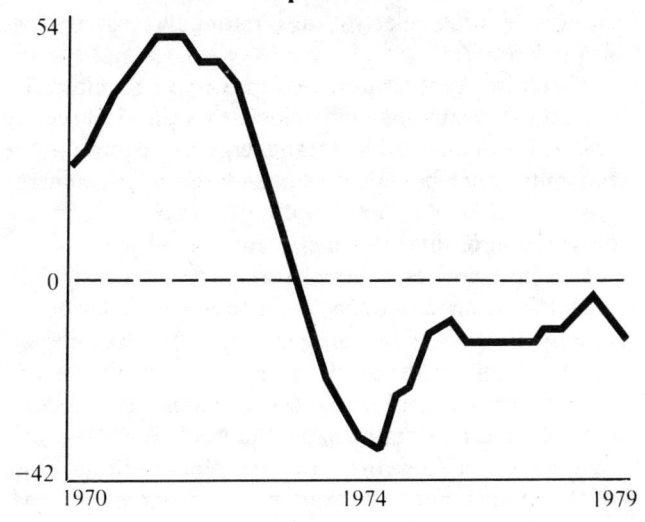

Figure 8
Free-energy ratio of the U.S. economy since 1970

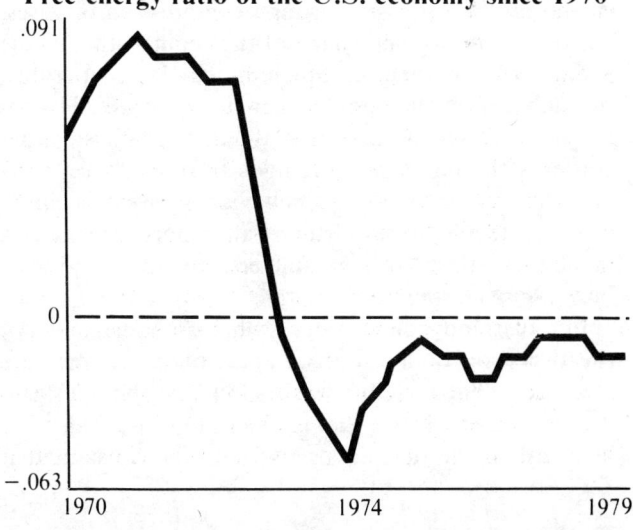

inputs rise spectacularly, thus inflating the cost of farm-sector V and C.

Therefore, another universal measure is required as a corrective, putting us much closer to a physical-science grasp of economics. The total energy throughput of the economy must be calculated, and the relative energy costs of S, C, V, and d must be computed as a distribution of this total energy throughput.

We have now established sufficient criteria to chart the path of an economy. We introduce the awesome-sounding term *hydrothermodynamics* to describe the overlap between the study of economic processes and the achievements of Hermann von Helmholtz and Bernhard Riemann in mathematical physics. What the term signifies is not so difficult to comprehend: In the sense of thermodynamics, we examine the economy's behavior at any point in time the same way we use the thermodynamic equations to measure efficiency of an engine producing work through compression of gases. However, the size and shape of the engine—that is, the economy—are themselves changing as it operates, through the introduction of new technologies. Hydrodynamics is the branch of mathematical physics that concerns the movement of fluids through space; thermodynamics concerns the behavior of systems under changing temperature. Virtually all important problems in physics affect both parameters, giving us the term *hydrothermodynamics*.

In a thermodynamic system, what is important is not the pressure, or amount of heat, or other absolute measure. What a scientist wishes to know about a steam engine is its efficiency, that is, the ratio of work done to heat lost to the outside atmosphere, the constant that describes what increase in pressure will cause a given amount of volume compression, and what temperature is required for the system to operate efficiently. The "phase space" in which a steam engine operates is created by the totality of these parameters; it produces a given amount of work with a certain volume of heat loss, at a given pressure and volume, at a certain temperature.

We measure the behavior of an economy in the same way. The ratios we described above, both in constant-dollar and energy distribution terms, are the equivalent of thermodynamic "phase" variables. Neither the absolute values of S', C, V, and d, nor the individual ratios as such, provide us with an accurate measurement. But the four ratios together define a "phase space," through which we can measure the economy's trajectory.

By reference to a "phase diagram" for the behavior of a gas under pressure available in any high school physics textbook, we can make this accessible to the nontechnical reader. An "ideal gas" follows Boyle's law, that is, its pressure multiplied by its volume are constant at a given temperature (Figure 9). In other words, any increase in pressure will reduce the volume, and vice versa. In the standard phase diagram, pressure is shown on the vertical and volume on the horizontal axis; lines of constant temperature, or isotherms, form a family of hyperbolae.

We can describe an economy as a force, like pressure, acting through a medium, like volume: a given amount of labor acting through a given capital stock at a specified productivity. *Temperature, which in thermodynamics is the efficiency measure of the system, is the economy's rate of realized technological progress, or the*

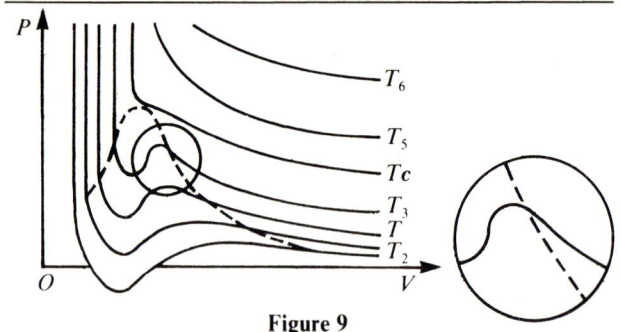

Figure 9
Phase diagram for an economy

By the same reasoning that underlies classical thermodynamics, it can be shown that an industrialized economy follows laws similar to those of a gas under pressure. Volume corresponds to the size of the labor force, measured by our "variable capital"; pressure corresponds to the input of capital at a specified productivity.

The "temperature" of the economy is the most important consideration. In gas dynamics, the temperature defines the efficiency with which the system produces work rather than waste heat. In economics, the equivalent of temperature is the *rate of depreciation,* or the rate at which old capital is replaced by new.

As in the case of a gas, lowering the depreciation rate corresponds to "cooling off" the economy, a process that can go on only so long before a "phase change" occurs, comparable to the liquefaction of a gas—known as depression.

The above diagram shows the standard physics-textbook diagram for a real gas. The inset shows in greater detail the dynamics of the phase change. It is known that some gases can be cooled below their normal condensation point. In this case, the lines of constant temperature on the phase diagram, or isotherms, do not behave normally, that is, pressure will rise *despite* a rise in volume, contrary to the classical inverse relationship between pressure and volume. These contradictory phenomena are associated with the point just before a phase change occurs. In the case of the economy, this property characterizes the situation immediately prior to a depression collapse.

rate at which old capital equipment is replaced with new: the rate of depreciation. These are "phase variables" defined geometrically as a "phase space." We examine the trajectory of a process through a geometry defined by the variables that properly characterize it.

We now measure the ratio-rates of change in both the four parameters and the values of S' corresponding to the transformations of the phase space defined by the four parameters of rates of change.

The resulting determination of the characteristic values of S' in that phase space states the problem of economic policy analysis in the terms of reference of the hydrothermodynamics of Helmholtz.

That defines the physical hydrothermodynamics of economic analysis.

The causal element "driving" the transformations proves to be advances in technology. Those advances are measured in terms of not merely the simple energy flux density, but rather negentropy flux density.

If F(E) defines energy flux density pure and simple, then the corresponding ratio, distributing F(E) over S', C, and V, defines a ratio corresponding to $S'/(C+V)$. The rate of increase of that derived ratio measures negentropy as negentropy flux density.

The corresponding measurement of progress in basic science and derived advances in productive technology is the correlated increase in the negentropy flux density of society.

In mathematical physics, this corresponds to the physical geometry outlined by Bernhard Riemann in his 1854 habilitation dissertation concerning "The Hypotheses Which Underlie Geometry."

The kind of physical geometries that correspond to

the principles of that habilitation dissertation has the following broad distinctions:

1. It defines a nested, causally interconnected manifold of phase spaces, such that the characteristic principle of physical action peculiar to one phase space differs from the characteristic principle of action in the others.

2. The phase spaces of such a manifold are counted in terms of their respective characteristics, denoted symbolically by the form *n+1, n+2, n+3,* and so forth.

3. That counting is ordered, such that each phase space so denoted is relatively degenerate with respect to the phase space that succeeds it.

4. The ordering of phase spaces is subsumed by a higher-order characteristic (relatively transfinite), associated with the characteristic action of *n+1*. That is, acting on any phase space of a characteristic denoted by *n,* the direction of action on phase space *n* is the emergence of a phase space of order *n+1.*

5. Therefore, as we encounter those regions of action in which *n* goes over into *n+1,* or the converse, the causal relationships associated with the higher-order principle [*n+1*], or *N,* determine the outcome of action in the one phase space in effects on the others. However, the characteristic principle of action peculiar to one does not determine (for example, mathematically) the effect in the other.

The higher-order characteristic of the manifold as a whole—[*n+1*] or *N,* the relative transfinite for the characteristics of all the included manifolds—is the physical-geometric correlative of the negentropy flux density we have designated for economic analysis.

The physical hydrothermodynamic domain defined for the study of the transformation of economic processes is a Riemannian multiply-connected manifold.

The study of the development of singularities and emergence of new phase spaces in economic processes corresponds to Riemannian "shock wave" physics in a matter analogous to Erwin Schrödinger's derivation of the de Broglie-Schrödinger analysis of the internal geometry of a "wavicle," and the related de Broglie prediction of the appearance of "solitons" and related phenomena.[1]

How the LaRouche-Riemann model works

The LaRouche-Riemann computer model employs the four ratios we described earlier to follow the trajectory of an economy or economic subsector. Its initial data base is the economy's tangible output. From this, it generates the ratios $S'/(C+V)$, S/V, C/V, and the depreciation rate. In the case of a multisector model it also calculates the distribution of tangible product through the different sectors in terms of sectoral surplus, C, V, and d, and the same ratios for each sector.

What concerns us is not the absolute values of these ratios but their rate of change with respect to one another. The computer calculates this rate of change in the form of differential equations for each of these ratios. The simultaneous solution of these differential equations establishes the economy's trajectory over time. It enables the operator to specify a required increase in the productivity of labor and learn the volume of investment in C, V, and d—providing that the operator can specify what technologies will be available in advance.

It also allows the operator to project the future behavior of the economy under different policy environments that imply different values for these ratios, and to forecast future economic behavior. The authors and their colleagues, as noted in the Introduction, successfully forecast the timing and extent of the present industrial collapse while other econometricians were predicting a "mild recession."

The simultaneous solution of these differential equations also allows the operator to chart the effect of new technologies on the economy as a whole. For example, if our industrial engineers tell us that a new process will double productivity in the steel industry, the LaRouche-Riemann model can calculate the effect on the total economy. If we wish to know what quantity and quality of surplus production we require to achieve fusion power by the 1990s, the LaRouche-Riemann model can find the optimal investment path to arrive at the specified state of the economy.

This method has already been applied to the economy of India, with results that have created a world uproar in development politics. Working closely with advisers to the Indira Gandhi government in India, the LaRouche-Riemann model showed how that economy could become an industrial power on the scale of the Soviet Union within forty years, or within two generations. The model specified the rates of growth in capital-intensive irrigation, nuclear power plant building, and industrial production required to achieve this. At this writing, the method embodied in this study is being incorporated into the current Indian five-year plan.[2]

In the case of the American economy, the LaRouche-Riemann model has also determined where Milton Friedman's depression will take us. The results are sobering. It shows us that we never really recovered from the 1975 recession, and that less than another year of Friedmanite policies will destroy the American economy's prospects for recovery altogether. By early 1981 or even earlier, the U.S. economy will be physically incapable of producing sufficient tangible wealth to meet its bare replacement needs. America will be finished as a major industrial power, and will not be able to recover except through foreign aid from the stronger Japanese and West German economies.

If the administration's policy to promote Schachtian forms of investment continues, the American economy will deteriorate even faster. Jimmy Carter or Ronald Reagan will crash into the same problem that should have toppled the Adolf Hitler regime in 1938: After years of misapplication of capital, the economy cannot continue producing armaments, let alone necessaries.

A series of quantitative measurements of the economy has been prepared, corresponding to the LaRouche method of analysis, to show all this in graphic detail.

Anyone who has visited an industrial city in the United States is struck by the state of deterioration of America's basic plant and equipment. Figure 7 measures how bad it really is. In constant dollars, productive investment has been stagnant for the last ten years, shown by the dashed line at the top. The Commerce Department deducts from this an inadequate measure-

Figure 10
Productive fixed investment

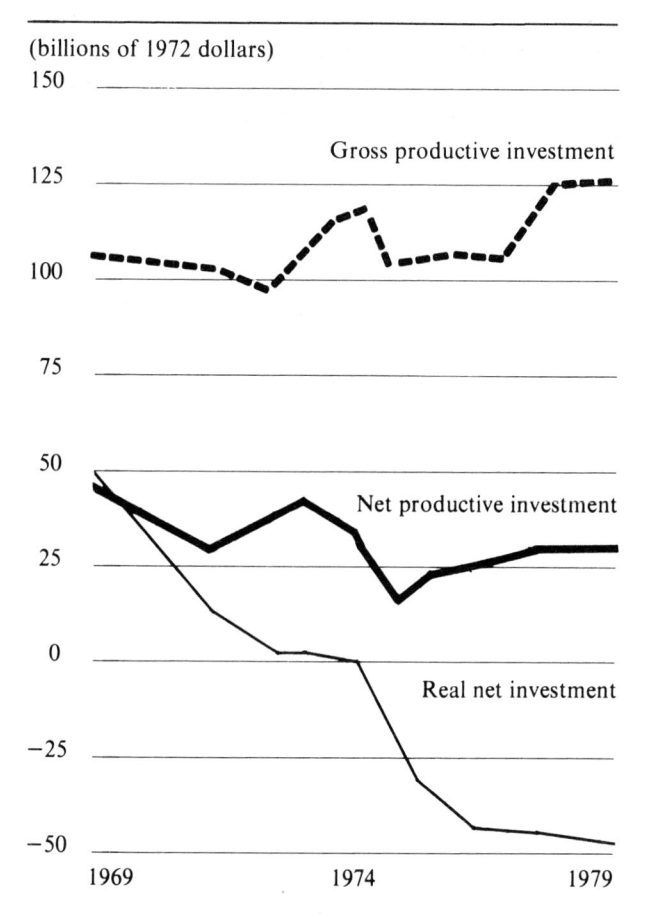

(billions of 1972 dollars)

The trend of gross investment is taken from the Bureau of Economic Analysis estimates adjusted for unproductive investment (like office buildings). Net investment is derived by adjusting for BEA capital consumption allowance. Real net investment is the gross adjusted by the model's capital consumption allowance.

ment of replacement costs, which fails to take into account the huge rise of replacement costs for plant and equipment under conditions of double-digit inflation. By calculating these costs and including a measurement of obsolescence, we show "real net investment," indicated by the dotted line at the bottom. By 1975, real investment was negative $10 billion a year in constant 1972 dollars. By 1979, it had fallen to negative $50 billion per year. In other words, America was underinvesting by a stupendous amount, losing that volume of its productive plant every year.

It should be no surprise that the growth rate of labor productivity has fallen from an average 3 percent per year during the 1960s to less than 2 percent after 1975, and to an annual rate of *decline* of 10 percent per year during the first quarter of 1980. The LaRouche-Riemann model calculates that real productivity has been falling by 3 percent per year since 1976—a lower estimate than the government's. The reason is that the Bureau of Labor Statistics calculates productivity in terms of *output per manhour*. There is a basic flaw in this measurement. Workers building a synthetic fuels plant, or retooling for antipollution devices, or digging holes in the ground and filling them up again, may increase their output per manhour. However, their output may be entirely useless in real economic terms. Instead of this measurement, the LaRouche-Riemann model uses the ratio S/V, or the amount of tangible surplus produced per employed worker. This measurement has been falling steadily.

To these measures of tangible product, we now add an energy measurement. Let us look at Figure 11 showing the energy intensity of the U.S. economy.

Figure 11
Apparent energy efficiency in U.S. economy

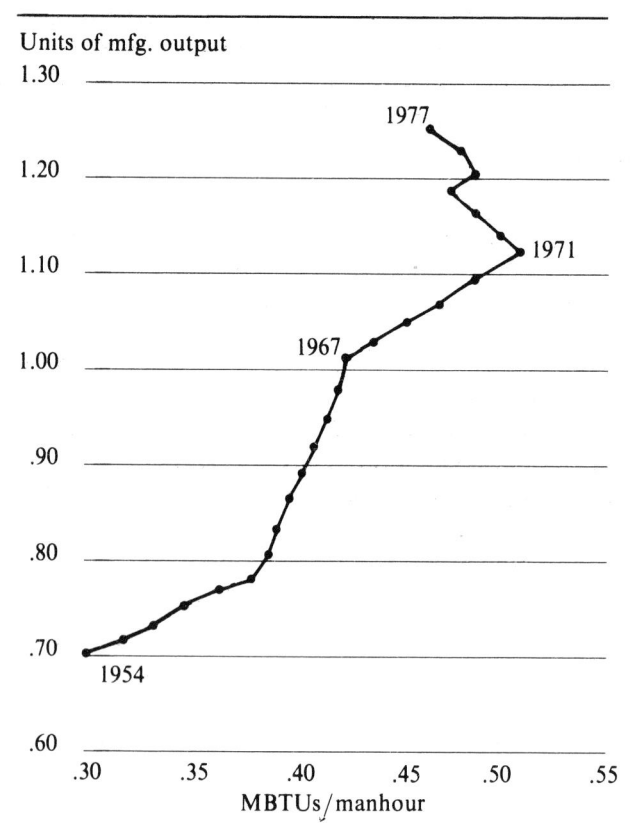

This graph shows the trajectory of a scalar measure of the energy balance in the U.S. economy over the past decade, plotting output per manhour against energy use (in million BTU) per manhour.

The Basis of Real Economics 293

It shows us that between 1954 and 1959, the economy expanded its quantitative use of energy much faster than the qualitative use of energy increased. In other words, energy intensity increased much faster than energy flux density. Between 1959 and 1967, under the technological spur of the National Aeronautics and Space Administration's space program, energy flux density, or the qualitative use of energy, increased at a faster rate than the mere scale of energy use. After 1967, the pattern reverted back to the qualitatively poorer circumstances of the period 1954 to 1959.

However, after 1971, an extraordinary thing occurred: The economy appears to use less energy while still expanding. This appears to violate the first condition we set forth, namely, that the total energy throughput of the economy must rise.

This two-dimensional view of things has been adopted by the environmentalist-leaning Kennedy Subcommittee of the Joint Economic Committee, the Department of Energy, professors Daniel Yergin and Robert Stobaugh of Harvard University, and a host of others. They argue that the economy can prosper, or at least survive, under conditions of enforced "energy conservation," that energy and economic growth have "decoupled," that is, are no longer related to each other.

Nothing could be further from the truth. If we use the method described earlier, the truth emerges. In Figure 12 we see a three-dimensional phase space, and a trajectory of the economy over time through these dimensions. An additional dimension has been added: the rate of capital formation (year-to-year change in capital stocks). As this trajectory, measured by the

**Figure 12
Actual energy efficiency
in U.S. economy**

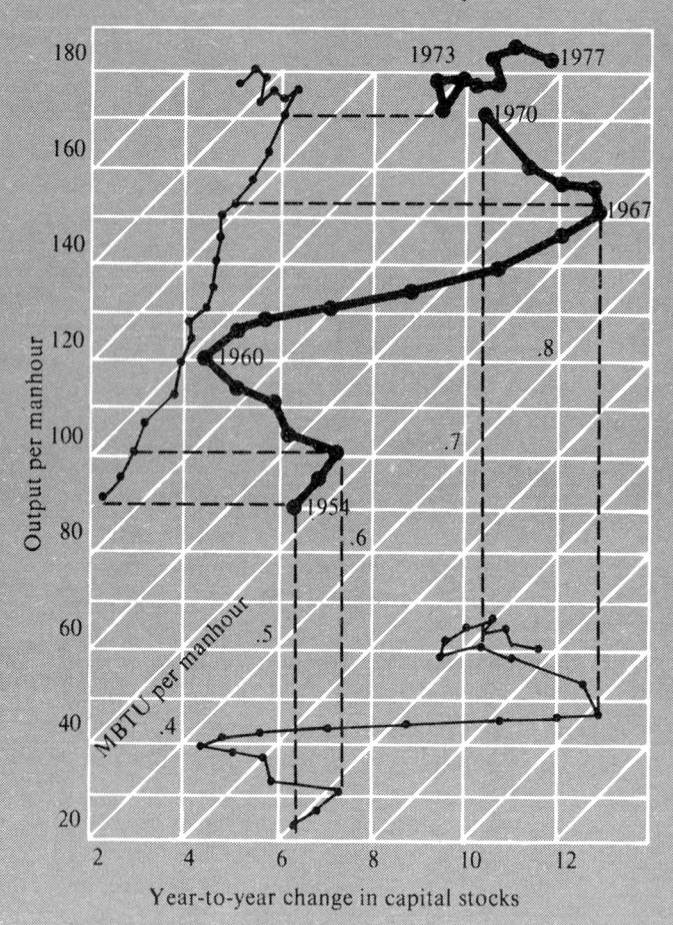

heavy solid line, moves "outward," capital formation is rising. We see that capital formation had collapsed during the period that the energy efficiency of the economy supposedly improved. What the decline in energy throughput shows us is that large sections of our primary metals and other energy-intensive heavy industry are being scrapped, in response to the Carter administration's conservation policy. Not only did the United States lose physical capacity, but nearly all investment was shifted into less capital and energy-intensive sectors, away from heavy industry. What the Carter administration considers a sign of improvement is, in fact, the alarming signs of crisis.

This is clear if we contrast the American picture with the same measurements for the healthier West Germany economy (see Figure 13). West Germany's energy use increases both in total amount and in efficiency throughout the same period. When we consider the qualitative aspects of the West German situation, the contrast is all the more striking. Because of gradual improvements in technology during the past fifteen years, West German steelmaking has become twice as energy-efficient; that is, its energy flux density has doubled. Even so, total West German energy consumption in manufacturing has continued to rise. The reason is that West Germany has oriented its capital investment increasingly toward the energy-intensive capital goods industries that the United States has neglected.

How long can America continue doing this? The LaRouche-Riemann computer simulation tells us that we are at the end of the road. Figures 7 and 8 showed the

Figure 13
Nominal West German energy efficiencies

Output per manhour in constant marks

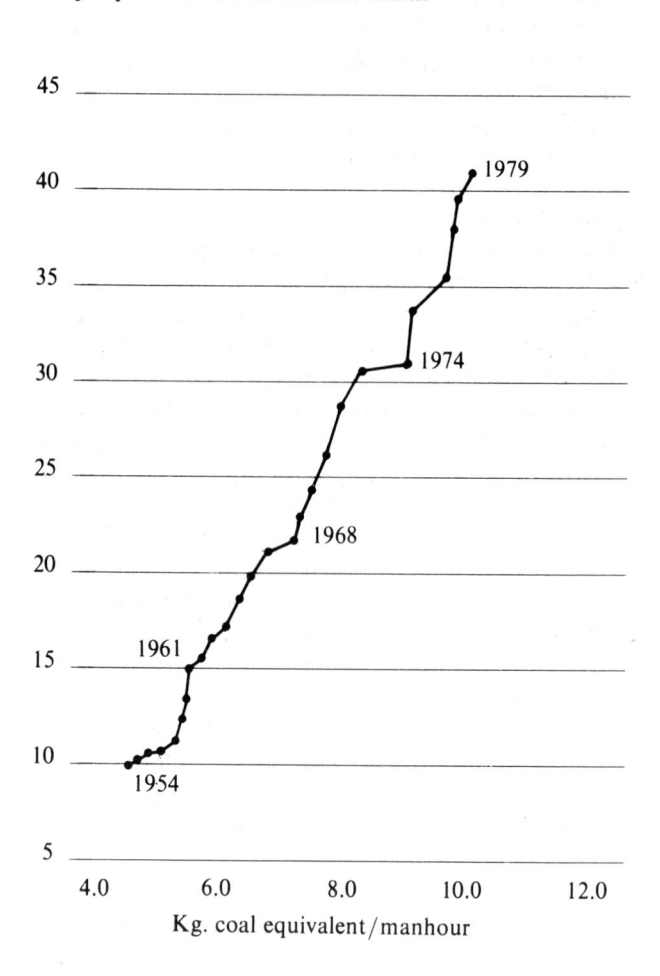

Kg. coal equivalent/manhour

real state of the American economy since 1970, taking into account the unmet depreciation costs of industry.

Figure 7, generated by the computer, shows reinvested profit between 1970 and 1979. Until 1972, the economy was rising, with a total volume of $54 billion in tangible goods available for reinvestment. After the 1974 recession, the economy contracted, in other words, the quantity of surplus for reinvestment, or S', became negative. However, during the entire period of so-called recovery, S' hovered about the zero line, and began to fall sharply downward in 1979.

Figure 8 is our "rate of profit," or potential growth rate measurement, $S'/(C + V)$. It shows that the U.S. economy began the 1970s with a potential growth rate of .091, or 9 percent per year, and finished with a potential growth rate of zero. That does not mean that the U.S. economy cannot grow. Rather, it means that the U.S. economy cannot grow at all *under present investment policies*. If we shift investment out of purely nonproductive categories such as antipollution devices, synthetic fuels plants, down-sizing automobiles, and apply the same resources to bring improved technology onto line, the American economy can restart economic growth—but only if we act quickly.

If the investment, or rather noninvestment, policies of the past five years continue for the next five years, the American economy will die. The LaRouche econometric team programmed the computer model to simulate economic conditions assuming that the key ratios behave as they did during the period from 1975 to 1979—a fairly optimistic assumption, considering that the Carter administration proposes to make things much worse. The result is shown in Figure 14, generated by the computer program: The U.S. economy will not recover from the present depression at any foreseeable point in the future. The fall into deep negative numbers of the surplus available for productive investment, of S', is so steep that the end of that fall projected by the computer to occur in 1985 is no longer meaningful.

Physicists call this condition "thermodynamic death"—the point at which a physical system can no longer produce the energy required to maintain itself. Past a certain point of no return late this year or early next year, it will be physically impossible for the economy to recover. The main bottleneck interfering with plans to build new steel plants is a shortage of basic steel. In 1979, America imported more manufactured goods than it exported, for the first time since World War I.

Even more dangerous is that the decline in education and the rock-drug counterculture are fast destroying an entire generation of what should be the most advanced labor force in the world. Physical constraints to economic recovery due to depleted capacity and the destruction of the labor force are evident when the economy is in a depression. Like Great Britain, the United States could limp along in a depressed state for some time to come—but never, unless we act now, regain international stature as an industrial power.

The LaRouche-Riemann model also specifies the minimum survival condition of the U.S. economy: We must immediately bring the rate of growth of labor productivity back up to the average level during the 1960s, our best previous period in the years after World War II. This is just barely possible. To achieve it, America

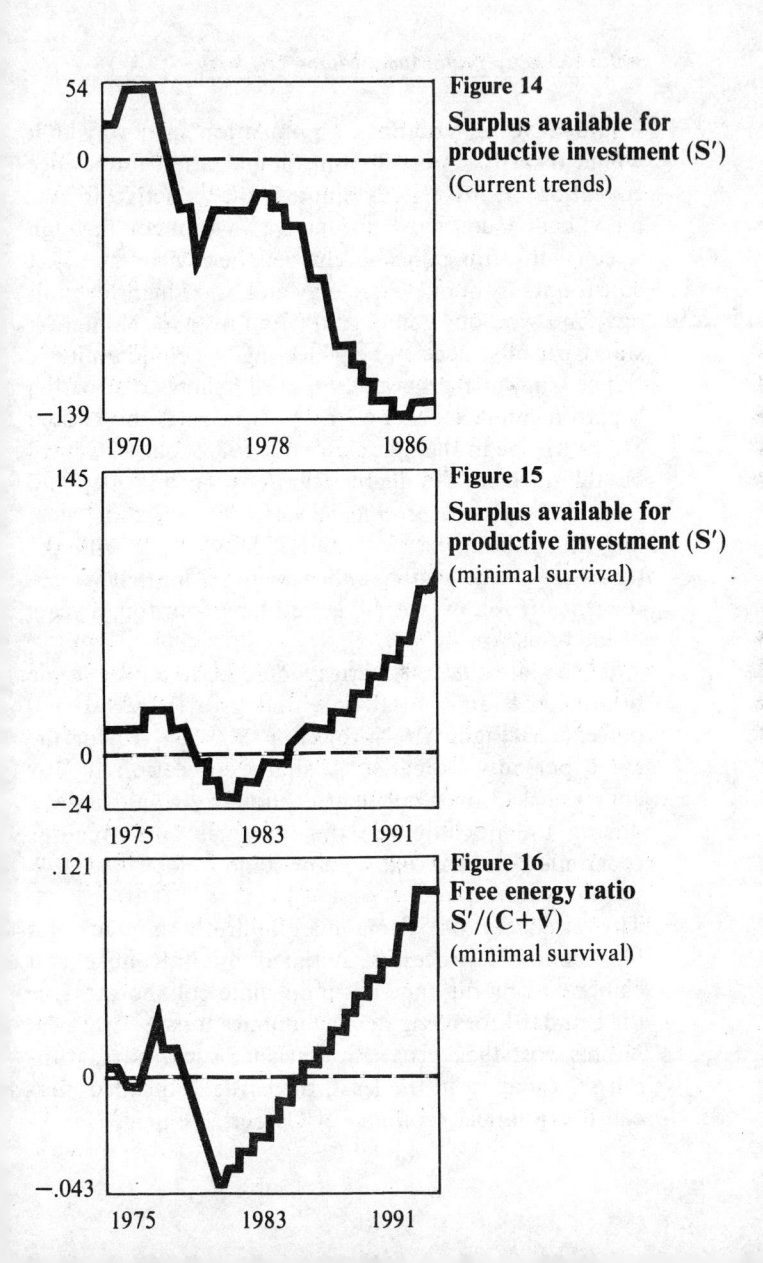

Figure 14
Surplus available for productive investment (S′)
(Current trends)

Figure 15
Surplus available for productive investment (S′)
(minimal survival)

Figure 16
Free energy ratio $S'/(C+V)$
(minimal survival)

would have to mobilize its population in a way that would dwarf the post-Sputnik mobilization for science education. If we strictly limited unproductive investment and encouraged productive investment through selective taxation policies, removed the environmentalist constraints from nuclear energy and other high-technology, and won our young generation over to the highest standards of science and engineering, we could do it.

The computer-generated Figure 15 shows that with a 3 percent annual productivity growth rate, the United States will be in the black by early 1983; that is, we will be able to meet the depreciation costs of industry and rebuild our basic productive capacity. What is most unsettling about this projection is how long it will take to get out of the trough; under the program that we can realistically follow, we will at best have four tough years ahead of us.

By the late 1980s, America would be in an economic boom, with an annual potential growth rate of 10 percent, as Figure 16—projecting $S'/(C + V)$ for the same period—indicates. A sharp correction in our course, based on competent economics, would unlock during the next decade the immense and precious economic potential that we now stand to lose.

The discovery of Riemannian hydrothermodynamics for economic processes, initiated by LaRouche and elaborated by him and his immediate collaborators, is the standard for competent economics today.

This post-1952 progress in science supersedes, without invalidating in the least, the earlier, so-called mercantilist political economy of Colbert, Leibniz, Hamilton, Chaptal, Ferrier, Dupin, Mathew Carey, Friedrich List, and Henry C. Carey. Insofar as those predecessor developers of the "anti-Adam Smith" American System of political economy progressed, they are as reliable today as they were in providing the unique policy guidance that made the former economic growth and greatness of the United States possible.

Their progress, as typified by Hamilton's 1791 *Report to Congress on the Subject of Manufactures,* succeeded in proving the correctness of their policy, and the wrongness of Adam Smith's doctrines, to the point of exposing the connection between scientific progress and rising intensity of per capita productive capital formation as the sole generator of the maintenance and increase of national gross and per capita wealth.

Any views explicitly contrary to such "mercantilist" policies are wrong to the point of being inevitably evil in their consequences.

The qualitative advantage of LaRouche's advances in economics over his American System predecessors is that LaRouche's breakthroughs opened the way for the efforts of himself and his collaborators to situate energy development policy rigorously within the systematic analysis of economic processes, and provide the basis for defining those directions of technological breakthrough and basic scientific research that lead economic development to desirable singularities in the further advancement of productivity.

The scientist whose development encompasses Riemannian physics of multiply-connected manifolds must quickly recognize that our use of the notion of negentropy flux density has an explicit application in assigning a sense of direction to scientific research. By using the fact that physical-science breakthroughs respecting the fundamental ordering of processes can be ranked in terms of the kind of phase spaces such successful discoveries describe, it is feasible today to define breakthrough areas in plasma physics, and in correlated matters of biological research that are crucial. By posing the kinds of solutions implied by the problems in terms of orders of hypothesis, we are implicitly stating which breakthroughs will enable qualitative transformations in the technology of production.

For example, the central problem of the frontiers of plasma physics today is that of gaining mastery over those singularities that yield "anomalous" existences analogous broadly to "solitons" within plasma regions. The investigation of coherent particle beams verges on the same point.

Therefore, it should be U.S. national policy to foster the development of a new generation of physicists oriented to the kind of Riemannian physics of a multiply-connected manifold we have alluded to here, giving those physicists the task-orientations coherent with the crucial areas of research and development in plasma physics and in correlated issues of the biological sciences. The new technologies derived from advances in this direction are to be the aspects of technological advancement that must be provided with the relatively greatest incentives.

That point of view among economic policy makers toward basic research and development will, in turn, foster the kinds of policy makers who will generate competent advice on all questions of policy formulation.

Then, why are otherwise serious people still occupying themselves with the Stone Age crudities of neo-Nazi monetarist Milton Friedman—with these other exciting and profitable concerns of real economics to be mastered for use?

Appendix

An interview with Milton Friedman on the Phil Donahue Show, April 16, 1980, Cincinnati, Ohio (selections).

Mr. Donahue: Ladies and gentlemen, I am pleased to present the number-one selling book in America, *Free to Choose*. It is number one on the *New York Times* Best Seller List ... and it is written by the Nobel Laureate, a man who will never be accused of making economics confusing, a man who has a reputation for not only saying what he thinks, but writing what he thinks, as he has done in this most important book. Please welcome the Nobel Laureate in economics, Milton Friedman....

And you also enjoy the prestige of the Nobel Prize. You are the counselor of Presidents and presidential candidates. It is really a wonderful spot to be in. You know, this is the last thing your mother would expect of "my son the economist," to have become a celebrity....

Let me see if I can express in very imprecise terms and very briefly the core of your statement here, a personal statement. We have too much government. We are not allowing the free enterprise system to work as your most favored historical figure, Adam Smith, suggested it would work if we just let things alone. We have too much government intervention. It is interrupting not only the wonderful work that the invisible hand does if we leave it alone, but it's also depriving people of personal liberties.

Mr. Friedman: Absolutely. That's a very good summary.

Mr. Donahue: Okay. Fill in the blanks for me.

Mr. Friedman: No, no, that's a very good summary. There is a very important role for government to play, but there's such a thing as too much of a good thing, and government has been growing beyond bounds. Right now, and to take the simplest measure, the government spending at federal, state, and local levels, amounts to over 40 percent of the income of the people of the country. If you go around and ask people, "Are you getting your money's worth for that 40 percent of your income which is being spent on your behalf, supposedly, by government," there are very few people who will say yes. And they are right. We're not getting our money's worth. Much of it is—it's not money that is being wasted. It's that it's being wasted in a very particular sense. You're spending money to do opposite things. Here at one place, you're spending—we're spending our money to try to propagandize us not to smoke. In another place, we're spending our money to subsidize the growing of tobacco. Now, what sense does it make to spend two streams of money like that and you can go over and over again and find exactly the same thing. The government is too big, it's too intrusive, it restricts what we can do. It's becoming our master instead of our servant, and we've got to react against it and cut it down to size.

Mr. Donahue: All right. Let's share with the people at home just—one of the statements of Adam Smith that you refer to in your book. . . . By pursuing his own interests, that is to say, his meaning the person engaged in free enterprise, the person who functions within the capitalist, free enterprise system, Adam Smith says, he frequently promotes that of the society more effectively than when he really intends to promote it. Smith says, "I have never known much good done by those who affected to trade for the public good." Meaning, spare me from the do-gooders. Spare me from the people who intend to do good. Smith is saying, if you seek, if you honestly seek your own self-interest within the free enterprise system, society will be the beneficiary.

Mr. Friedman: That's right.

Mr. Donahue: That's a hard thing to—

Mr. Friedman: I've never known much good done. No, I don't have to see it. I've never known much good done by those who affected to trade—affected, note he doesn't say did trade—affected to trade for the public. Now, that word affected is a very important point, because you must realize that people don't always express their real interest or their real values. They say what they think will be attractive to the public in life. Let me give you a very simple example right now. General Motors, one of our major corporations, has come out against the deregulation of the trucking industry. The trucking industry today is grossly over-regulated. It never should have been regulated at all. We never should have had it brought under the Interstate Commerce Commission. It was brought under the Interstate Commerce Commission not to protect the consumer, but to protect the railroads at the time from the competition of trucks when they were first introduced in the twenties. Right now there is a move underway to deregulate trucking the way airlines have been deregulated. Nobody doubts that the deregulation of airlines was a very good thing for everybody. The deregulation of trucking would be an equally good thing. There are literally billions of dollars being wasted because of the monopoly in trucking.

Mr. Donahue: But you're talking about fees when you talk about deregulation. I assume you would still have some monitor on weight. And can the trucking industry benefit by using highways that I am paying for and may not be using the merchandise—

Mr. Friedman: They don't, they don't now. You now have a gasoline tax which covers the cost of the highways. It is appropriate to charge for the use of highways, of course. They ought not to get a subsidy. I am opposed to subsidies, and I'm opposed to the opposite of excess taxes. But they do now pay for the use of the highway through the gasoline tax, and they should continue to do so. As to weight limits, that really has nothing to do with the ICC. That has to do with the capacity of different roads.

Mr. Donahue: I want to understand you, though, that you're not such a purist as to be impractical. You don't think anybody's truck should drive over anybody's pavement if the construction isn't prepared to accept the weight.

Mr. Friedman: No, no, of course not.... But that applies not only to trucks. It applies to private cars. It applies to a private recreational vehicle. But what you ought to do is to allow anybody who wants to go into the business of trucking to do so. You know, there are people today who receive $100,000 a year to give somebody else permission to use their ICC right to carry trucks—to carry freight from one place to another, people who make a very good living without owning a single truck. The total value of these special permits, which have been given to trucking enterprises to carry freight, amounts, literally, to billions of dollars. Now, General Motors and the trucking industry, when they come down to Washington and say, "We ought to continue regulation," do they say we ought to continue regulation in order to promote our interest? Huh-uh. What do they say? They say the public will be hurt. They are affecting to trade for the public good, but do you think they're kidding themselves?

Mr. Donahue: They're saying, "We don't want the wonderful individual people in middle America to be hurt." And you're saying that's not what they're—

Mr. Friedman: They know. They're not stupid.

Mr. Donahue: They're not Santa Claus?

Mr. Friedman: They're not Santa Claus. They are people who are promoting their interests, and they're affecting to trade for the public good because that's the way to get things done. Nobody ever goes up to Congress and says, "Look, vote me a big bonanza of $100,000 because I'm a good man and I deserve $100,000 out of the public purse." No. He says, "You should subsidize X, Y and Z because the poor middle-class Americans, who are the poor people in the slums, will be benefited by it." So, you have two classes of people; the so-called do-gooders; you have the honest, sincere people, and they invariably end up being the front men for private interests they would never knowingly support.

Mr. Donahue: What's an example of that?

Mr. Friedman: An example of that are the nineteenth-century Ralph Naders who got the Interstate Commerce Commission established. They got the Interstate Commerce Commission established, supposedly, to protect the consumer. No, no. They, the do-good reformers, the Ralph Nader types, were sincere. They were interested in promoting the interests of the consumer, and they were complaining that the railroads were monopolies, and they were charging too high freight rates, and we had to get the government in in order to eliminate that exploitation of the consumer. But who benefited from it? The ICC was set up. The do-gooder, well-meaning reformers went on to their next reform—the railroads took over the ICC. And they use the ICC to keep out competition, to raise rates rather than lower them. They used it in the 1920s to get the control of ICC extended to trucking because that was the most dangerous source of competition. So those well-meaning reformers, not because they were bad people, but they ended up being the front men for special interests. And you have that over and over again.

Mr. Donahue: All right. All right. I know you've heard these—

Mr. Friedman: Incidentally, I should point out that this little picture on here is Adam Smith.

Mr. Donahue: Yes. You have the Adam Smith tie on. . . .

How do you prevent monopoly? You have to have constraints on monopoly. And isn't United Air Lines too big? And look what happened when they went on strike. And should Pan Am absorb National Air Lines? We're going to have three airlines when it's all over, and we're all going to be beholden to them. Everybody's going to be impersonal. You can see it now on the airlines. Nobody looks you in the eye anymore, and they're giving paper cups in first class.

Mr. Friedman: Well, personally, I don't see any objection to paper cups.... But let's go back. The problem with the kind of statement you're making is to distinguish what's true from what's not true. The plain fact is that the main restriction on the number of airlines has been the Civil Aeronautics Board. From the time the Civil Aeronautics Board took over control of the airlines in the 1930s until now—until the deregulation—they did not authorize a single new trunk line—

Mr. Donahue: Because they were owned by the airlines who didn't want more competition.... The government became then an agency to help existing airlines not to have to compete.

Mr. Friedman: Exactly, exactly. Now what happened with deregulation?

Mr. Donahue: You filled every seat in the airplane.

Mr. Friedman: And you had new airlines come in. The number of airlines has gone up, not down. It is true that there are some proposals to merge United and National, but there are also ... a bunch of new airlines that are coming out. Here's World Airways, whom you've never heard of before that's offering these cheap fares.

So the fact is that the best protection of the consumer,

the best offense against monopoly is—Let me put it another way. There's an old saying. "If you want to catch a thief, you set a thief to catch him." If you want to catch a businessmen monopoly, you set another businessman to break it down. You don't send a government civil servant after them. The most effective antimonopoly legislation you could possibly have would be free trade.

Mr. Donahue: Okay. Now, answer this practical question, Professor Friedman.... There are some angry people who would say, "Come down from your academic tower, and tell us how we're going to get automobile dealers who really care about servicing the car, as much as they care about selling the car." Tell us how we're going to get automobile dealers who sell us safety with the same vigor that they sell us cosmetics.

Mr. Friedman: Well, if the public at large really wanted to buy safety, rather than cosmetics, it would be in the self-interest of the automobile dealers to sell them safety. You have had some automobile companies that have concentrated on selling safety, and they have not done very well in the sales.... Let me give you a very simple example. You have the so-called superba car, which is built by the Checker Company that produces Checker cabs. They emphasize safety. It's the safest car probably there is built in America. They haven't been able to sell very many. The problem with your talk is that you're not talking in terms of what the consumer really wants, as judged by what he's willing to pay for. You're talking in terms of what you think he ought to want.

Mr. Donahue: So the underpinning underneath your statement is, "The stupid public want landau tops and colors, and they buy—They put blue lights on these cars in the showrooms, and everybody says, 'Yeah. I want one of those.' " Like Pavlov's dog.

Mr. Friedman: No, no, No, siree. No, siree. I'm not going to call them stupid. The public is entitled to buy what it wants to buy. Who am I to say whether those tastes are better or worse than my taste. Who am I to say?

Mr. Donahue: What's your conclusion on a person who's more interested in the style of a car than whether or not the baby's protected after the collision? That's stupid.

Mr. Friedman: Well, I think he has every right to pursue his own objectives and his own tastes, and I have every right to try to persuade him he's wrong. But if I can't persuade him, do I have the right to force him? Don't bring in the baby because that raises another, and an extraneous and very difficult issue, 'cause I will agree with you. He does not have the right—

Mr. Donahue: To put a baby like an egg in a crate and—

Mr. Friedman: That's right. That's a different question. The third party effect is different.

Mr. Donahue: I trust you wouldn't pass a law to oblige babies to be constrained in cars?

Mr. Friedman: No, I probably would not. But I think, though, I would—

Mr. Donahue: You're not very comfortable in saying no to the question.

Mr. Friedman: No, no, no. I'm comfortable. But what I would do is, I would say that any parent ought to be subject to suit and to being sent to jail, if a child has been damaged because of that parent's failing to—

Mr. Donahue: Right. Are you willing to pay the prosecutor that it's going to take to develop the evidence that the mother didn't place the baby properly in the car, and the bureaucracy that will accompany the enforcement of the law which says that you can go to jail if you don't—

Mr. Friedman: Yes, yes. Unfortunately, I have to pay for it. I'm not, as I say, I'm not an anarchist. I'm not an anarchist.

Mr. Donahue: So there are limits to your free—Okay.

Mr. Friedman: I believe that government has a very important role, but it's a limited role. And because we've been trying to extend the role, we haven't been doing what government ought to do as well as it does, as it should. We've been doing a terrible job on what ought to be the first function of government. The first function of government is to protect the nation against foreign enemies, and to protect individual citizens against assault by their fellow citizens. And we've been doing a terrible job on both ends.

Mr. Donahue: And in that goal you are aligned with John Stuart Mill?

Mr. Friedman: Absolutely.

Mr. Donahue: Here it is, John Stuart Mill says, "The sole end for which mankind are warranted—" This looks grammatically incorrect, but stay with us. "Individually or collectively, in interfering with the liberty of action of any of their number is self-protection. The only purpose for which power can be rightfully exercised over any member of a civilized community against his will, is to prevent harm to other." The only part of the conduct of anyone—I'm sorry. "His own good, either physical or moral, is not a sufficient warranty."

Let's understand that. For my own good, the government cannot pass what would be called forcible action. In other words, a person ought to be able to kill themselves if they want.

Mr. Friedman: The right to commit suicide is a natural human right.

Mr. Donahue: It's your life.

Mr. Friedman: It's your life.

Mr. Donahue: And you don't want the government to spend any money to prevent you from doing that.

Mr. Friedman: Absolutely, no. Obviously, I, as a friend of yours, will try to prevent you. If you were a friend of mine and you suddenly got to a bridge and were going to jump over, I would certainly rush over and grab you and pull you off. And I would—

Mr. Donahue: But you don't want public money to keep me from doing it.

Mr. Friedman: Well I would go farther. No, no. I want to go farther on a personal basis. I would reason with you. I would argue with you. But let's suppose after I had reasoned with you, after I had argued with you, I had failed to persuade you. Do I have the right to use force to prevent you from disposing of your own life?

Mr. Donahue: I think you do. I think you do.

Mr. Friedman: I certainly do not. I certainly do not. And you do not. And certainly, you do not have the right to put your hands in the pockets of other people in order to prevent somebody from doing something in his own value system. Now, you know, it's an interesting thing. Every time you bring up issues like this, people don't recognize what's been happening. Where is the rate of suicide highest? Is it in the countries that are free enterprise countries, or is it in socialist countries? Sweden has the highest rate of suicide of any of the Western countries the last time I looked at the figures. Maybe they've changed. Why? I don't mean why, but it's an interesting thing, an interesting observation, that Sweden is one of the most government-controlled governments—socialist countries in the world. But that hasn't prevented people from committing suicide.

Mr. Donahue: Yes. But the problem with your—

Mr. Friedman: But look. Take the simpler cases. Don't take the—

Mr. Donahue: This point has to be made. The problem with your point is that this is hardly anymore the best representative example of what the free enterprise system ought to be. So, you, yourself are America's severest critic. You think we've blown Adam Smith's theory here in America. So, we should have people jumping off bridges left and right here, not because it's a bad—

Mr. Friedman: We do. We do.... Look at the number of—

Mr. Donahue: Well, but that contradicts the point you just made.

Mr. Friedman: No, no. It doesn't because we have become so socialist. Look at the extent to which people are—

Mr. Donahue: Oh, I see. I see. All right.

Mr. Friedman: —opting out of the world, by going in for drugs, by going in for various other activities of this kind, which are a delayed form of committing suicide. One of the problems of our society is that by having all responsibility assigned to the government, we have removed the pressure on individuals to be responsible for themselves, to feel that they have a set of values that they are entitled to pursue, so that—

Mr. Donahue: I assume then that if somebody wants to smoke marijuana, that's their business, too.

Mr. Friedman: That's his business. Absolutely.

Mr. Donahue: Are we going to take that to heroin, and addiction?

Mr. Friedman: Absolutely. Let me go back on that one because that's a very interesting thing. Even if on ethical principles, you believe it is right to prevent somebody else from smoking marijuana, as a matter of expediency, it's a terrible mistake.

Mr. Donahue: And so's jumping off the bridge.

Mr. Friedman: No, no. I don't mean that. I mean, it's a terrible mistake for society to render heroin illegal, because that increases the harm which heroin does. Why do we have so much crime in the inner cities and in the cities? Over 50 percent of it is attributed to crime for the sake of acquiring money to buy heroin.

Mr. Donahue: Because the price—

Mr. Friedman: Why is heroin so expensive? Because it's illegal. We went through this with Prohibition. Whether you believe it's right or wrong to prevent people from drinking alcohol, we had the experience with Prohibition in which we found that it did more harm than good. . . . More important, the basic respect for law was eroded. Law-abiding people who would never ordinarily have broken the law, broke the law in order to get a drink.

Mr. Donahue: Because they knew that the law enforcement agencies could not possibly enforce, with any efficiency, the Prohibition laws.

Mr. Friedman: But the reason they couldn't enforce it was because it wasn't publicly backed. If 90 percent of the public had been in favor of the Prohibition law, you could have enforced it.

Mr. Donahue: But I'm promising you, 90 percent of the public right now is in favor of enforcing prohibition against heroin.

Mr. Friedman: And you cannot enforce it. I agree. I was understating my case. Even with 90 percent of the people, you can't enforce it, and it does vastly more harm today because it is illegal, than it would do if it were legal. Let me point out for a moment that more lives are lost each year through drinking alcohol than through heroin. . . . If you're going to make the case for preventing heroin on the basis of saving lives, there's a much stronger case for prohibition of alcohol.

Mr. Donahue: But there would be some who would argue that to relax law enforcement, or to take away law enforcement pressure on heroin trade is to ensure that heroin deaths will meet and exceed alcohol deaths.

Mr. Friedman: On the contrary. It would reduce the number of heroin deaths. Why would it reduce the number of heroin deaths? In the first place, many of the deaths come from impure or adulterated heroin, or needles that are contaminated. In the second place, as we found in Prohibition, the fact that Prohibition encouraged alcoholism rather than the opposite. To the young people, in particular, it became an adventure to go out and get drunk, to go to a speakeasy. Today, with heroin illegal, it pays a heroin pusher to create an addict because given that it's illegal it's worth his while to spend some money on getting somebody else hooked because once hooked, he has a captive audience. If heroin were readily available everywhere, it wouldn't pay anybody to create an addict because the addict could then go anywhere to buy it. You have had experience with this. Britain has had legalized—not heroin in general, but they have had an arrangement under which certified addicts can get heroin from physicians on prescription. And it's done very much less harm than our system has. So, I have no apologies for believing that far less harm would be done to this country by legalizing heroin than is now being done by trying to enforce heroin prohibition.

Mr. Donahue: I assume, like the baby in the car, you would support legislation prohibiting the sale of heroin and other addictive substances to juveniles.

Mr. Friedman: Well, that's a very hard question. There is a different case for juveniles. But whether you could really handle the question, that's a question of expediency, not of principle. If I thought I could enforce it, I would be willing to say that for juveniles. But I'm not sure I could enforce it, and I'm not sure when I looked into it I wouldn't decide I did more harm than good, even there.

Mr. Donahue: You'll agree that this is the issue that lays bare the whole notion of your personal statement, and this is where we get to the practical realities of sweat and blood everyday life, with parental anxiety. Where are my kids? What are those sirens? Who's selling what to whom? What are they doing in the car? Who's sniffing, smoking, drinking? What is happening out there? And for all of the adulation that you've received, standing ovations everywhere you go, this is a very difficult platform for you to speak from.

Mr. Friedman: I don't believe so. I don't believe so,

because I believe it corresponds to the real understanding and interest and beliefs of the vast majority of the American people. I think that you have to distinguish between the attitudes of the public at large, and the attitudes of a relatively small group of people who have been trying to persuade the public to have different views.

Mr. Donahue: I know that, Dr. Friedman, and—

Mr. Friedman: Look at Prohibition. . . . Why did you get it adopted in the first place? If the people in this audience, who are predominantly female, will pardon me, it was only adopted because the young males were away in France during World War I, and the women of the country voted in Prohibition. Now that's neither good nor bad. It's a pure statement of historical fact.

Mr. Donahue: Let's not miss the irony here. The irony is that you are the darling of the conservatives. Is there anybody left who doesn't think we have too much government? And you are as eloquent a spokesman against that abuse as there is walking around today. You are also on record as supporting the candidacy of Ronald Reagan.

Mr. Friedman: Yes, indeed.

Mr. Donahue: Do I have to tell you what happens to Ronald Reagan's candidacy if he so much breathes agreement to the statement you've just made about drugs?

Mr. Friedman: Well, fortunately, one of the great virtues of being a college professor is that you can say exactly what you believe and what you mean. And I'm not running for office. I'd never run for office. I have no desire to run for office. And so, I regard it as a great luxury that I can be irresponsible. . . .

Audience: Since you do like Ronald Reagan, and let's say he wins the election and he chooses you as his chief economic adviser, what would you do to restore our economy back on the right track? And would you put us on a gold standard, or could you put us on a gold standard?

Mr. Friedman: Number one, I have been offered the chairmanship of the Council of Economic Advisors in the past, and I have refused it, and I guarantee you I would refuse it again.... I believe that I, personally, can be more useful outside the government than I can inside. It's a very important job. There are many able people who can do the job. I don't believe that's the way I can use my abilities and my interests most effectively. And I want to remain irresponsible....

But number two. Let me answer your second two questions. What measures should the government take to try to restore economic health to the United States? Let me say first, you're not going to do it overnight. We've gotten into our present pickle because of three decades of mismanagement of the economy, and we are not going to get out of it in six months. But what you have to do is, number one, you have to move to cut down government spending, to hold down the rate of growth of government spending in dollars, and to cut it in terms of pursestring power. Number two, you have to have a restrained monetary policy, not a shock treatment, not a real cut in the quantity of money, but to hold down and have a gradual reduction in the rate of monetary growth.

Number three, you have to eliminate as many of the regulations that now bedevil the economy as you possibly can. The most important area there is the energy area. We have created the energy mess because of governmental intervention. The most effective measure we could take for both foreign policy and domestic policy would be to get rid of the Department of Energy, to get rid of this mislabeled windfall profits tax, to let the private enterprise economy go to work to produce the energy that we need.

Now, on your last question, I do not believe it is either feasible or desirable to establish a gold standard under current circumstances. The gold standard served well in the nineteenth century. If you could restore the conditions of the nineteenth century, namely, a situation in which federal government spending was 3 percent of national income, I'd be in favor of a gold standard.

Notes

Introduction: Milton Friedman Is a Hoax

1. Milton Friedman, *Freedom to Choose* (Chicago: University of Chicago Press, 1979), pp. 34-35.
2. Konstandinos Kalimtgis, David Goldman, and Jeffrey Steinberg, *Dope, Inc.* (New York: New Benjamin Franklin House, 1978), pp. 106-112.
3. David Goldman, "Carter Let the World's Biggest Drug Bank into the U.S.," *War on Drugs* (July 1980) 1:22-27.
4. Milton Friedman, *Capitalism and Freedom* (Chicago: University of Chicago Press, 1962).
5. *The New York Times*, October 17, 1976, Financial section, p. 16.
6. Milton Friedman, *Essays in Positive Economics* (Chicago: University of Chicago Press, 1953), p. 319.

Chapter one: What Is Fascist Economics?

1. Burton C. Klein, *Germany's Economic Preparations for War* (Cambridge, Mass.: Harvard University Press, 1951).
2. Milton Friedman, *Studies in the Quantity Theory of Money* (Chicago: University of Chicago Press, 1956).
3. Ibid., p. 155.
4. Ibid., p. 151.
5. Ibid.
6. Friedman, *Studies in Money*, p. 137.
7. Ibid., pp. 132-135.
8. Ibid.
9. H. R. Trevor-Roper, N. Cameron, and R. H. Stevens, *Hitler's Table Talk* (London: Weidenfeld and Nicholson, 1953), p. 65.

10. Ibid., p. 155.
11. Ibid.
12. Konstandinos Kalimtgis, "Hitler's Final Solution," *The Campaigner* (Feb.-March 1975), p. 35.
13. Ibid., p. 36.
14. Ibid.
15. Friedman, *Studies in Money*, p. 155.
16. Edward Norman Peterson, *Hjalmar Schacht: For and Against Hitler* (Boston: Christopher Publishing, 1954), p. 297.
17. Konstantin George, "Planning Crises: From Nuclear Disaster to Nuclear War," *The Executive Intelligence Review* (April 12, 1980) 7:16-29.
18. David Goldman, "Carter's Schachtian Budget Proposal," *Executive Intelligence Review* (Feb. 12, 1980) 7:6-8.
19. Peterson, *Schacht*, p. 175.
20. Ibid., p. 170.
21. Friedman, *Essays in Economics*, p. 135.
22. Peterson, *Schacht*, p. 172.
23. Jacques Rueff, *The Age of Inflation* (Chicago: Regnery, 1964), p. 68.
24. As quoted in Kalimtgis, "Hitler's Final Solution."
25. Friedman, *Studies in Money*, p. 155.
26. Rueff, *Age of Inflation*, p. 12.
27. Jacques Rueff, *The Monetary Sins of the West* (New York: Macmillan, 1972), p. 53.
28. *The New York Times*, October 17, 1976, Financial section, p. 16.
29. Friedman, *Essays in Economics*, p. 14.
30. Milton Friedman, *Milton Friedman's Monetary Framework: A Debate with His Critics* (Chicago: University of Chicago Press, 1974), p. 27.
31. Ibid., p. 3.
32. Ibid., p. 18.
33. John Maynard Keynes, *The General Theory of Employment, Interest and Money* (New York: Harcourt, Brace and Co., 1964), p. 131.
34. Friedman, *Studies in Money*, p. 83.
35. Ibid., p. 34.
36. Ibid., p. 46.

37. Milton Friedman and Anna Jacobson Schwarz, *A Monetary History of the United States 1867-1960* (Princeton, N.J.: Princeton University Press, 1963), p. 700.
38. Friedman, *Monetary Framework,* p. 38.
39. Friedman, *Studies in Money,* p. 233.
40. John Kenneth Galbraith, *Money: Whence It Came, Where It Went* (New York: Houghton Mifflin, 1975), pp. 343-364.

Chapter two: Rueff versus Friedman

1. G. R. Taylor, ed., *Hamilton and the National Debt* (Boston: D. C. Heath, 1950).
2. Jacques Rueff, *Complete Works,* vol. III, chapter 3. This and other quotations from Rueff in this chapter are drawn from soon-to-be-published translations of Rueff's work by the Lehrman Institute in New York City, which has graciously permitted their use. For purpose of location, the volume and chapter numbers in the forthcoming complete works of Rueff are given.
3. Ibid.
4. Ibid.
5. Ibid.
6. Ibid.
7. Ibid.
8. Ibid.
9. Rueff, *Complete Works,* vol. III, chapter 4.
10. Rueff, *Age of Inflation,* p. 21.
11. Friedman, *Essays in Economics,* p. 135.
12. Jacques Rueff, *The Gods and the Kings* (New York: Macmillan, 1973), p. 193.
13. Quoted in Jacques Cheminade, "Friedrich List und die Neue Weltwirtschaftsordnung," *Internationale Bulletin,* 1979.
14. Ibid., p. 14.
15. The authors are indebted to research conducted by Susan Johnson of the *Executive Intelligence Review* for the real story of the Marshall Plan.

16. Immediately after the war, America faced the predictable sort of shortage of almost all forms of capital goods for civilian production. Conventional economic wisdom was that any export of these goods to Europe would represent a sacrifice to the American economy, and, therefore, that the Marshall Plan should foster European self-sufficiency. This argument held true only under the assumption that America did not require a vast, basic renewal of industrial capacity that dated back to the 1920s, the sort of renewal that Germany and Japan had to undertake because the war had obliterated their existing industry. In this circumstance the roots of America's 1960s economic decline are apparent.
17. Friedman, *Essays in Economics,* pp. 157-203.
18. Ibid., p. 202.
19. Ibid., p. 200.
20. *Papers and Proceedings of the 80th Annual Meeting of the American Economic Association.* Wisconsin, 1968, p. 365.
21. Reported by former Nixon aide William Safire in his memoir *Before the Fall* (New York: Doubleday, 1975).
22. Rueff, *Monetary Sins of the West,* p. 91.
23. Ibid., p. 40.
24. Ibid., p. 44.
25. Ibid., p. 96.
26. Ibid., p. 41.
27. Ibid., p. 44.
28. Ibid., p. 45.
29. *Papers,* American Economic Association, p. 366.
30. Since 1970, the Eurodollar market, or the deposits of dollars held in banks outside the United States, principally in London and the Caribbean, has grown from less than $100 billion to *$1.2 trillion.* The market turns over, that is, the total volume changes hands, about every two weeks. The Western European monetary authorities have for some years called for some form of controls on this market, which operates without any official scrutiny to speak of.

    For an account of the 1773 crisis, see David Goldman, "How the City of London Got Through the Revolutionary War Crisis," in *New Solidarity,* December 15, 1977.

31. Employing the LaRouche-Riemann computer model, Dr. Steven Bardwell has demonstrated the existence of an optimum level of capital transfer from the industrial to the developing countries.
32. Lyndon LaRouche, *How the International Development Bank Works* (New York: Campaigner Publications, 1975).
33. Ibid.
34. Linda Frommer, "How British Jacobinism Destroyed the French Revolution," *New Solidarity*, June 11, 1977.
35. Only one American economist upheld Rueff's position. In a series of public debates with Columbia University Economics Department chairman C. Lowell Harriss, a collaborator of Friedman, Queens College economist Abba Lerner, and others, LaRouche warned that the August 15 decision would steer the United States into depression. "They're a bunch of cowards," LaRouche said of the Nixon administration. "If they had any guts, they would have devalued the dollar against gold"—Rueff's proposal—"instead of floating," that is, letting the value of the dollar fluctuate arbitrarily. "But they did exactly what the British did with sterling in 1931, and it's going to have the same results."
36. Richard Nixon, *Memoirs* (New York: Grosset and Dunlap, 1978), p. 477.
37. According to Safire's account of the Camp David meeting that produced the August 15 decision, Nixon acted in fear of Reuss on that issue.

Chapter three: The Fraud of Free Enterprise

1. Elie Halevy, *The Growth of Philosophical Radicalism* (New York: Augustus Kelley, 1949), p. 304.
2. Kalimtgis et al., *Dope Inc.*
3. Disraeli maintained that Shelburne was the most important and least appreciated figure in eighteenth-century English politics. He represents Shelburne fictionally in his novel *Sybil*.

4. David Hume, "On Miracles," in Hume, *Philosophical Works,* T. H. Green and T. H. Grose, eds. vol. IV (Berlin: Scientia Verlag Aalen, 1964).
5. Ibid.
6. Charles W. Hendel, ed. *David Hume's Political Essays.* (New York: Liberal Arts Press, 1953), p. ix.
7. Christopher White, *The Noble Family* (New York: Campaigner Publications, 1977). *The Works of Ossian, the Son of Fingal* (London: 1975).
8. The first German translation of Ossian appeared in 1768, a mere three years after it first was published in London, as "The Poems of Ossian, an ancient Celtic poet, translated by the Vienna Jesuit Michael Denis." Johann Gottfried Herder, who usually knew better, gave the forgery credibility in his classic "Ossian and the Songs of Ancient Peoples," in 1773. Herder attacked Denis's translation on the grounds that it did not do justice to the "original."
9. Hume, *Philosophical Works,* vol. IV, p. 415.
10. Ibid., p. 421.
11. See Frederick Ryan, *The House of Temple: A Study of Malta and Its Knights in the French Revolution* (London: Burns, Oates, and Washbourne, 1930).
12. Disraeli, *Sybil.*
13. See Ly Siou Y, *Les grands courants de la pensée économique chinoise dans l'antiquité et leur influence sur la formation de la doctrine physiocratique* (Paris: Jouve et Cie., 1936).
14. Virgile Pinot, *La Chine et la formation de l'espirit philosophique en France* (Paris: Librairie Orientaliste Paul Geuthner, 1932), p. 9.
15. Goldman, "How the City of London."
16. Adam Smith, *Wealth of Nations* (New York: Modern Library).
17. Alexander Hamilton, *Report to Congress on the Subject of Manufactures,* in Nancy Spannaus and Christopher White, *The Political Economy of the American Revolution* (New York: Campaigner Publications, 1977), pp. 375-441.
18. Adam Smith, *The Theory of Moral Sentiments.*
19. According to Jack Beeching, *The Chinese Opium Wars* (London: Hutchinson, 1975).
20. Goldman, "How the City of London."

21. A sort of Scots mafia directed by the intermarried Scots-Dutch Hope and Baring families became the leading practitioners of the opium trade, including such names as Jardine, Matheson, Keswick, and Hutchinson.
22. Halevy, *Growth of Radicalism,* p. 75.
23. Ibid., p. 147.
24. Frommer, "How British Jacobinism."
25. Halevy, *Growth of Radicalism,* p. 30.
26. Cited in Lyndon LaRouche, *How to Defeat Liberalism and William F. Buckley* (New York: New Benjamin Franklin House, 1979), p. 15.
27. Halevy, *Growth of Radicalism,* p. 113.
28. Smith, *Wealth of Nations.*
29. This is the closing sentence of Smith's entire work.
30. The Smith proposal was made first by Shelburne's correspondent Dean Tucker before the Seven Years' War.
31. Vincent T. Harlow, *The Founding of the Second British Empire, 1763-1793* (Toronto: Longman's Ltd., 1965).
32. Donald Phau, "The Treachery of Thomas Jefferson," *The Campaigner* (March 1980) 13:4-32.
33. Kalimtgis et al., *Dope, Inc.,* p. 39.
34. Ibid., p. 40.
35. As cited in unpublished report, Kathy Burdman, New York City, 1979.
36. Ibid.
37. Ibid.
38. Smith, *Wealth of Nations.*
39. Harlow, *Second British Empire.*
40. See Kalimtgis et al., *Dope, Inc.,* Part III.
41. In other words, the East India Company network had total command over world trade in Asia, while the City of London, by trade war against its rival France, had the monopoly of trade financing in Europe.
42. The relative position of narcotics in international trade only fell behind petroleum for the first time in 1973. Otherwise, for more than a century the dope trade has been the world's largest business, according to the authors of *Dope, Inc.*
43. John Maynard Keynes, *Essays in Biography* (New York: W. W. Norton, 1951), p. 100.

44. P. Straffa, ed., *The Works of David Ricardo* (London: Cambridge University Press, 1950-1955), vol. II, p. 288.
45. Keynes, *Essays in Biography,* p. 84. The other "fairy godmother" was Hume's intimate friend, Jean-Jacques Rousseau, reports Keynes.
46. Straffa, *Ricardo,* p. 287. The Malthus book is contained in the Ricardo set with Ricardo's marginal notes.
47. Ibid., p. 292.
48. Rosa Luxemburg, *The Accumulation of Capital* (London: 1951), p. 375.
49. Halevy, *Growth of Radicalism,* p. 304.
50. Ibid., p. 50.
51. Keynes, *Essays in Biography,* p. 103.
52. Keynes, *General Theory,* p. 363.
53. Henry Carey, *Principles of Political Economy* (Philadelphia: 1831), vol. I, chapter 2.
54. Aristotle, *The Politics,* chapter 1, section 8.
55. Ibid., chapter 1, section 11.
56. Criton Zoakos, "Aristotle, Political Warfare, and Classical Studies," *The Campaigner* (Sept.-Oct. 1978) 11:43-73.
57. Hume, *Philosophical Works,* vol. IV, p. 318.
58. In Karl Marx, *Critique of Political Economy* (Chicago: Clark Kerr, 1904), p. 246.
59. Leland H. Jencks, *The Migration of British Capital to 1875* (New York: Barnes and Noble, 1973), p. 59.
60. Marx, *Critique,* p. 246.
61. Warren Hamerman, "America's Unpaid Debt to European Republicans," *The Campaigner* (April 1980) 13:4-19.
62. Jencks, *British Capital,* p. 62.
63. Sir John Clapham, *History of the Bank of England* (London: Cambridge University Press, 1966), vol. II, p. 185.
64. Karl Marx, *Capital* (London: Lawrence and Wishart, 1972), vol. III, p. 556.
65. Ibid., p. 554.
66. Allen Salisbury, *The Civil War and the American System* (New York: Campaigner Publications, 1978), p. 16 and *passim.*
67. Richard Freeman, "The Specie Resumption Act," *New Solidarity,* July 28, 1980.

Chapter four: Oxford Monetarism and Hitler's Vienna

1. Criton Zoakos, Translator's Preface to Plato's *Timaeus*, *The Campaigner* (February 1980) 13:33-35.
2. E.g., Cleon Skousen of the Freeman Foundation.
3. Unpublished report by Laurie Sloane, New York City, 1979.
4. Ibid.
5. Wesley Clair Mitchell, *The Backward Art of Spending Money* (New York: Augustus Kelley, 1950), p. 183.
6. Ibid., p. 187.
7. Ibid., p. 181.
8. Jeremy Bentham, *Panopticon.* (London: T. Payne, 1791).
9. Mitchell, *Spending Money,* p. 187.
10. Ibid.
11. Ibid., p. 354.
12. Ibid., p. 359.
13. Keynes, *Essays in Biography,* p. 274.
14. Ibid., p. 285.
15. Ibid., p. 284.
16. Ibid., p. 262.
17. Ibid., p. 260.
18. Ibid., p. 279.
19. Ibid., p. 229.
20. Mitchell, *Spending Money,* pp. 164-165.
21. Ibid., pp. 149, 176.
22. Edward Pease, *The History of the Fabian Society* (New York: International Publishers, 1926), Appendix I by G. B. Shaw.
23. Ibid., p. 275.
24. Ibid., p. 276.
25. Ibid., p. 278.
26. See Carol White, *The New Dark Ages Conspiracy* (New York: New Benjamin Franklin House, 1980), pp. 64-69 and *passim.*
27. Ludwig von Mises, *The Austrian School of Economics,* (New York: 1939), p. 10.

332 The Ugly Truth About Milton Friedman

28. Kathy Burdman, unpublished report, New York City, 1978.
29. Ibid.
30. Uwe Parpart, "Riemann Declassified: His Method and Program for the Natural Sciences," *Fusion* (1979) 2:24.
31. Burdman, unpublished report.
32. Burdman, unpublished report.
33. Vivian Zoakos of the Society for Platonic Humanism has documented this in a paper to be published in *The Campaigner* late in 1980. One of the most uncontestable pieces of evidence was reported this year by violinist Yehudi Menuhin, who saw during a trip to China a set of bells, whose tones spanned four octaves, and which were in perfect well-tempered tuning.
34. White, *New Dark Ages,* chapter 1.
35. Mises, *Austrian School,* p. 25.
36. Ludwig von Mises, *Theory of Money and Credit* (London: 1912), p. 81.
37. Ibid., p. 21.
38. Friedrich von Hayek, "Geldtheorie und Konjuncturtheorie," in *Beiträge zur Konjunkturforschung* (Vienna: Oesterreichisches Institut für Konjunkturforschung, 1929), no. 1, p. 87.
39. Ibid., p. 145.
40. Ibid., p. 170.
41. Ibid., p. 189.
42. Friedman, *Essays in Economics,* p. 136.
43. Friedrich von Hayek, *The Road to Serfdom* (London: 1944), p. 21.

Chapter five: Monetarism Invades America

1. Kathy Burdman, unpublished report, New York City, 1978.
2. Ibid.
3. J. Laurence Laughlin, "Hamilton as a Political Economist," *The Journal of Political Economy* (December 1894) 3:302.

4. Ibid., p. 303.
5. Mitchell, *Spending Money*, p. 78.
6. Ibid.
7. Thorstein Veblen, *The Theory of the Leisure Class* (Chicago: University of Chicago Press, 1899).
8. Robert Heilbroner, *The Worldly Philosophers* (New York: Simon and Schuster, 1961), p. 199.
9. Thorstein Veblen, *Absentee Ownership and Business Enterprise* (New York: Viking Press, 1924).
10. Heilbroner, *Worldly Philosophers*, p. 194.
11. Ibid., p. 210.
12. Ibid.
13. Mitchell, *Spending Money*, p. 169.
14. Ibid., p. 171.
15. Ibid., p. 160.
16. Ibid., p. 283.
17. Wesley Clair Mitchell, *A History of the Greenbacks* (Chicago: University of Chicago Press, 1903).
18. Burdman, unpublished report.
19. Ibid.
20. Mitchell, *Spending Money*, p. 278.
21. Mises, *Austrian School*, p. 34.
22. Wesley Clair Mitchell, *Business Cycles and Unemployment* (New York: National Bureau of Economic Research, 1923).
23. John Kenneth Galbraith, *The Great Crash* (London: Hamilton, 1953), p. 23.
24. Ibid.
25. In the *Journal of Law and Economics*, October 1967.
26. The actual story of the Crash of 1929, as told here, and the correspondence quoted here can basically be found in two sources: Stephen V. O. Clarke, *Central Bank Cooperation, 1924-31* (New York: Federal Reserve Board of New York, 1967); and Sir Henry Clay, *Lord Norman* (London: Macmillan, 1957).
27. Rueff, *Age of Inflation*, p. 9.
28. Ibid., pp. 10-11.
29. Ibid., p. 12.
30. Hayek, *Road to Serfdom*.
31. Friedman, *Capitalism and Freedom*, p. 45.
32. Ibid., p. 54.

33. Ibid., p. 50.
34. Friedman, *A Monetary History*, p. 809.
35. Ibid., p. 812.
36. Ibid., p. 810.
37. Kalimtgis et al., *Dope, Inc.*, p. 216.
38. White, *New Dark Ages*, chapter 4.

Chapter six: The Undead of Economics

1. *Executive Intelligence Review* obtained from a member of the society its 1978 membership list. This document is not public record, but *EIR* will make it available to bona fide researchers. During the preparation of this book, William Baroody, Sr. died.
2. Angelika Beyreuther prepared quotations from Coudenhove-Kalergi's works for this and related projects. See White, *New Dark Ages*, p. 377, note 52, for a detailed listing of Coudenhove's work.
3. White, *New Dark Ages*, chapter 4.
4. H. G. Wells, *After Democracy, Addresses and Papers on the Present World Situation* (London: Watts and Col., 1932), p. 24.
5. In a letter May 10, 1933.
6. H. G. Wells, *The World Brain* (London: Methuen and Co., 1938), pp. 7-23.
7. Unpublished letter in H. G. Wells Archives, University of Illinois at Urbana.
8. Unpublished report by Carol Cleary, New York City, 1979.
9. Friedman, *Essays in Economics*, p. 14.
10. Mitchell, *Spending Money*, p. 169.
11. Wells, *World Brain*, p. 23.
12. Marilyn Ferguson, *The Aquarian Conspiracy* (New York: St. Martin's Press, 1980), p. 49.
13. Hayek, *Road to Serfdom*, p. 21.
14. Ibid., p. 235.
15. Ibid., p. 236.
16. Charles Markmann, *The Buckleys—A Family Examined* (New York: William Morrow and Company, 1973).

17. From the files of the Latin America desk of the *Executive Intelligence Review*.
18. Unpublished research by James Cleary, New York City, 1978.
19. *El Día*, Mexico City, September 8, 1978.

Chapter seven: The Worst Economist in the World

1. In conversation with a colleague of the authors.
2. Mises, *Theory of Money*, p. 81.
3. Friedman's "technical brilliance," and his Nobel Prize, are based on work in price theory, also the title of a Friedman volume not cited in this book. The technique of price theory reaches the outer extremes of irrelevance to the real world. In a nutshell, Marshallian price theory assumes that the lower the relative price of an item, the more people will have of it, and the higher the price, the less of it, all other things being equal—the "downward sloping price curve." Most of contemporary economics is built around the idea of holding everything constant and changing a single price or supply of a single commodity, and seeing what happens. The idea that a single process could introduce coherence into the mass of such changes is out of the realm of Friedman's imagination. Friedman is an extremist in the pursuit of incoherence, compared to Marshall or traditional price theorists. His first great "technical" essay, published in 1947, asserts that you cannot hold real income constant and alter a single price, because even that one price change will alter real income, and so forth. This extraordinary piece of flummery occurs in "The Marshallian Demand Curve," in *Essays on Economics*.
4. Galbraith, *Money: Whence It Came*, pp. 279-280. Galbraith, who worked with Friedman directly on the 1930s National Resources Planning Council described the conspiracy as follows: "In the summer of 1940, a few days after the fall of France, I was summoned to Washington

by [Federal Reserve Research Director Laughlin] Currie. Leon Henderson had just been placed in charge of prices in the recently revived National Defense Advisory Commission. It was potentially—and, as matters developed in practice—a powerful position. . . . Currie wanted a reliable disciple to be at hand. I was such. From this came my wartime responsibiliity for price control. A couple of years earlier, also at Currie's behest, I had directed a large review of the public works experience of the 1930s for the National Resources Planning Board [where Friedman was staff economist at the time]. . . .

"Later, in the '50s when Currie came under heavy and richly unjustified attack as an alleged Communist agent, I came across letters from him, long forgotten, urging the importance of getting 'our people' into one or another agency of the Administration. . . . It occurred to me that I would have difficulty persuading one of the congressional committees then searching out Communists of this meaning."

5. Nixon, *Memoirs*, p. 43.
6. Lyndon LaRouche, *The Power of Reason* (New York: New Benjamin Franklin House, 1979), p. 137.
7. The leading figure whom von Hayek looked toward for advice on this matter was Walter Lippmann. Lippmann's 1936 book, *The Good Society*, proposed "progress by liberation," arguing that "the method of human progress is to liberate human energies," foreshadowing the 1980 *Aquarian Conspiracy*.
8. *Business Week*, November 1, 1976.
9. Friedman, *A Monetary History*, p. 612.
10. Ibid., p. 613.
11. *The New York Times*, March 31, 1964.
12. *The New York Times*, October 25, 1964.
13. Leonard Silk, *Nixonomics* (New York: Praeger, 1972), p. 7.
14. As quoted in Silk, *Nixonomics*.
15. Ibid., p.11.
16. *National Review*, August 16, 1971.
17. Document of the Organization of American States, 1976.
18. *Business Week*, January 11, 1976.

19. Ibid.
20. *Business Week*, June 2, 1975.
21. *La Prensa*, Lima, Peru, January 16, 1977.
22. *Institutional Investor*, March 1979.
23. Ibid.
24. Kalimtgis et al., *Dope, Inc.*, Part II.
25. The overthrow of Nicaraguan dictator Anastasio Somoza may have reduced this somewhat.
26. London *Economist*, March 26, 1980.
27. London *Economist*, March 18, 1980.

Chapter eight: The Basis of Real Economics

1. For basic treatment of the soliton, see Steven Bardwell, "Elementary Plasma Physics from an Advanced Standpoint," *Fusion* (November 1978) 2:18-42.
2. Uwe Parpart et al., *The Industrialization of India, Executive Intelligence Review Special Report* (February 1980).

   For in-depth discussion of the LaRouche-Riemann model see: Uwe Parpart and David Goldman, "Energy Conservation: Building Inflation into the Economy," *Executive Intelligence Review* (March 18, 1980) 7:16-29; David Goldman et al., "LaRouche-Riemann model Forecast: Can the U.S. Economy Survive the Depression?" *Executive Intelligence Review* (May 6, 1980) 7:16-35. For a basic theoretical treatment of the principles behind the LaRouche-Riemann model see Lyndon LaRouche, "The Fallacy of Scalar Elementarity," *Fusion* (November 1979) 3:48-57. For a primer on the science of economics as defined in this book see Lyndon LaRouche, *Basic Economics for Conservative Democrats* (New York: New Benjamin Franklin House, 1980).

Index

A

Adams, John Quincy, 90
Addams, Jane, 170, 171, 237
Adenauer, Konrad, 63, 78, 210
Alexander the Great, 128
Allende, Salvador, 253, 254, 255
Althusser, Louis, 89
American Enterprise Institute, 209
Anderson, Martin, 10
Argoud, Colonel, 226
Aristotle, 97, 217; on wealth, 131-132; *Politics,* 131, 217
Aspen Institute, 80
Astor, John Jacob, 120
Austrian Institute for the Study of Trade Cycles, 163
Aveling, Edward, 147

B

Bakunin, Michael, 171
Balfour, Lord Arthur, 143
Barahona, Pablo, 255
Baring, Francis, 99, 111, 123
Baruch, Bernard, 182, 212
Baruch, Kuntner, 183
Begin, Menachem, 53, 232, 260-261
Bentham, Jeremy, 6, 17, 94, 96, 99, 103, 114-115, 119-120, 124-125, 127-128, 129, 134-135, 143, 146, 149, 151, 153, 161, 174-178, 220, 274; *Defense of Usury,* 115; *Panopticon,* 150, 176; *Principles of Morals and Legislation,* 149

Beveridge, Sir William, 215
Biddle, Nicholas, 181
Biffen, John, 266, 268
Blavatsky, Madame, 143
Blavet, Abbé, 103
Bleiberg, Robert M., 209
Böhm-Bawerk, 161, 174, 180
Bolingbroke, Lord, 103
Brandeis, Louis, 171
Brandt, Karl, 247
Brandt, Willy, 89
Brookings Institution, 238
Buckley, William F., 22, 209, 224, 227, 247-252; on Friedman, 252
Bukharin, Nikolai, 180; *The Economic Theory of the Leisure Class,* 180
Bulwer-Lytton, Edward, 144-145; *Rienzi,* 144
Burns, Arthur, 79, 181, 234-236, 243, 244, 247, 250, 251; on 1952 recession, 242-243
Burr, Aaron, 120
Bush, George, 251
Butler, Nicholas Murray, 212, 215, 216, 235

C

Campbell, Glenn, 209
Canning, George, 135
Cantor, Georg, 15, 158
Carey, Mathew, 63, 121, 301
Carey, Henry, 63, 75, 121, 129, 131, 139, 160, 170, 172, 301

Carnegie Foundation, 212
Carnap, Rudolf, 217, 218
Carnot, Lazare, 75, 76, 90, 115, 158, 160
Carter, James Earl, 9, 21, 24, 35, 36, 38, 41, 42, 43, 44, 46, 259, 280, 289, 295, 297
Carteret, John, 103
Carver, Lord, 82
Castro, Sergio de, 255, 258-259
Cecil, Sir Robert, 211
Center for Documentation and Information, (Madrid), 225, 227
Center for Strategic and International Studies, 24
Chamberlain, Houston Stewart, 155, 156, 166, 205, 210
Chamberlain, Neville, 205, 214
Chaptal, Claude, 75, 76, 77, 244, 301
Chatham, Lord, 118
Churchill, Winston, 87, 183, 187, 190, 195, 198-200, 211, 213, 239-240; on Black Thursday, 187
Clapham, Sir John, 223
Cleveland, Harlan, 80
Clive, Robert, 110
Cliveden Set, 142; also see *Roundtable*
Club of Rome, 71, 125
Cobden Club, 120, 170, 172
Colbert, Jean-Baptiste, 62, 71, 75, 90, 300
Confucius, 105
Conti, Prince de Bourbon, 103
Coolidge, Calvin, 172
Coudenhove-Kalergi, Count Richard, 207-214, 218, 220-225, 228, 235; on the League of Nations, 211; on the Pan-European Union, 210-211
Council on Foreign Relations (New York), 78
Courant, Richard, 216

D

Danton, Georges Jacques, 89, 146
Dawes, Charles, 198
de Gaulle, General Charles, 13, 62, 63, 64, 75, 77-78, 84-85, 87-90, 210, 224, 226
deBroglie, Louis, 13, 75, 287
DeGrelle, Leon, 225
Debré, Michael, 89
Descartes, René, 100
Dewey, Thomas, 235
Dillon, C. Douglas, 86
Director, Aaron, 237, 242
Director, Rose, (Mrs. Milton Friedman), 237
Disraeli, Benjamin, 99; on Lord Shelburne, 103
Dewey, John, 172-174, 176, 178-181, 208, 212, 214-218, 220, 234; on labor power, 176
Dollfuss, Engelberg, 213
Dorfman, Joseph, 175; on Veblen, 175
Dundas, Henry, 112, 122, 123
Dundas, Robert, 112
Dunne, Peter, 249
Dupin, Charles, 75, 76, 77, 301; on labor, 76

E

East India Company, 2, 6, 97, 99, 108-112, 120-122, 123, 126-129, 131, 137, 139, 253-254, 274
Eden, Anthony, 86
Edgeworth, F. X., 148, 153
Edinburgh, 101, 120, 124
Ehrlich, Simeha, 260-261
Eisenhower, Dwight D., 86, 90, 233-235, 242, 243, 247
Elizabeth, Empress, 95, 155, 156, 157, 159, 208
Engels, Frederick, 138

European Monetary System, 12, 79, 83-84
Exter, John, 209

F

Fabian Society, 141, 144, 154, 156, 170, 171, 180
Federal Emergency Management Agency, 35-36, 44, 182
Federal Reserve Board, 35, 36, 50, 135, 182, 185, 186, 187, 188, 189, 195, 196, 197, 198, 199, 204, 243, 250, 251
Ferguson, Marilyn, 221; *The Aquar ian Conspiracy,* 221; on H. G. Wells, 221
Feulner, Edwin J., 210
Field, Marshall, 171
Fisher, Irving, 58
Forbes, William Hathaway, 120
Forbonnais, 76-77, 104; on wealth, 76-77
Ford, Gerald, 3
Fowler, Henry, 82, 88
Franklin, Benjamin, 13, 62, 75, 90, 104, 111
Friedman, Milton, 1, 2, 3, 6, 7, 8, 9, 10, 11, 12, 13, 14, 15, 17, 19, 20, 22, 23, 24, 26, 27, 28, 29, 31, 32, 33, 37, 45, 46, 47, 48, 49, 51, 53, 54, 55, 57, 60, 61, 64, 67, 69, 70, 74, 75, 78, 79, 81, 82, 83, 84, 86, 88, 90, 91, 93, 94, 95, 96, 97, 101, 107, 123, 129, 131, 132, 133, 139, 140, 141, 142, 144, 148, 153, 155, 164-65, 166, 170, 178, 179, 180, 183, 184, 203, 204, 206, 208, 209, 219, 220, 223, 224, 225, 227, 228, 229, 231, 232, 233, 235-243, 247, 248, 249, 250, 251, 252, 253, 254, 255, 256, 258, 259, 260, 261, 264, 265, 266, 268, 273, 274, 275, 289, 303; *Capitalism and Freedom,* 6, 51, 221, 237, 241, 248; *Essays in Positive Economics,* 51; *Free to Choose,* 2, 4, 51, 237, 305; "The Methodology of Positive Economics," 51, 157, 219; *Milton Friedman's Monetary Framework,* 51; *A Monetary History of the United States,* 51, 53, 58, 204; *Studies in the Quantity Theory of Money,* 5, 26, 27, 46, 59, 239; *Taxing to Prevent Inflation,* 238; on Chile, 255-256, 257; on the Depression, 203; on drugs, 3-4; on economic policy, 9; on economic theory, 52, 53, 219; on floating rates, 82-83; on Henry Simons, 186; on Hong Kong, 4; on liberalism, 7; on the national purpose, 6; on Nazi Germany, 27-28, 29-30; on money, 28, 54-55, 57-58

G

Galbraith, John Kenneth, 32, 191-193; *The Great Crash,* 191; on the 1929 crash, 191, 192
Gandhi, Indira, 288
Garrison, James, 226
Gauss, Karl, 157
Gay, Edwin, 182-184
George III, King of England, 110, 111, 118
George, Lloyd, 195
Giscard d'Estaing, Valéry, 89, 210
Goebbels, Joseph, 261
Goldman, David, 5; *Dope, Inc.,* 97-98, 142
Goldman, Emma, 171
Goldwater, Barry, 8, 248, 249
Gomez, Laureano, 227; on Hitler, 227

Göring, Hermann, 24-25, 29, 30, 33, 49, 205, 214, 226; on Russia, 30-31
Greenspan, Alan, 3
Grey, Albert, 143

H

Haberler, Gottfried, 247
Hamilton, Alexander, 12, 13, 16, 62-63, 71, 96, 111, 120, 135, 173, 182, 244, 300, 301; *Report on Public Credit,* 62, 71; *Report to the Congress on the Subject of Manufactures,* 14, 106, 301; on money, 62-63; on value, 106-107
Hanotaux, Gabriel, 160
Hapsburg, Otto von, 207, 208, 210, 224-225, 228
Harding, Warren, 197
Harlow, Vincent, on East India Company, 123-124
Harper, William Rainey, 172
Harrison, George L., 188; on the 1929 credit squeeze, 188
Hastings, Warren, 110
Haushofer, Col. Karl, 142, 205; *Zeitschrift für Geopolitik,* 213
Hayek, Friedrich von, 81, 95, 154, 164-167, 175, 202-203, 208, 215-216, 221-224, 235, 239, 242, 247-248, 273; *Monetary Theory of the Trade Cycle,* 163; *The Road to Serfdom,* 166, 221, 239; on the Depression, 163; on government intervention, 166-167, 221-222; on liberalism, 242; on the trade cycle, 164
Heller, Walter W., 238
Helmholtz, Hermann von, 282, 285
Henri IV, King of France, 90
Heritage Foundation, 209, 233
Herzl, Theodore, 95, 210
Hettinger, Albert J., Jr., 204
Hirsch, Fred, 85
Hirst, Josiah, 189-190; on the 1929 crash, 189-190
Hitler, Adolf, 2, 9, 10, 19, 20, 24, 29, 33, 46, 48, 49, 50, 59, 108, 132, 142, 144, 155, 156, 166, 179, 182, 191, 198, 201, 202, 205, 212, 213, 214, 222, 227, 229, 235, 239, 289; *Mein Kampf,* 142, 213; on currency stability, 29
Hongkong and Shanghai Bank, 5, 120, 124, 146
Hook, Sidney, 10
Hoover, Herbert, 172, 185, 186, 212, 234
Hoover Institution, 10, 16, 25, 141, 209
House, Colonel Edward, 212
Howe, Geoffrey, 232, 233, 266, 268, 272
Hull House, 170-172, 176, 237
Hume, David, 93, 94, 96, 100-102, 104, 114, 116, 119, 126, 132, 133, 137, 149, 178, 179; *Treatise on Human Understanding,* 100; on money, 132-133
Hurtado, Alvaro Gomez, 226, 227, 229; on drugs, 226
Hurvitz, Yigal, 261
Hutchins, Robert, 218; *International Encyclopedia of Unified Sciences,* 218, 219, 220

I

Initiatives Committee for National Economic Planning, 11, 179, 184, 239
International Monetary Fund, 78-79, 80-81, 82, 86, 88, 89, 234, 240, 244

J

Jackson, Andrew, 139
Jardine Matheson, 123, 146
Jefferson, Thomas, 116, 120, 169
Jevons, William Stanley, 59, 146, 148, 150-151, 152, 154, 156, 162, 175, 216; *The Coal Question: An Inquiry concerning the Progress of the Nation and the Probable Exhaustion of our Coal Mines* 151-152; *Theory of Political Economy,* 151, 156
Johnson, Lyndon, 82, 249, 250
Joseph, Keith, 266
Jowett, Benjamin, 94, 142-143, 146, 148, 152

K

Kaldor, Nicholas, 32
Kalimtgis, Konstandinos, 5, 31; *Dope, Inc.,* 97-98, 142; on Nazi Germany, 31-32
Kemmerer, Donald, 209
Kennan, George, 80
Kennedy, John F., 55, 210, 226, 238, 293
Keynes, John Maynard, 10, 56, 61, 70, 74, 80, 81, 88, 125, 131, 151, 152, 199, 204, 238; *General Theory,* 10; on Thomas Malthus, 125
Kipling, Rudyard, 145, 205
Klein, Burton, 26-27, 31-33, 184; *Germany's Economic Preparations for War,* 25; on Hjalmar Schacht, 26-27
Klein, John J., 26, 28
Knight, Frank, 223, 236-237
Kraus, Karl, 156, 157, 159
Kuhnwald, Gottfried, 215
Krushchev, Nikita, 86

L

Lafayette, Marquis de, 111, 160
Lamont, Thomas, 195
LaRouche, Lyndon H., 10, 12, 13, 14, 15, 22, 47, 66, 70, 73, 75, 77, 78, 79, 84, 88, 90, 158, 241, 289, 301; *Mathematical Economics,* 87; *The Power of Reason,* 241; on McCarthyism, 241
LaRouche-Riemann econometric model, 15, 280, 287, 288, 291, 295, 297, 298
Laughlin, J. Lawrence, 172, 173, 180, 182, 186
Lavoisier, Antoine, 114
Lee, Arthur, 120
Leibniz, Gottfried Wilhelm, 90, 300
Leontief, Wassily, 11, 32, 184, 239, 240
Lerner, Abba, 10, 12, 17; *The Economics of Control,* 11; on Hjalmar Schacht, 11
Levi, Edward H., 209
Lincoln, Abraham, 16, 121, 139, 160, 180
Lippmann, Walter, 223
List, Friedrich, 63, 75, 77, 160, 161, 166, 167, 170, 172, 301
London School of Economics, 154, 155, 166, 180-181, 216
Louis XIV, King of France, 75
Louis, XV, King of France, 112-113
Louis XVI, King of France, 113
Ludwig I, King of Bavaria, 156
Luxemburg, Rosa, 128; on the East India Company, 128

M

Mach, Ernst, 95, 157-159, 163, 216-217; *Science of Mechanics,* 157; on science, 157-159

Mackinder, Halford, 142, 156, 166, 205, 213
Macpherson, James, 101-102
Mahler, Gustav, 159
Malthus, Parson Thomas, 124-125, 127-131, 136, 152, 163, 273; *Essay on Population,* 125-126, 131; *Principles of Political Economy,* 126-127; on capital investment, 126-127
Marat, Jean-Paul, 89, 114, 115, 146
Markmann, Charles, 224; *The Buckleys—A Family Examined,* 224
Marshall, Alfred, 59, 146, 148, 153-155, 177, 178, 181; on money, 153
Marshall, George, 79
Martin, William McChesney, 243, 250
Marx, Eleanor (Aveling), 147
Marx, Karl, 104, 138, 147, 154
McCracken, Paul, 249
McDowell, Edwin, 209
McKinley, William, 160, 171, 172, 173, 243
Medaris, John B. 234
Mefo-Institut, 24, 44
Mellon, Andrew, 172, 197
Mencius, 105
Menger, Karl von, 150, 156, 157, 160, 161, 174, 180, 216, 217; *Investigations on Method,* 157; *Principles of Economics,* 156
Metternich, Prince Klemens, 145, 155
Mill, James, 94-95, 97, 124, 127-129, 134; *A History of British India,* 127, 128
Mill, John Stuart, 6, 70, 94-97, 124, 136, 137, 154, 314; on credit to industry, 137
Miller, G. William, 41
Milner, Lord Alfred, 143, 161

Mises, Ludwig von, 81, 95, 157, 161, 162, 164, 165, 166, 167, 175, 185, 203, 208, 215-217, 221, 225, 227, 228, 235; *Omnipotent Government,* 222; on production, 161-162
Mitchell, Wesley Clair, 79, 95, 148, 149, 150-151, 153, 155, 162, 175, 176, 177, 179, 180, 181, 182, 183, 184, 185, 186, 203, 212, 215, 220, 234, 235, 236, 237, 239, 242; "The Backward Art of Spending Money," 177-178; *Business Cycles,* 181, 185-186; *A History of the Greenback,* 180; on Bentham, 149, 150; on labor power, 177; on money, 151, 153, 177-178; on Thorstein Veblen, 173-174
Monge, Gaspard, 75
Mont Pelerin Society, 5, 95, 207-217, 221, 224, 227, 228, 229, 235, 237, 242, 266
Morris, William, 144, 147, 154, 170-171, 174
Mosley, Sir Oswald, 199
Mussolini, Benito, 11, 146, 179, 198, 205, 213, 229

N

Nader, Ralph, 310
Nagy, Ferenc, 226
Napoleon, 125
National Aeronautics and Space Administration, 16, 23, 234, 240, 244, 247, 293
National Bureau of Economic Research, 95, 148, 162, 183, 184, 185, 186, 203, 204, 212, 223, 234, 236, 237, 238, 247, 275, 279
Naumann, Werner, 226
Necker, Jacques, 112, 113
Newton, Isaac, 149, 157, 158

Nixon, Richard M., 3, 20, 53, 78, 83, 86, 89, 90, 240, 241, 247, 249, 250-252, 273; on post World War II America, 240
Norman, Montagu, 20, 188, 195, 196, 197, 199, 200, 201; on the 1929 crash, 188, 201; on tight credit, 196

O

Order of St. John of Jerusalem, 99, 102, 104, 114, 144-145
O'Sullivan, John, 232

P

Paish, F. W., 238
Palmerston, Lord, 120, 124, 144, 146, 253
Pan-European Union, 141-142, 148, 167, 207, 210, 211, 212, 213, 216, 224, 225
Pasos, Luis, 228
Patton, Jacob, 121, 122; on England vs. America, 121
Pechman, Joseph, 238
Peel, Sir Robert, 134, 136, 181
Permindex (Permanent Industrial Expositions), 210, 226
Peterson, Edward Norman, on the Nazi economy, 33
Petty, William, 119, 130
Pforr, Franz, 145
Pinochet, Augusto, 2, 7, 23, 229, 253-255, 259, 264
Pipes, Richard, 25
Pitt, William, 99, 111, 112, 113, 118, 125, 133, 273
Plato, 143
Popper, Karl, 217, 223
Pope Paul VI, 78, 90; *De Populorum Progressio*, 88
Pre-Raphaelite Brotherhood, 95, 143-145, 175

Q

Quesnay, François, *Despotism in China*, 104; *Tableau Economique*, 104

R

Reagan, Ronald, 1, 25, 209, 247, 289, 321
Rees-Mogg, William, 272
Reuss, Henry, 36, 90, 136, 252
Rhodes, Cecil, 143, 156, 171
Ricardo, David, 6, 14, 74, 94, 96, 124, 126, 129-137, 139-140, 150, 163, 173, 177, 178, 181, 266; *Principles of Political Economy*, 129, 131; on money, 133, 135
Riemann, Bernhard, 14, 15, 77, 157, 158, 215, 216, 282, 285, 300; *The Hypotheses Which Underlie Geometry*, 285
Robinson, John, 111
Rockefeller, John D., 171
Roll, Sir Eric, 80
Roosa, Robert U., 86
Roosevelt, Franklin D., 79, 87, 237-241
Rossetti, Dante Gabriel, 144
Rostow, Walter, 25
Rothbard, Murray, 225
Rothschild, Baron Albert de, 156, 159
Rothschild, Evelyn de, 268
Rothschild, Julie de, 156
Rothschild, Louis, 210
Roundtable, 141, 142, 143, 156, 161, 166, 183, 190, 195; also see *Cliveden Set*
Rousseau, Jean Jacques, 104
Rudoff, Crown Prince, 157

Rueff, Jacques, 13, 22, 47, 49, 61-64, 66-70, 73-79, 83-85, 90, 91, 104, 142, 182, 201; *The Age of Inflation,* 48; on Adolf Hitler, 48; on credit, 84; his emergency economic plan, 65-68; on fascist economics, 47, 49; on Germany's 1931 currency crisis, 202; on gold, 85; on inflation, 73; on science, 75-76

Ruskin, John, 94, 95, 141, 142, 143-147, 154, 156, 160, 170, 171, 174, 180, 205; on education, 147

Russell, Bertrand, 53, 217, 218, 223

S

Sada, Andres Marcelo, 227, 228
Saenz, Orlando, 259
Samuelson, Paul, 8, 101, 248, 249; on Friedman, 8, 101, 248-249
Sartre, Jean-Paul, 89
Saulnier, Raymond, 242
Schacht, Hjalmar, 5, 10, 11, 19, 20, 22, 23, 24, 25, 26, 29, 31, 32, 33, 35, 36, 38, 43, 44, 45, 46, 48, 49, 53, 64, 66, 142, 161, 184, 186, 191, 198, 199, 200, 201, 202, 205, 211, 212, 213, 214, 225, 235, 264; on German economy, 46, 48
Schiller, Friedrich, 148
Schlesinger, James, 25
Schmidt, Helmut, 210
Schmöller, Gustav von, 160, 161, 167
Schönberg, Arnold, 95, 159
Schrödinger, Erwin, 287
Sharpe, Myron E., 11
Shaw, Clay, 226
Shaw, George Bernard, 144, 146, 154, 171, 174, 180; *Man and Superman,* 154
Shelburne, Lord, 89, 99-100, 102-104, 108, 110-116, 118, 119, 121, 123

Silk, Leonard, 249; on 1970 economic crisis, 250-251; on Milton Friedman, 51-52
Simon, William, 3
Simons, Henry, 164, 186, 203, 223, 236, 242
Skorzeny, Otto von, 207, 225, 226
Smith, Adam, 6, 14, 16, 94, 96, 97, 100, 101, 104, 110, 112, 114, 115, 117, 119, 120, 123, 124, 130, 173, 301, 306, 307, 310, 316; *Theory of Moral Sentiments,* 107; *Wealth of Nations,* 102, 103, 105, 108, 115, 116, 117, 118, 123; on colonial policy, 116, 117, 118; on the East India Company, 123; on moral indifferentism, 107; on value, 105
Society of Jesus, 99, 100, 102
Sombart, Werner, 184; *High Capitalism,* 184; *A New Social Philosophy,* 185
Speer, Albert, 29, 30, 31, 49, 206; on arms production, 31
Stead, William, 171
Steinberg, Jeffrey, 5; *Dope, Inc.,* 5, 97, 98, 142
Stewart, Dugald, 120, 124, 169
Stigler, George, 209, 235, 241, 242
Stimson, Henry, 50
Stobaugh, Robert, 293
Strauss, Franz-Josef, 207
Strauz-Hupe, Robert, 247
Strong, Benjamin, 195, 196, 197, 200
Sullivan, Laurence, 111, 112
Szilard, Leo, 214, 215, 218

T

Teller, Dr. Edward, 158
Tennyson, Lord Alfred, 145
Thatcher, Margaret, 2, 232, 266, 268, 270, 272

Thurn und Taxis, Max von, 208, 223
Tobin, James, 8, 55-57, 131
Townsend, Lord, 117
Toynbee, Arnold, 143
Triffin, Robert, 81, 88
Trudaine, Daniel-Charles, 104-112
Truman, Harry S., 78, 240
Tufts, Charles, 172
Turgot, Anne Robert, *Reflections on the Formation and the Distribution of Wealth,* 104, 105

U

University of Chicago, 26, 54, 74, 93, 96, 141, 144, 148, 154, 155, 164, 170, 171, 172, 173, 175, 176, 178, 179, 180, 183, 186, 208, 209, 217, 218, 219, 223, 228, 235, 237, 238, 253, 256, 269

V

Veblen, Oswald, 215; on recruitment of German scientists, 215
Veblen, Thorstein, 148, 170, 172-176, 179-180, 215; *Absentee Ownership and Business Enterprise,* 175; *Theory of the Leisure Class,* 174; on credit, 175; on labor, 174, 175
Velasco, Gustavo R., 228
Vergennes, Comte de, 90
Victoria, Queen of England, 155
Vienna School, 74, 81, 95, 105, 148, 155, 157, 162, 185, 214, 216

Volcher, Paul, 1, 15, 20, 22, 35-40, 43, 46, 83, 252, 259, 267
Voltaire (François Arouet), 104

W

Wagner, Richard, 101, 144, 154, 156, 159, 209, 210, 213; *Art and Revolution,* 154
Warburg, Max, 50, 186, 210, 211, 214
Warburg, Paul, 50, 173, 182, 185, 186, 202, 211-212
Washington, George, 12, 119
Webb, Beatrice, 144, 170, 171, 174, 179, 180, 199
Webb, Sidney, 144, 154, 155, 171, 174, 180, 199
Wedekind, Frank, 95
Wells, H. G., 214, 218, 219, 220, 221, 223; *The Open Conspiracy: Blueprints for a World Revolution,* 221, 223
White, Carol, 205; *The New Dark Ages,* 142
Wilde, Oscar, 143, 144, 147, 154; *The Soul of Man under Socialism,* 147, 154
Wilson, Woodrow, 182, 212
Wiseley, William, 82
Witte, Count Sergei, 160
Wittgenstein, Karl, 53, 159
World Bank, 125

Y

Yergin, Daniel, 293
Young, Owen, 212